38 Basic Speech Experiences

38
BASIC SPEECH EXPERIENCES

Tenth Revised Edition

by
Clark S. Carlile, *Professor Emeritus, Idaho State University*
and
Dana V. Hensley, *Wichita Collegiate School*

Consulting Editor
Susan Redding Emel, *Baker University*

Cover:
Todd R. Kinney

Layout & Design:
Todd R. Kinney
Tara Schmitz

Photo Credits:

Baker University, 93, 105
College of Southern Idaho, 157
R. Steve Dick, University of Kansas University Relations, 110
Susan Redding Emel, 20
Focused Images, Inc. xii, 96, 135
Scott Harper, University of Kansas University Relations, 79
Todd Kinney, 37
Kansas State University Photo Services, 100, 151
KTKA Channel 49, Topeka, KS vi, 119, 189
Lawrence, Kansas Chamber of Commerce, 139
Tom Moore, 87
Ann Carlin Ozegovic, 163
Pittsburg State University, 30, 69, 122
University of Kansas Sports Information, 56
James Vequist, 72, 75, 82, 182
Linda Webb, 160
Mike Yoder, Lawrence Journal-World, 146

Tenth Revised Edition

© 2003 Clark Publishing, a division of Perfection Learning® Corporation.

Perfection Learning® Corporation
1000 North Second Avenue, P.O. Box 500
Logan, Iowa 51546-0500
Phone: 1-800-831-4190 • Fax: 1-800-543-2745
perfectionlearning.com
Printed in the U.S.A.

2 3 4 5 6 JO 06 05 04 03 02

ISBN 0931054-53-2 Hardcover
ISBN 0931054-54-0 Papercover

FOREWORD TO THE TENTH REVISED EDITION

This tenth edition was written as Clark Publishing, Inc. celebrated its 50th anniversary. This is the book that launched the company. Fifty years and 36 books later, 38 Basic Speech Experiences is still the company's top seller. This book was originally written for students and teachers who want to learn and teach public speaking by the simple process of giving speeches. The tenth edition maintains that purpose.

As we prepared this golden anniversary edition, we knew we shouldn't mess too much with a good thing. However, we also knew that times have changed and the type of speeches given in the "real world" have changed as well. We still have 38 speech activities, but several are new and others combine two experiences from previous editions. For example, the development of new technologies has resulted in computer-generated visual aids. Speeches using this type of visual are commonplace in the business world and in education. Thus, a new chapter was added on "Computer Assisted Presentations" Chapters on "The Nominating Speech" and "Accepting a Nomination or Office" were combined into one chapter as were other pairs of speeches.

The book is now organized into six units with unit introductions. We have updated bibliographies, activities, assignments, and included new speeches. Some of the best examples of model speeches from past editions remain. Topic suggestions were updated and moved from an appendix to the chapters to which they relate. The biggest change, however, is in the book's appearance. The hardcover edition is four-color with numerous photographs and illustrations. The softcover version has some key illustrations and photos. Student activities and assignment sheets are in a separate teacher's manual for the hard cover version and in an appendix in the softcover text. All forms may be duplicated for classroom use.

The revision remains committed to the original concept of providing speech teachers and students with self-contained, basic speech experiences since the assignment sheets and outlines do not have to be used — students can prepare their own.

To those teachers who are plagued by the everlasting question of "What shall I assign my students for their next speeches?" this text provides thirty-eight completely worked-out projects. These speech projects are of the kind a student will be asked to continue in real life situations when students are no longer enrolled in a speech course. They are practical because they meet the needs of students who will be tomorrow's business and social leaders. The teacher may assign any one of the speaking experiences and know that the student will have all the information needed *in the assignment* in order to prepare and present a dedication speech, a eulogy, a sales talk, an after dinner speech, a panel, a debate, a speech to inform, or any one of dozens of others.

The text is adaptable and flexible. Any sequence of assignments or modifications a teacher desires may be scheduled. Any basic speech text may be used as a supplement. The teacher's manual contains a complete bibliography of speech textbooks.

Students' jobs are made easy because they know from each assignment what they must do to fulfill adequately the purpose of a specific speech. They know because the assignment specifies clearly what they must do. The requirements, such as time limits, outlining, organizing, and research materials, are not easy. They are not intended to be easy, but they are basic to all good speech making.

A speech course, well taught, and earnestly applied by the student, does more than train a person for public speaking. With this training comes the feeling of self-adequacy and high self-confidence that can last a lifetime. Enjoy the new 38 Basic Speech Experiences!

CLARK S. CARLILE
Professor Emeritus, Idaho State University

DANA V. HENSELY
Wichita Collegiate School

TABLE OF CONTENTS

PROLOGUE

UNIT I — Getting Your Feet Wet

UNIT II — The Basics

UNIT III — Business and Career Speaking

UNIT IV — Special Occasion Speeches

UNIT V — Contest Speaking

UNIT VI — Speaking for the Mass Media

PROLOGUE

HOW TO PREPARE A GOOD SPEECH

The first law of good speaking is adequate preparation. Preparing a good speech is like preparing to run a four-forty yard dash in a track meet. Each requires many trial runs before the event actually starts. To attempt a speech without preparation is just as foolhardy as to attempt a quarter-mile run without practice. The well-trained and conditioned racer makes it look easy, just as does the well-prepared speaker. To an uninformed person, both the speaker and the racer may appear to be performing effortlessly and impromptu, yet in most cases nothing could be further from the truth. Only many hours of intense preparation make it possible for the good speaker and the good athlete to display great ability. If there is doubt about this point in anyone's mind, then *ask the person who makes speeches or who runs races.*

There are several essentials which should be considered at this time in order to explain adequate speech preparation. They are:

I. CHOOSE AND DEVELOP YOUR TOPIC CAREFULLY

A. *Be sure you can find sufficient material on your subject,* otherwise your speech may be too short, devoid of quantity as well as quality.

B. *Be sure the subject you plan to discuss is appropriate to you, your audience and the occasion.* Any subject not adjusted to these three factors simply is inadequate. If you are in doubt, consult your instructor.

C. *Be certain that your subject can be adequately discussed in the time allotted* for your speech. Preliminary investigation, narrowing the subject, and a few "trial runs" will clear up doubts about this phase of preparation.

D. Since it takes time for ideas to grow and develop, *weigh carefully the time you allow yourself for preparation*, otherwise your speech may not be past the rough draft stage when you present it, and frankly an audience dislikes seeing a practice run when it comes to see a finished product.

E. The importance of selecting a suitable subject need not be stressed since it is so obvious; however, *you should decide whether your topic is too technical, trivial, trite or broad*. If it falls into any one of these categories, then it must be altered accordingly or a new topic chosen.

F. The *title of your speech should be provocative, brief, relative to your subject, and interesting.* It is one of the first things your audience will read about in the papers or hear before you speak. A good title can add immeasurably to the initial interest in your speech.

II. THINK OF YOUR AUDIENCE

Even though you may be preparing a speech to fulfill a class assignment, the *primary reason* anyone speaks in public is *to communicate with an audience*. In order to do that well, it is important to think about your audience through every step of the preparation of the speech.

A. *Understand how communication works.* Early scholars once thought of communication as the simple process of speakers trying to "hit the target" (the audience) with their ideas. We now know it's not nearly that simple at all.

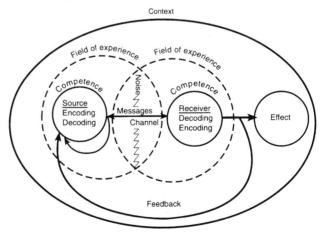

From Shockley-Zalabak, P. (1988). *Fundamentals of Organizational Communication*. New York: Longman, p. 25.

Communication between any two people involves the simultaneous sending and receiving of messages which require encoding and decoding skills on each end. So, while you may be speaking, your audience is sending messages to you at the same time through nonverbal means. *Messages* are the thoughts and feelings we have that we express through commonly agreed upon *codes*, or languages and behaviors. If we want to communicate about a "tree," for example, with an English-speaking audience, we must use the word t-r-e-e because it is the commonly agreed upon code for that plant. Communicators encode the messages they wish to send, and must decode the messages they receive, as accurately as possible. All communicators must be skilled at selecting the proper code for each of their expressions if they are to be successful.

But encoding our messages for successful communicating is complicated by some key factors:

1. **Noise** is anything that interferes with clear communication. Noise can be physical, such as air conditioner or heating units turning off and on, trucks roaring down the road outside the room where you speak, or someone tapping a pencil on a desk while you are speaking; it can be psychological, as is the case when audience members are bored or are worried about something irrelevant to your speech; or it can be physiological, as when a room is too cold or too hot, or the volume of your voice is too loud or too soft, thereby distracting the listener from what you are saying. A speaker must anticipate the potential for noise in the speaking situation and do whatever can be done to minimize those problems.

2. **Fields of experience** provide the reference points for each communicator to know how to decode messages and assign meaning to them. Each person's set of reference points is collected from the time and environment(s) in which s/he has lived. This means, then, that every person's field of experience is at least slightly different from everyone else's. Sometimes the differences are quite large; in which case we speak of "communicating across cultures." There is no real way to know the full scope of information in someone else's field of experience. As a speaker, you must try to evaluate the fields of experience of the potential audience, anticipating as best you can what the audience may know about the topic, what their attitude may be toward the topic and what factors may make them favorable or unfavorable to the speaker's point of view.

For example, if you are speaking to a group of residents at a retirement village you may be able to assume that as a general population they would not be very familiar with the music of teenagers today. Therefore, using song lyrics from the hottest group on the charts to illustrate a point you are trying to make might not be the most effective way to communicate because it is not likely that the song will be in your audience's fields of experience. It would be better to try to find music or poetry that may be more familiar to them that will make a similar point for your speech.

It will be important to know what your audience does *not* have in their fields of experience in order to plan the scope of an informative presentation. However, evaluating the audience's experiences becomes even more important with an increasingly controversial topic for your speech, or the increasing importance of persuading listeners to your point of view. In these cases you not only want to discover symbolic codes you share with them, but you will also want to be aware of their sensitivities in order not to offend them while you are trying to persuade them.

3. **The context of a communication exchange** includes the wide range of environmental and chronological factors that are operating when the communication transaction takes place. As such, it can influence the effectiveness of the communication act and must be understood in order to be used to maximum benefit by the competent communicator. The context of the transaction would include the historical, seasonal, and temporal setting in which the act takes place; the geographical location; the culture or co-cultures in which you are speaking, recent news events, etc. A competent speaker must take the context into consideration in a similar manner as you would the audience's fields of experience in order to maximize the effectiveness of your communication efforts.

B. *Understand how credibility is achieved for the speaker.* The listeners alone determine whether or not a speaker has credibility, as well as the amount. Therefore, a speaker must utilize as many resources as possible to encourage the audience to view them as credible on their chosen topic. *Credibility* is the perception that a speaker is a knowledgeable, trustworthy, and dynamic communicator. Listeners want to know that the speaker thoroughly understands the topic about which they are speaking, have the audience's best interests at heart, and feel strongly about what they are saying. It is important for the audience to feel the speaker is making good use of their listening time and energies.

A speaker can have credibility with the audience even before the speech is given. First, if the speaker is known by the audience, credibility may be assigned in accordance with the degree of likability perceived by the listeners. Additionally, if there is a formal introduction of the speaker, the introduction can serve to build credibility for the main speaker by relating their accomplishments and interests in the topic to be addressed.

But often, neither of these opportunities precedes a speaker's presentation. The speaker is neither known, nor introduced. In these cases, it is important to fill the speech with credibility-building materials and opportunities. You should begin as early in the speech as possible to seek credibility from the audience. In the introduction to the speech you can tell why you are qualified to speak on the topic by stating your experience with, your research on, or your interest in the topic you are about to address. References to shared experiences or history with the audience can serve to establish common ground with your listeners.

In the body of the speech you may continue to build your credibility by being well organized and clear in presenting your ideas. Using *transitions*, *signposts*, and *internal summaries* will help you maintain that clarity and help your audience to keep up with your ideas as you speak. In addition to being organized, you will need to be thorough in your treatment of the topic, avoiding any glaring omissions while keeping within your time limits. This requires the art of being concise!

Citing credible sources is another way to enhance your trustworthiness in the body of the speech. Expert sources are an excellent way to show you are not alone in your ideas. If the expert is unknown to the audience, you will need to briefly give their credentials to help orient your audience to the source's authority. Be sure to avoid experts who may have a conflict of interest within the subject they discuss. For example, the recent Congressional testimonies of tobacco industry officials that cigarettes (more specifically, nicotine) are not addictive has proven to be unreliable due to the tremendous investment these individuals have in the continued success of their industry.

Finally, you may build credibility through your delivery of the speech. Movements and gestures that are natural and relate directly to what you are saying give the impression that you are energetic and involved in your topic. Eye contact is especially important in the dominant culture of the U.S.—it says that you can "look us in the eye" and enhances your trustworthiness. Above all, sincerity is the key to sustaining credibility. If you are not sincere, the audience will sense it immediately and everything you say from then on will be suspect to them. Perhaps you can recall your own experiences with sincere speakers. Careful selection of your topic can go a long way toward helping you demonstrate your sincerity.

C. *Understand the basic ethics of communicating with others. Ethics*, put simply, is a set of beliefs about what is right or wrong. We generally say that communicating the truth is ethical; obscuring the truth is unethical. Listeners will judge speakers based on whether or not they believe the speaker is trying to reveal, or to cover up, the truth. *Plagiarism* is the practice of representing the work or words of others as one's own. A speaker must take careful notes when researching for a speech, attributing all borrowed material to the original authors or sources as you speak to avoid plagiarism.

III. MASTER THE MECHANICS OF SPEECH PREPARATION

Now that you have considered your subject and analyzed your audience, you are ready to begin the mechanical preparation of your speech. Here are the steps to follow:

A. *Decide on the purpose of your speech,* that is, what do you want to accomplish with your speech? What reaction do you want from the people who hear you? Do you want them to understand an idea better? To become stirred up and aroused about something? To perform an act, such as to vote for or against a candidate or contribute to a fund or join an organization? In your own mind it is absolutely essential that you know definitely what you want your listeners to do as a result of your speech. If you don't have this point settled, then you really don't know why you are giving your speech or why you organized it the way you did or why you are telling your audience "thus and so." In reality you don't know what you want and nobody else does. You cannot expect your audience to get anything from your speech if you yourself don't know what you want them to get. One of the most pronounced causes of poor speaking lies in the elementary act that the speaker has nothing in mind to accomplish with the speech. This need not happen if you decide on a purpose and direct all efforts toward achieving it.

With your purpose clearly in mind, determine what aspect of your topic will fulfill that purpose most completely. Identify the main ideas you think must be communicated for your purpose to be fulfilled. You should narrow those ideas down so that you have no more than two to five main points. Typically, an audience will not remember more than that.

B. Considering your main ideas, *carefully craft the thesis of the speech.* The thesis is usually a one-sentence statement that clearly and concisely explains what you are going to talk about in your speech as explicitly as possible. For many speeches, the thesis tells the listener exactly what your position is on the topic you will be discussing. Do not rush the development of this important part of the speech preparation process: a strong thesis statement can provide the basic "blueprint" for your entire speech, making it much easier to fill out the rest of the speech as you go on.

Tips for testing the strength of your thesis statement:

— Make your thesis a complete sentence, not a sentence fragment.
— Be sure to form your thesis as a declarative sentence, not as a question.
— Be sure your thesis does not imply you will discuss more than you can cover in your allotted speaking time.
— Your thesis should say enough to distinguish your presentation of this topic from anyone else's.

C. Your next step is to *gather material for your speech.* Once you have determined your main ideas and your thesis, you will need to provide a variety of supporting materials to help explain your ideas to the audience and to provide evidence in support of your arguments. This requires a search for information from respected sources on your topic. While you are gathering basic information on your topic, you will also want to look for appropriate quotations, statistics, examples or anecdotes, visual aids, models and other materials that can be used to both illustrate your ideas and hold your audience's attention.

With a little planning ahead, you can determine what kinds of supporting materials would be ideal for your speech, then conduct a search for those specific materials. *Quotations* or testimony, gives your idea the authority of an expert or other credible opinion on the topic besides your own point of view; it shows the audience that you are not alone in your thinking on this topic. Using Abraham Lincoln's famous line from the Gettysburg Address, for example, "...[G]overnment of the people, by the people, and for the people..." in a speech that argues in favor of allowing a particular rule to be voted on by the whole school, lends Lincoln's reputation as a statesman and as one of our greatest Presidents in support of your point.

Statistics, including charts and graphs that put numerical concepts in a visual format, help the audience gain a perspective on an idea for the purposes of comparison. Often, listeners feel that putting ideas in numerical form helps them understand the range and depth of the topic you are presenting. Instead of saying that a particular company expected "a lot of layoffs" soon, the audience gets a better idea of the impact of lost jobs when they are told to expect about 100 layoffs.

Examples or anecdotes are brief stories or illustrations that make the topic more personal to the listeners, more vivid to the audience's imagination. A statement that "Drunk driving kills innocent people" has a much greater impact if a story is told of an actual person whose life was lost due to the actions of a drunk driver. It ties an abstract statement to an actual face and name, making the same point more memorable.

Many people learn best when they can visualize the idea a speaker is trying to convey. Here is a case where a picture can literally be worth 1,000 words. Selecting *visual aids* for your speech can make the difference between what the audience remembers about your presentation and what they don't. Visual aids can come in a variety of formats: photographs (enlarged sufficiently, or placed on a transparency); video tape segments (carefully cued and timed to be presented as efficiently as possible—nothing allows an audience's mind to wander more quickly than having trouble with starting or stopping your video!); computer-drawn graphics and lettering for charts and illustrations; selected objects such as equipment you intend to demonstrate; even other persons who may assist you in demonstrating a movement or process. The keys to successful use of visual aids are: 1) good planning so that the visuals actually add to what you are saying; and 2) practice in presenting the visual aids to help anticipate any problems that might arise regarding placement of the visuals or operation of the equipment needed to display them.

A *model* is a particular type of visual aid that is used to help explain items or ideas that are either too large or too small to be brought into the room in which you are presenting your speech. A model would be a useful way to discuss a disease's effect on a particular organ in the human body. It would also be one of the easier ways to show key features

of a space shuttle. Models allow the audience to see things "up close" that they might not be able to see otherwise.

Other types of supporting materials that can enhance your speech and illustrate what you are saying include *definitions* which can come from dictionaries, from experts on the topic, or from telling how something operates in order to be called by that name. *Song lyrics, poetry, and dramatic lines* can help an audience feel the emotions involved in a particular issue.

Consult the next section entitled "Where To Go To Find Sources and Materials." Having located various materials, take comprehensive notes on what you decide to use. Be sure to indicate sources exactly and completely. This includes the specific names of the magazines or books the material was taken from, titles of articles, authors' full names, dates of publication, and chapters or pages where the material was found. If a source is a person, identify the source completely by title, position, occupation, etc. The data, telling exactly where you got your material, will prove most beneficial when someone later asks you where you found your material. The validity of your remarks will be no greater than the sources you use.

D. Once you have gathered the basic information and supporting materials, *organize the material* in an orderly and logical sequence. This means putting your thoughts in an order that your audience will not only be able to follow with ease, but one in which they may even be able to anticipate where you will go next.

There are several methods of organizing your thoughts that draw upon an audience's natural sense of how ideas logically flow from one another. Main points ordered *chronologically* follow a time sequence pattern such as past, present, and future. Demonstrating a process in which the steps must come in a particular order is also an example of chronological order, such as how to bake a cake. Because you would not put the ingredients in the oven before you have gathered them and mixed them, the steps fall in a chronologically-organized pattern. Telling a narrative also falls in a chronological pattern because you would not want to tell the happy ending before you've introduced the characters or described how they all fit in the story.

Another naturally related organizational pattern is *spatial*. This method of organizing ideas follows the order in which each main point would occupy physical space in relation to the others. For example, you might describe the effect of a disease on the human body from the head, through the shoulders, through the torso, down through the legs. Or you might discuss a current trend in the United States by looking at the trend on the west coast, through western states, through the center of the country, through the midwest, and finally throughout states on the eastern seaboard. When the spatial arrangement follows a physical placement pattern familiar to your audience, they are better able to follow the flow of your ideas as well.

A third method for organizing your main ideas is called *problem/solution*. Using this pattern, you begin by presenting the materials that define and illustrate a particular problem, then you follow that with information and/or arguments you have regarding a solution or multiple solutions to that problem. An example of the use of this organization pattern would be a speech that begins by discussing the problems associated with a limited supply of human organs for transplantation, and then presents current solutions being considered to relieve this problem such as signatures on driver's licenses, transplants from other animal species, and redesigned priority assignment systems for those in need of transplants.

A fourth method of organizing speeches is very similar to the third. Ordering your material in a *cause/effect* pattern means that you identify the cause of a particular problem, then you identify the effects resulting from that cause. A speech using this pattern, for example, would be one that begins by discussing what is known about the causes of the El Nino weather phenomenon, and then reports the effects of that weather pattern on people across the western hemisphere.

A fifth organizational pattern used to structure speech materials is called *topical*. This particular pattern is used when no other logical relationship pattern between your ideas can be identified. It is the organization of ideas in the order of the topics you wish to cover. For example, an informative speech on different breeds of dogs might group the varieties of dogs into categories based on what the breeds were designed to do: hunting breeds, working breeds, and companion breeds.

As you can see, each of these topics would be important to cover in such a speech, but they do not naturally connect to each other in any particular order. Therefore, when using the topical organizational pattern, the speaker should be aware that the audience may not be able to anticipate the next main point. In order to make up for that lack, a speaker can provide extra assistance to the listener such as parallel language. In the example of the dog breed speech, the first sentence of each main point would be constructed with similar language: "Hunting dogs provide their owners with excellent tracking and retrieving skills... Working dogs provide their owners with valuable assistance in tasks of strength and perseverance... Companion dogs provide their owners with friendship and loyalty." Such repetitive phrases signal the audience that you are shifting to another key area of information.

One special organization pattern for persuasive speaking is called *Monroe's motivated sequence,* or *the motivated sequence,* and is discussed in fuller detail in Chapter 9.

The best way to achieve organization that is progressive and unified is to prepare a complete sentence outline of your speech. For a fuller understanding of a complete sentence outline, study the example in "Preparing Speakers Notes." A complete sentence outline will assist in formulating and crystallizing complete thoughts prior to presenting the speech. Without this procedure you will discover it is exceedingly difficult to prepare and present a quality speech.

E. Your next step in speech preparation is *wording the speech*. Here you must decide what words you will use when you expand your complete sentence outline into a full speech. To get in mind the words you want to use, employ the methods best suited to you; however, two recommended methods follow.

One method for wording your speech is to rehearse aloud from your complete sentence outline or other outline until you have attained a definite mastery of the words you plan to use. It is wise to memorize the introduction and conclusion although you should not memorize the rest of your speech word for word. You should, of course, memorize the sequence of your main points irrespective of how you practice. The number of times needed for *oral rehearsal* will depend solely on you, but probably it will be at least four to six times and quite possibly even more, regardless of what method you use. In any case, if you plan to use notes while speaking, be sure to use the final copy of your speaking notes during your last few rehearsals. *Consider tape recording* your first or second practice to determine what changes in wording are necessary for clarity of ideas.

A second method for wording your speech is to write it out in full, then read your manuscript aloud several times to master the general ideas and the necessary details. After doing this, construct a set of very brief notes containing only the main ideas of your speech and *rehearse aloud* from them until you master the general wording and the order of the main points. Do not rehearse by mumbling in a monotone or by "thinking about" your wording.

One of the best ways to rehearse a speech is to stand before a mirror so that you may observe your posture and other body language. Some students object to using a mirror saying that it bothers them to observe themselves. This is a flimsy excuse since those same students know they must speak before their classmates who will be forced, through courtesy, to observe them while they stumble through actions, gestures and various postures which they themselves couldn't bear to see reflected in a mirror. A few "trial runs" before a mirror will vastly improve most speeches and speakers. A video tape is unexcelled in giving feedback.

F. Finally, preparing for a quality speech involves the *development of a positive mental attitude about the entire speaking situation.* You will be wise to expect nervousness and stage fright during the first few speeches. You should realize quite clearly that although stage fright will largely disappear after a reasonably short while, nervousness just before speaking probably will not. You should look upon it as a form of energy that will keep your speaking on a more vigorous plane than would otherwise be possible were you entirely devoid of nervous feelings. Your attitude should tell you that *you will gain self-confidence and poise* as you make more speeches, but do not expect a miracle. Your mental attitude should be one in which you recognize your own weaknesses, but you are not morbidly disturbed because you aren't a great success on the first attempt. You should be willing to seek advice from the instructor, to make honest efforts toward a more adequate preparation of speeches since this is the greatest guarantee for good speaking, and gradually as you progress you should take pride in your own personal improvement and feelings of self-confidence. Every beginning speaker should look forward to a feeling of adequacy and personal satisfaction, for if you do and if you possess a healthy mental attitude, you are sure to attain these goals—and a good speech.

WHERE TO GO TO FIND SOURCES AND MATERIALS

One of the biggest problems confronting students in speech courses is that of finding materials on subjects which interest them. Actually this problem is easy to solve if the student is willing to "look around a bit" to find sources of information and to read what is found. In preparing a speech, students should not say they cannot find enough material unless they have actually checked all of the possible sources.

The question which occurs most often concerning source materials is: "Where do I go to find these materials?" Aside from one's personal experience and interviews with business people, teachers, parents, and friends, there is one great source, the greatest and most valuable of all, namely, the library or media center. Here a person can find just about anything desired, provided a willingness to look for it. It may well be admitted that whatever a person is hunting for will not be "growing on trees." It will be in books, magazines, newspapers, and pamphlets—often filed away on unfrequented shelves in the library, but it will be there. To find these forgotten sources or others, there is one sure method—ask the librarian to help locate materials for the speech. In most cases, a librarian will provide more materials in ten minutes than the student can digest in several hours. Libraries also frequently provide access to Internet and CD-ROM based resources. Your librarian will be able to explain to you what is available on-line.

Besides going to the librarian for assistance, there are many sources which an individual can check out. A person should learn what these sources are and how to use them in order to find speech materials quickly. A representative group of these research tools is listed below:

1. THE CARD CATALOGUE: Check here for title and/or author of materials kept in the library.

2. ENCYCLOPEDIAS:
A. General:
(1) Britannica: general information.
(2) Encyclopedia Americana: general information.
(3) Collier's Encyclopedia: general information.

B. Special:
(1) International Encyclopedia of the Social Sciences: relates to social sciences.
(2) Afro-American Encyclopedia: history, great personalities, literature, art, music, dance, athletic accomplishments of Black people from ancient to modern times.
(3) The Encyclopedia of Education: concerns the history and philosophy of education.
(4) The Encyclopedia of Religion: contains articles concerning all the religions of the world.
(5) Mythology of All Races: just what the title implies.
(6) Encyclopedia of Asian History: information about Asian countries and their history.
(7) Cambridge History of Latin America.
(8) Encyclopedia of Latin American History and Culture.
(9) McGraw Hill Encyclopedia of Science and Technology: information on all branches of sciences, agriculture, and technology.
(10) Grzimek's Animal Life Encyclopedia: volumes on lower animals, insects, fishes, mammals, and birds.

3. YEARBOOKS:
A. Americana Annual: a source of current events.
B. Britannica Book of the Year: a record of events from 1937 to date.
C. World Almanac and Book of Facts, from 1868

crammed full of information, largely statistical on hundreds of subjects.
D. Stateman's Yearbook: statistical and historical information of the states of the world.
E. The Costeau Almanac: an inventory of life on our water planet.

4. HANDBOOKS:
A. Chronology of World History: a history of the world in chronological outline.
B. Political Handbook of the World: concerns party programs, world leaders, and the press.
C. The Westpoint Military History Series: military history from ancient to modern times.

5. INDEXES:
A. Poole's's Index to Periodical Literature: covers years up to 1906; useful for finding old material on hundreds of topics.
B. Reader's Guide to Periodical Literature: covers years since 1900; lists sources of information in practically every field.
C. New York Times Index: lists information which is to be found in copies of the *New York Times*.

6. BIOGRAPHICAL DICTIONARIES:
A. Newsmakers: published three times per year with information about politicians, business leaders, and movie, television, and rock music stars in headlines today.
B. Dictionary of American Biography: an encyclopedia of American biography of deceased persons. Kept up to date with supplements.
C. Who's Who: principally English biographies and a few internationally famous names.
D. Who's Who in America: brief biographies of notable living persons of the United States.
E. National Cyclopedia of American Biography: the most complete list of famous Americans living and dead available in any one source.
F. Encyclopedia of World Biography.
G. Current Biography: short biographies of people in the news.
H. Contemporary Authors: current writers of fiction, non-fiction, poetry, journalism, drama, motion pictures, and television.

7. SPECIAL DICTIONARIES:
A. Partridge. A Dictionary of Slang and Unconventional English.
B. Mawson. Dictionary of Foreign Terms.

8. QUOTATIONS FROM LITERATURE:
A. Stevenson. The Home Book of Quotations: approximately 50,000; arranged alphabetically by subject.
B. The Oxford Dictionary of Quotations.
C. Bartlett's Familiar Quotations: traces quotations to their sources in ancient and modern literature.

9. GOVERNMENT PUBLICATIONS: These materials cover almost unlimited fields. Ask the librarian or media specialist about them.

10. COMPUTER-BASED RESEARCH: Many libraries now have computer networks that will assist in accessing material you may need. Your librarian should be able to help you. There are also many sources of information that can be accessed through a home computer if you have a telephone modem and subscribe to an on-line service. Search engines such as Yahoo and Alta Vista as well as archives from sites such as *The Christian Science Monitor* (http://www.csmonitor.com), CNN Interactive (http://www.cnn.com), C-SPAN (http://www.c-span.org), The National Archives (http://www.nara.gov), and the Library of Congress (http://www.loc.gov), are helpful sources. CD-ROMS such as Microsoft Encarta that often come bundled with most new computers, provide the same basic information as encyclopedias.

11. THERE ARE MANY OTHER SOURCES: Available on the above subjects and subjects not included here. Ask the media specialist for assistance in locating them.

12. INTERVIEWS. Original research in which you interview experts can be one source of material that is overlooked by many students.

HOW TO BEGIN A SPEECH:
THE INTRODUCTION

An **introduction** to a speech is what a coat is when you go outside in the winter—it is a necessity. Without it you might become ill. A speech without an introduction is ill. It has been said that every speaker has the audience's attention upon rising to speak and if attention is lost it is after the speaker begins to speak; hence, the importance of the introduction becomes apparent.

There are several purposes speakers normally wish to achieve by means of their introductory remarks in order to be most effective. These purposes may be listed as follows:

I. One purpose of the introduction may be to *gain attention, arouse the interest and excite the curiosity* of listeners. This may be effected in numerous ways.

A. The speaker may refer to the occasion and purpose of the meeting with a few brief remarks explaining and commenting on why the audience is gathered on this occasion. A speaker may refer to the audience's special interests and show how the subject is connected with these interests. In no way should a speaker apologize for a speech.

B. The speaker may *pay the audience a genuine compliment* relative to their hospitality, their interest in the subject to be discussed, or the outstanding leadership of the group sponsoring the speech. The sincerity of the speaker should be genuine since the audience's judgment of the speech will be strongly influenced by the opening phrases.

C. The speaker *may open by telling a story* (human interest, humorous, exciting, etc.) that catches interest and arouses curiosity. The story should be linked to the subject. If the story is not related to the subject, it should not be told.

D. The speaker *may refer to a recent incident with which the audience is acquainted.*
For example:

"Three persons were burned to death a week ago because a school building had improper fire escape exits."

This paves the way for the speaker's discourse, the need for a new school building.

E. The speaker *may use a quotation to open remarks* and set the stage for the introduction of ideas. The quotation should be relevant to the subject and be tied to it with a few brief explanations.

F. The speaker *may refer to a preceding speaker or communication event* in order to secure interest and attention; however, too much elaboration should not occur. For example, the great orator, Anna Howard Shaw opened her famous speech on "God's Women" this way:

"The subject, God's Women, was suggested to me by reading an article in a Chicago newspaper, in which a gentleman defined God's Women. It has always seemed to me very remarkable how clear the definitions of men are in regard to women, their duties, their privileges, their responsibilities, their relations to each other, to men, to government, and now to God; and while they have been elucidating them for years, we have been patiently listening."

G. The speaker *may put pertinent and challenging questions to the audience* to arouse their curiosity. "Did you know that...? Do you want this to happen to you?", etc. These questions should have a bearing on the material which is to follow, otherwise they will be just so much noise.

H. Various combinations of the above suggestions may provide an effective introduction. The combinations which should be used will depend on the audience, occasion, speaker, speech and environment.

II. A second purpose of the introduction may *be to prepare and open the minds of the audience for the thoughts which are to come*. This is particularly necessary if the audience is hostile. It may be accomplished by giving background and historical information so that the audience can and will understand the subject. This purpose may be further achieved if the speaker establishes a right to speak by recounting the research done on the subject, by naming prominent persons associated with the endeavor, and by modestly telling of certain honors, offices and awards received as a result of accomplishments in fields closely related to the topic.

III. A speaker's third objective of an introduction may be to *indicate the direction and purpose of the speech and the end it will reach*. This may be achieved by stating generally the subject and by announcing and explaining the thesis of the talk. To give only a simple statement of the topic is not enough. It is uninteresting and in most cases dull. An appropriate and interesting exposition of any general statement of the subject should be made in reference to the topic. In other words, to announce only the title of a speech and to consider this an adequate introduction is a grave mistake. An example of a speech that forecasts is as follows:

"Ladies and Gentlemen: I have chosen to speak with you today on the subject of crime, which is costing our nation untold billions of dollars annually. It is my desire to explain to you the causes of crime as well as some forms of prevention. It is only when crime is understood that people are enabled to combat it and decrease its scope."

There are a few points to remember when preparing and delivering an introduction. Dullness and triteness, undue length of opening remarks, false leads that are not followed up, suggestive or risqué stories which are used only to fill time, or a mere announcement of the topic should all be avoided. Any apologies or remarks which might be construed to be apologies for the speech should definitely be omitted. There is nothing so invigorating, so appreciated, so likely to secure good will as an introduction which provides an original, fresh and sparkling meeting between the audience and the speaker and the subject. Work for it.

Generally speaking, an introduction is prepared last. This is practical because a speaker needs to have the *body of the talk outlined and the ideas developed* and ripe before determining how they should be introduced. The length of an introduction may vary considerably; however, it should not comprise more than one-fourth of the entire speech. It may comprise much less.

One more important aspect of the beginning of a speech is the speaker's behavior before taking the platform and after getting there. Speakers sitting on stage in full view of the audience should remain comfortably and calmly alert, yet politely seated. People are carefully appraising the speaker while they wait. When the speaker is introduced, he or she should rise easily without delay or noise and move to the appropriate place on the platform. After arriving there, the speaker should take a few seconds to deliberately survey the scene. Then after addressing the person presiding and anyone else who should be acknowledged, the speaker is ready to begin the introductory remarks.

HOW TO END A SPEECH: THE CONCLUSION

A day is never ended without a sunset of some kind. If the sunset is captivating, the entire day is often long remembered because of its impressive ending. A speech is much the same. It must have an ending, and to be most successful the ending should be impressive.

The **conclusion** brings together all the thoughts, emotions, discussions, arguments, and feelings which the speaker has tried to communicate to the audience. The closing words should make a powerful emotional impression on the listeners, since in most cases logic alone is insufficient to move an audience to act or believe as the speaker suggests. The conclusion is the last opportunity to emphasize the point of the speech. It should be a natural culmination of all that has been spoken. It should not contain weak, insipid remarks which are begun or ended just as the speaker starts a hesitant but very obvious journey away from the podium.

The conclusion should be, without exception, one of the most carefully prepared parts of a speech. Just when it should be prepared is largely a matter of opinion. Some authorities advise preparing it first because such a practice enables a speaker to point the talk toward a predetermined end. Other speakers suggest preparing the conclusion last because this procedure allows a person to draw their final words from the full draft of the speech. A third approach is to prepare it along with the introduction after the body is developed in order to coordinate both. Regardless of when a conclusion is prepared, there is one point on which all authorities agree, and it is that the conclusion must be carefully worded, carefully organized, carefully rehearsed and in most cases committed to memory or nearly so. The conclusion should be brief, generally not more than one-eighth to one-tenth of the entire speech, perhaps less, depending on the speech, the speaker, the audience, the occasion and the environment in which the speech is delivered. A conclusion should never bring in new material, since an action requires a discussion of the new material which in turn unnecessarily prolongs the speech. Also the introduction of new material brings about an undesirable anticlimax and frequently irritates an audience because a speaker runs past a perfect place to stop.

When a speaker moves into the conclusion, it should be obvious that it is the closing remarks. The speaker's intentions should be so clear that it is not necessary to say, "In conclusion..."

The importance of the delivery of a conclusion cannot be overemphasized. The total person—mind, body and soul—must be harmoniously at work. The eye contact should be direct, the gestures and actions appropriate, the posture alert, and the voice sincere, distinct and well articulated. The speaker's effort in delivering the conclusion may be likened to a foot racer who culminates an entire race in one great, last surge of power while lunging toward the tape—and victory.

Now that you have been told what should be contained within a conclusion, there remains one major question: "How do you actually go about attaining these ends, i.e., what methods should be used?" There are numerous ways to develop a conclusion. Some of the better known are listed on the following page.

A. *Summary* is a method often utilized in closing a speech. It is sometimes expressed by restatement of the speech title, of the purpose, of some specific phrase that has been used several times in the speech, by an apt quotation, either prose or poetry, which adroitly says what the speaker wishes to be said, or by any other means which tends to bring the main point of the speech into final focus for the audience. An example of a brief summary to conclude the speech is:

"As you can see, interviewing for a job can be made much easier if you prepare yourself well in advance by learning about the company, knowing your own strengths and weaknesses for the job, and by building up your self-confidence before you go in."

B. *Recapitulation* may be used in longer formal speeches when it is necessary to restate points in a one, two, three order. The danger of this method is that it may become monotonous and uninteresting. Short speeches do not require this type of conclusion, since the points are easily remembered. A short speech may close with the last main point if it is a strong point. Usually, however, more is needed to close a speech, even a short one.

"To be sure that we all understand my reasons for believing as I do, let me restate my main points. First, world federation is the only type of government which will save the world from destroying itself. Second, world federation is the only type of government which is acceptable to the several nations, and third, world federation is the most democratic type of world government yet conceived by humans. It is for these reasons that I favor the establishment of a world government."

C. *A striking anecdote, an analogy, or a simile* may be employed as closing remarks, or any one of them or a suitable combination of them may be interwoven with the summary or recapitulation type of conclusion. One conclusion which utilized the analogy for a speech concerning our children in crisis is:

"Just as a wind snuffs out the light from a candle, the winds of turmoil and discontent in our cities are snuffing out the lives and potential light of too many innocent youth. It is time to act to save our children."

D. *An emotionalized or idealized statement of the thesis* may serve as a useful conclusion. If the topic were "Our country's future" a conclusion could be:

"I want the legacy of this generation of Americans to be one of viewing progress as a never-ending process. I want us to be able to show that we recognized those things that must remain unchanged, and we preserved them. And that we had the foresight to determine what needed to be altered, and we did it. Let us take our place among other generations of Americans who made decisions not just for today, but for tomorrow. And not just for themselves, but for all Americans."

E. There may be a *powerful restatement of the thesis*. If the subject were "Volunteerism Can Change a Life," the final words could be:

"Volunteerism, giving of your talents to improve someone else's condition, can change a life. In fact, it can change yours as well as the lives of those you help."

F. *A vivid illustration of the central idea* may fittingly conclude a speech. For example:

"Millions of Americans have been mesmerized by the talent, agility, and record-breaking perseverance of Chicago Bulls' basketball star Michael Jordan. So the next time you think about all the money he makes, the fame he has received, the charities he has supported, the advances he's made for his sport, just remember that he built his career on the solid foundation of a college education."

G. *A call for action* from the audience may clinch a speech. It must of course pertain to the ideas of the speaker. This is an excellent type of conclusion, particularly when the purpose has been to stimulate or to get action from the audience. If a speech were on "Building Good Government," a conclusion could be:
"Let us no longer sit here doing nothing while the professional politicians corrupt our government and squander our money. Let's go out one by one, by two's and three's or by the hundreds and vote for better, more representative government. Let's do it tomorrow—it's election day and our only hope!"

One final word of warning is this: When the speech is finished, the speaker should hold the floor for a second or two (this cannot be stressed enough), before leaving the podium. Display or frivolity of any kind on the part of the speaker after the speech may sharply alter many good impressions which were made while on the platform. A person should not let actions portray a self-assessment of the speech. The audience will decide this point.

PREPARING SPEAKER'S NOTES

There are two ways to prepare your speech notes. You can put a few words on a card or sheet of paper, or you can prepare a sentence outline.

I. Below is a sample copy of notes a speaker might use in presenting a five to six-minute speech on body language. Each word stands for an idea, each word is large enough to be easily seen at a glance, and the actual size of the note card is about equal to that of a post card. Speaking notes should serve *only as a guide*, not as a crutch. The actual speech should be in the mind of the speaker, not in a mass of notes.

Hold your card of notes by the lower corner between your thumb and forefinger.

BODY LANGUAGE

1. MOVEMENTS TALK
2. EVERYONE USES
3. HELPFUL
4. CAN IMPROVE
5. BORN WITH

II. In the next column is a sample of a complete sentence outline. If you will study it carefully, you will note that every statement is a complete sentence. There are no incomplete sentences. There are no compound sentences. The outline is logically organized and divided into three parts: the introduction, body, and conclusion.

There are numerous ways to develop an outline and numerous sections into which it can be divided. The method followed by any one person is a matter of choice. If your instructor prefers a particular method of outlining, find out what it is. The important point to remember when constructing an outline (which is the skeleton of a speech) is that it must *make sense—logical sense*, which is easily followed. It takes time and effort to construct a complete sentence outline; yet the time and energy one spends in building a good outline will pay big dividends in improved speaking.

At the top of your outline include the following information:

Type of speech:_____(Informative)_____.

Name:_____(Your Name)_____.

Purpose of this speech: (What do you want your audience to learn, to think, to believe, to feel, or do because of this speech? e.g., I want my audience to have a better understanding of body language).

Title: BODY LANGUAGE
Introduction:
I. Your physical movements talk for you.
   A. They tell secrets about you.
   B. They tell what kind of person you are.
   C. I will discuss the behavior we call body language.

Body:
I. Everyone uses movements with spoken words.
   A. They are part of natural behavior.
      1. People are unaware of their movements.
         a. Posture reflects inner thoughts.
         b. Eyes, hands and feet talk eloquently.

II. Body language can be helpful.
   A. It can make a person attractive.
      1. Movements can reflect honesty.
      2. Appearance can bring favorable responses.
      3. Behavior patterns can make friends.
   B. Employers observe body language.
      1. They make judgments from what they see.
      2. They hire or reject an applicant by watching movements and posture.
III. Body language can be improved.
   A. A person can enhance personal appearance.
   B. Anyone can strive for better posture and walking habits.

Conclusion:
I. People are born with body language.
   A. It influences life.
      1. It speaks louder than words.

COMMUNICATION – A FEW IDEAS ABOUT IT

Communication may not be what you think. So let's first agree on what it is. Basically whenever you do anything (intentionally or not) that people interpret, they receive a message from you. Most people think communication occurs only when someone speaks, yet you know how people gesture with their hands, nod their heads, move their legs or shoulders, smile or frown, raise eyebrows or wiggle their noses all while they talk. These physical movements which you see often tell more than what is said with the speaker's words. Actually we *express feelings and ideas* two ways simultaneously. One way is with words or verbal communication and another is with bodily movements or nonverbal communication. It is almost impossible to talk without accompanying nonverbals; thus, we often send out messages we do not intend to send because of nonverbals. An example would be an individual who claims with words to be unafraid, but you know the person is scared to death by observing nonverbals. An embarrassed or frightened person often communicates feelings through actions.

The point is, communication occurs anytime someone else sees and/or hears you. What you communicate may be what you intended, or it may not be. However, words are one of your most powerful communication devices.

I. MEANINGS CHANGE OVER TIME

As a small child learning to talk, every word you learned had a special meaning to you because of your association with it. The word "puppy" meant only your puppy because to you there was no other. And so it was with all your words. Each had your own special meaning, and every time you spoke, your words referred to the meaning you gave them. This remained true as you grew from childhood and will remain true all your life. Your words now carry broader meanings because you have learned there are many kinds of puppies but you still attach your meaning to your words. The trouble in trying to convey (symbolize) your ideas to someone else is that for every word you speak, listeners interpret it with their special meanings which are different from yours. When this happens they do not fully understand you. It means that you communicated something but not exactly what you intended.

II. MEANINGS ARE ENCODED AND DECODED TO BE SHARED

The process of putting words together in phrases and sentences to represent feelings and ideas is called encoding. Listeners interpret your words by sorting out ideas they create in their minds, which is called decoding, somewhat like figuring out a message sent in secret code.

Still another way you communicate when talking is by how loud, how fast, how high or low your voice is. All reflect meanings about things *for which you have no specific words*. People hearing you usually can tell by your vocal variety whether you are happy, sad, tired or angry. A good example would be the way a friend greets you with, "Good morning." You know instantly something is bothering the person because of voice quality. Perhaps your friend muttered, possibly had a frown or they walked slowly. But the feeling was communicated whether intended to or not. Because people don't have words to completely express all their thoughts and feelings, they use vocal variety and thousands of muscular movements in addition to their words.

You also tell people all about yourself by your appearance. Your clothes, hair and personal hygiene tell who you are. Think about how you are describing yourself.

III. MEANINGS SHOULD BE ENCODED AND DE-CODED AS PRECISELY AS POSSIBLE

Since words have different meanings for the speaker and the listener, the question arises, "How does one talk to be understood more precisely?" Perhaps the best way is to use accurate and specific words. For example do not say, "It was bright colored." Instead say, "It was red and orange." Instead of, "He was a big man," say, "He was six feet three inches tall and weighed 225 pounds." Omit words such as pretty, nice, beautiful, bad, good, great, very, most, much, fast, slow and similar terms with generalized meanings. In other words say specifically what you mean, use correct grammar, articulate clearly, and pronounce distinctly. And finally, say it in as few words as possible. Don't make a listener decode fifty words to get your message when you can say the same thing using twenty-five.

Now in a broader sense you hear much about business, social, political, economic, and educational communication. It's popular to say, "Pat didn't communicate," to explain misunderstandings; however, it would be more appropriate to say, "Pat wasn't specific," or "Pat wasn't definite," or "Pat wasn't accurate," or "Pat used technical language," or "Pat wasn't complete." You could say in many instances, "Pat didn't speak plainly," or "Pat wrote sloppily and misspelled words," or "Pat did not signal (communicate) the message in time" (too early or too late.)

IV. UNDERSTANDING MEANINGS REQUIRES CAREFUL, INTENTIONAL LISTENING

On the other side it can be said that some people don't listen to understand but instead to argue and talk about their own thoughts. They don't read carefully, or they hear and read only a part of what is said and pretend they heard and read everything. Thus they only partially decode messages they receive and foolishly wonder why they don't understand.

Here's an interesting device. Next time you argue with someone try to restate their point of view so they will say, "That's exactly what I mean." Have them restate your views likewise. Do this on every point of disagreement then each will know what the other is talking about. Continue your discussion only if you both can do this.

We can summarize these remarks when we say communication can be improved by being definite, specific, accurate and complete in speaking and writing. When receiving messages we must listen, observe and read carefully and completely. It's that simple. Add to these communication principles, attentiveness, appropriate bodily movements and gestures, a clean and neat personal appearance and an earnest desire to understand or to be understood.

KEEPING A RECORD OF YOUR LEARNINGS AND PROGRESS

Communication skills are critically important in every profession and career. It is important to keep records of your training and development of these skills as you go along in order to have a well-documented **portfolio** to demonstrate your abilities when that becomes necessary.

Portfolio materials from speaking exercises should include video tapes, audio tapes, typed outlines, and professional-looking visual aids you may create. Further, you will want to include evaluation forms from instructors and your own self-evaluations that will indicate the improvements you make over time. All of the exercises in this text will make good material for your oral communication portfolio.

Elements of your portfolio may be stored in a variety of ways: tapes, photographs, or scanned materials on a computer disk. What matters most is that you maintain and continuously update your records to keep your best examples in good order for those with whom you choose to share them.

HOW TO RECORD A SPEECH FOR THE PORTFOLIO

First, decide if you will use audio or video to record the speech. Be sure your have sufficient preparation and rehearsal before you record.

Ask your instructor how close to stand to the microphone; however, ten inches is generally considered a good distance. If you use notes, avoid rustling them near the microphone. Any sound they make will be picked up and magnified by the recorder. When one piece of paper is finished, place it quietly behind or to the side of your other papers.

Begin the recording by saying, "This is (your name) speaking on (date)." After your first sentence, go ahead with your talk. Speak in your natural voice as you normally would. Be careful not to vary the distance from the microphone by moving around the room or your recording may be loud at first, then weak. Also avoid coughing, clearing your throat, sneezing, or shouting into the "mike."

While speaking, be sure to watch your progress so that you may be sure to finish before your time or tape runs out.

EVALUATING YOUR OWN WORK

Points to look for when evaluating your recorded speeches should fall into two basic areas: content and delivery. To evaluate the content, check to see that as many sources as possible are used and properly cited, your organization is clear and easy to follow, your introduction is attention-getting and logically structured, your conclusion summarizes your main ideas and provides a memorable final thought.

To evaluate your delivery, listen for vocal qualities that are desired (fluency, variety in pitch, clear articulation, good volume and rate) and undesired (harsh tones, nasality, vocal fillers such as "um," and stumbles over words). If the recording is on video, notice the level and frequency of eye contact, whether your gestures and movements are adding to the meaning of what you are saying or whether they are indicating nervousness, posture, and presentation and explanation of visual aids.

Self-evaluation is a key component of the total portfolio. Having a record of your communication skills development and progress will capture the richness, breadth, and depth of your learning. This information will be especially valuable to you as you seek jobs, scholarships, and acceptance into colleges or groups.

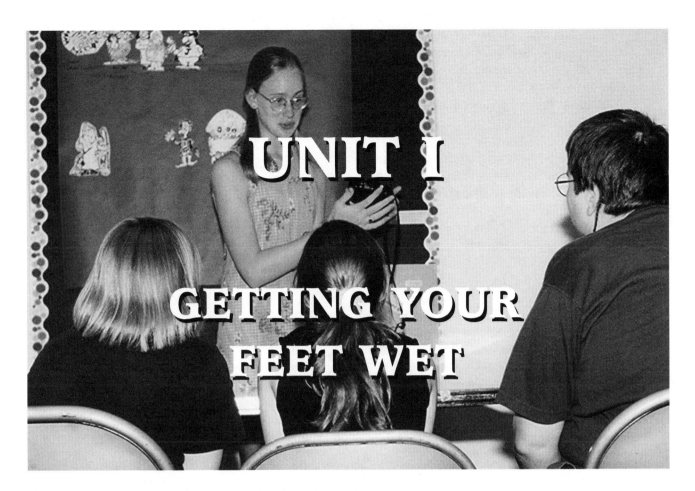

UNIT I

GETTING YOUR FEET WET

"I am **SO** afraid to give a speech!" Any time a public speaking class is required at a high school or university, the teacher is bound to hear this statement every semester. Even more students likely experience the fear without saying so aloud.

If such a statement resonates with you to any degree, you will find that this unit will help you begin to overcome those concerns. Public speaking is not, ideally, about performance. Rather, it is about being able to express your ideas to a group of others in a clear manner that communicates both your feelings and your thinking about a particular topic. Sooner or later we all find ourselves either wanting or needing to share our ideas and emotions with other people.

This unit begins the book because it contains assignments that are made of the most basic building blocks of speech preparation. Public speaking differs from interpersonal conversation in its level of formality, its relatively extended preparation, and the intentional construction and elaboration of ideas over more than a few seconds at a time. In this unit the following principles will be explored:

1) *Speak about something you know.* It is important to choose topics you are either already familiar with, or have an interest in learning more about so that you will have a variety of resources of information from which to draw your speech. In fact, you should not only know more on the topic than most of your audience members will know, but you should also know more than you will have time to present. This will ensure, for your audience, that you will present to them the best of the available material on the topic. It also allows you to be prepared in the event that any questions arise. *The Introductory Speech* takes advantage of the fact that there is one subject you already know more about than any other person: yourself. With that wealth of knowledge easily available, you can begin to experience the public speaking process right away.

2) *Speak with authority.* Audiences generally do not like to listen to speakers who can babble on about topics they really know nothing or very little about. In formal public speaking, it is important to learn to tell your audience as directly as possible how you come to know what you know. One of the best ways to speak from authority is deliver a *Speech of Personal Experience.* This type of speech has the additional benefit of introducing the novice speaker to the feeling of speaking with confidence because it is *your* experience about which you are speaking.

3) *Understand how communication apprehension works, and look for solutions that fit your personal needs as a speaker.* Many (if not most) people experience some level of this concern on a regular basis even if they speak in public frequently. In fact, many speakers hold that *some* level of nervousness actually has a positive effect on a presentation because it keeps you alert and animated. The most important way to deal with speech anxiety is to be thoroughly prepared, which this book is designed to teach you. However, in addition, it can be very helpful to discuss feelings of nervousness with persons who may actually deal with it on a regular basis to learn from their experiences. The *Speech on Communication Apprehension* is designed to help you learn from others and to take the opportunity to identify your own concerns and possible solutions.

4) *Speak with enthusiasm.* No one likes to hear speakers who sound as if they are bored with their own speaking. In fact, several studies have shown that speakers who are not dynamic suffer a loss of credibility with their listeners. One way to begin to experience the feeling of being a dynamic speaker is to select a topic that you already know gets your energies flowing, such as—a pet peeve or strong opinion. *The Pet Peeve or Opinion Speech* is designed to take advantage of those types of topics in order to provide you with a dynamic opportunity. You will notice a distinct difference in how you present a speech topic you feel strongly about and one about which you are unsure or undecided.

5) *Communication occurs on two levels: verbal and nonverbal.* Humans have the ability to send messages through verbal and nonverbal means. Using both channels allows more opportunities for the message to be displayed, thus enhancing the chances of creating shared meanings with the listener. But occasionally these two channels contradict each other: a speaker will be saying exciting, vivid words; but the volume may be low and gestures minimal or absent. When verbals and nonverbals contradict, studies show that listeners tend to believe the nonverbal messages are more reliable because they are harder to control than verbal ones. For this reason, it is important to pay careful attention to the movements and gestures that you may need to enhance the words you have carefully selected for a speech. *The Speech to Develop Body Language* is an assignment that will focus your attention on this very important aspect of speech delivery.

6) *One of the most important purposes for public speaking is to share information.* Sharing information and ideas is such a valuable part of a well-functioning society that the right to do so is protected by the United States' Constitution. Presenting information publicly can be done in several forms. One of the most familiar forms is *The Demonstration Speech,* in which the information you are imparting can be illustrated visually in several sequential steps that build on one another. This chapter will provide you with an opportunity to provide information through this particular format.

There's no better way to begin to learn the art of public speaking than to jump right in with the support of your teacher, classmates, and textbook. As in any art form, the more experience you have actually doing speeches, the more fully you will be able to learn and refine your skills. Good luck!

1

INTRODUCTORY SPEECH

Time Limits: 1-2 minutes.

Speaking notes: See the end of the chapter.

Outline your speech: Prepare a 75-150 word complete sentence outline.

Question: Does one ever overcome nervous tension before giving a speech?

Answer: Probably not entirely. Without some nervous tension you might end up with a lifeless speech.

Key Words:
Audience
Introductory statement
Summarizing statement

Student Expectations: In completing this assignment, each student will:
> ➤ *Organize familiar material in a format to present to others*
> ➤ *Experience speaking in front of an audience to become aware of aspects of effective delivery such as eye contact, volume, gestures, and vocal variety*
> ➤ *Get a feel for presenting ideas in front of a group*

PURPOSE OF YOUR FIRST SPEECH ASSIGNMENT

This speech is your first to be presented in this course. Your first speech gives you a chance to stand before your classmates and to tell them something about yourself. You are not expected to give a long biographical account of your life. By answering the questions at the end of this assignment, you introduce yourself to your audience, and you make your first speech. You will get the feel of standing on your feet and talking before a group of people. Since you must start somewhere, this experience will provide a good beginning.

HOW TO PREPARE FOR YOUR FIRST SPEECH

One reason for making this speech is to let the **audience** get acquainted with you. Another pur-

pose of this experience is to give you an opportunity to learn what it is like to see many people sitting before you waiting to hear what you have to say. Study the questions at the end of this assignment. Decide generally how you will answer them. It will help you to practice aloud several times by standing in front of a mirror while you speak. Do not memorize your answers word for word, since this would make your remarks sound like a recitation.

NERVOUSNESS SHOULD BE EXPECTED

Some students get a thrill from public speaking; others get a scare. Actually the scare is only a feeling that comes to a speaker because the adrenal glands are functioning more than they usually do. Because people dislike these feelings, they say they are scared. Instead of being scared of *speaking*, they are scared of a normal physical action taking place within themselves. They associate this feeling with speechmaking and, tying the two together, say, speaking "scares" them.

Just as a balloon can land anywhere once launched, being a skilled public speaker can take you places you never imagined.

To be scared is normal. To be nervous is normal. To be tense is normal. You must experience these feelings; otherwise you would be as lifeless as an old shirt. These feelings are present in football players before and during a game. Great actors have them. Great speakers have them. Nervousness is the high octane gas which provides these persons with the drive to give life to their performances. They want a normal amount of it because they use it. You see, they *control* their nervousness (energy) and that is all you need to do. Do not try to *rid* yourself of nervousness entirely; you will gain control of this power. As you give more speeches throughout this course, you will discover your control growing stronger—and that is what you want.

HOW TO PRESENT YOUR FIRST SPEECH
Look at the questions at the end of the assignment. On a note card jot down your answers in brief phrases. Take this with you when you speak.

When your name is called walk quietly to the front of the room. Do not do anything to call unnecessary attention to yourself. When you get there,

stand politely on *both* feet. Keep your weight on both feet or on one foot placed slightly forward.

Let your hands hang loosely at your sides unless you care to bring the one holding your notes up in front of you. It is certainly permissible to place a hand on a tabletop, or a chair back, if you do not call attention to the act. Grasp your notes lightly between the thumb and index finger. Do not palm them, roll, crumple, twist, or disfigure them in any way by continuous handling. When you refer to your notes, raise them high enough that you do not need to lower your head to glance at them.

If you feel like moving around a few paces, do so naturally, without shuffling or scraping your feet, or without continuous pacing. When you are not changing positions, stand still and keep your feet quiet.

When you begin your speech, talk with your normal voice just as you would if you were telling about yourself to a group of good friends. Good speaking is good conversation. Make an **introductory statement** for a beginning. Show some interest in your remarks. Be sure that everyone can hear you. Look your audience directly in the eyes; however, avoid a shifty, flitting type of gaze that never really stops anywhere. You may look at certain persons in different parts of the group, since you cannot very well look at everybody during the short time you are speaking.

When you are ready to close your remarks, conclude with a brief **summarizing statement**. Pause at least two seconds after your final words; then go easily and politely to your chair. Do not rush or hurry or crumple your notes into a wad and shove them in your pocket. Upon reaching your chair, avoid slouching down in it, sprawling out, heaving a big sigh and in general going through a pantomime which says in effect, "I'm glad that's over!" You may feel that way; however, this is one time that advertising does not pay. Sit comfortably in your chair and remember that you are still giving impressions of yourself. If you have done your best, no one will complain.

Answer the questions below on a note card or sheet of paper with a few brief words or phrases. Use the answers as the basis of your presentation.

1. My name is (what shall we call you?)
2. When and how did you spend your childhood? Explain.
3. Tell about your hometown or neighborhood.
4. How do you spend your spare time?
5. Who is your role model? Why?
6. What is your favorite sport? Why?
7. Conclude with a summarizing statement about your school plans.

CHAPTER 2

SPEECH OF PERSONAL EXPERIENCE

Time limits: 3-4 minutes.

Speaking notes: 10-word maximum limit.

Source of information: Use your own personal experience.

Outline of speech: Prepare a 50-100 word complete sentence outline to be handed to your instructor when you rise to speak. Your instructor may wish to write comments on it regarding your speech.

Question: How can you improve pronunciation?

Answer: Keep a dictionary handy. Carry a small one with you. Read aloud fifteen minutes daily making sure of all pronunciation.

Key Words:
Confidence
Convince
Entertain
Inform
Persuade or arouse
Preparation
Purpose

Student Expectations: In completing this assignment, each student will:
- ➤ *Determine the desired purpose of the presentation to be created*
- ➤ *Analyze the occasion for the presentation of this speech*
- ➤ *Select an appropriate topic for the identified occasion*
- ➤ *Adapt the speech material to the identified occasion*
- ➤ *Outline the speech in detail*
- ➤ *Identify and rehearse appropriate gestures to enhance the message*
- ➤ *Determine and rehearse appropriate enthusiasm for the topic*

PURPOSE OF THIS ASSIGNMENT

You take a step forward in your speaking experience when you present a speech of personal experience. While this speech is essentially about yourself, it still requires definite **preparation** and interesting presentation. You should learn the importance of these two requirements early in your speech training. Aside from becoming acquainted with these aspects of speechmaking, you should feel increased **confidence** and poise as a result of this speech experience. Your ease before the group should improve noticeably. By giving your best to this speech you will achieve a credible improvement and desirable personal satisfaction.

EXPLANATION OF A SPEECH OF PERSONAL EXPERIENCE

A speech of personal experience may be one of any four basic types. The speech may be given to: (1) **inform,** (2) **persuade or arouse,** (3) **convince,** or (4) **entertain.** The specific *purpose* of your remarks will determine which of these types you plan to present. If you want to tell a funny or amusing personal experience, you will plan to *entertain* your listeners. If you wish to tell about your stamp collection, your purpose will be to *inform* your listeners. It is advisable to confine your efforts to one of these two kinds of speeches.

This speech requires thorough preparation. You must know the order in which you plan to tell of your experiences. You also need to know how you will tell them, that is, the words you will use. *This does not mean you are to memorize your speech.*

Unlimited occasions for a speech of personal experience occur at all kinds of meetings—such as before school assemblies, clubs, business meetings, religious gatherings, and other groups. You might have heard such a speech from a war veteran, a war correspondent, from a missionary, a newspaper reporter, a great athlete, or from persons such as yourself who tell what has happened to them. Topic suggestions for a speech of personal experience are given below.

HOW TO CHOOSE A TOPIC FOR A SPEECH OF PERSONAL EXPERIENCE

If you have had an exciting experience, select it for your speech. Whatever you decide to talk about should be vivid in your memory and quite clear. As you think about it you may feel prickly chills race up your spine, you may laugh, you may feel sad. But whatever it is, the experience should be personal.

Do not stall before making a choice of topic because you do not know anything interesting to talk about. This is an old, worn-out excuse. The topic that you choose may not be interesting in itself. It is your responsibility to plan to tell the personal experience in an interesting way. You can do this with a little effort. Choose a topic without delay, and then read the rest of this assignment to find out how to prepare and present a speech on the topic you have chosen.

A *speech of personal experience allows you to relive an adventure.*

SOME TOPIC POSSIBILITIES

Moving
Flying
Sports
Summertime Activities
Friends
An Embarrassing Experience
Family
Accidents
Movies
Travel
Holidays
First Job

HOW TO PREPARE A SPEECH OF PERSONAL EXPERIENCE

First, decide on your purpose for giving this speech. Do you want to inform your listeners? Do you want to entertain them? It will be wise to work toward one of these ends for this speech. Having decided this point, your next step is to find out how you go about informing or entertaining. You may do this by reading the chapters in this text dealing with these types of talks.

Now let us assume that you know generally what is expected of you when you give your speech. Let us assume, too, that you have your purpose constantly before you (to entertain or to inform). Now develop your speech in the following order:

I. Outline your speech in considerable detail. This means that you must set up the order of events you want to talk about.

   A. Be sure your outline places these events in their most effective order throughout your talk. A little thought about arrangement will tell you how to place your ideas.

   B. In arranging what you will talk about, include your own personal feelings and reactions, the activities of other persons or animals, and objects that made your experience thrilling, exciting, funny. This will add interest.

II. *Practice your speech aloud* before friends and in front of a mirror. Do this until you have memorized the *sequence* of events, *not the words*. You will quite naturally tend to memorize certain words and phrases, and this is all right. But do not under any circumstances memorize the whole speech word for word. Every time you rehearse you will tell the same things, but never with exactly the same words. Each rehearsal will set the pattern of your speech more firmly in mind until after several practices (the number depends on the individual) you will be able to present your speech with full confidence and the knowledge that you know what you are going to say. That is, you know the events and feelings you are going to talk about and describe.

III. Make a final evaluation of your speech before marking it "ready for presentation." Ask yourself the following questions and be sure that your speech answers each question adequately:

   A. Does your speech merely list a series of persons, places, things, and times without telling what happened to these persons and things? (You should vitalize these persons and things by describing what happened and by pointing out unusual or exciting incidents, such as

dangers or humorous occurrences.) Avoid unnecessary details.

   B. Is your speech about *you only*? If so, you can improve it by talking about the influences that were operating in your presence. For example, if you rescued a drowning person, do not be satisfied to say, "I jumped in and pulled him out." Tell what he was doing, describe his struggles, tell how deep the water was, how far he was from shore, recount your fears and other feelings as you pulled him toward shore, tell how the current almost took you under, demonstrate the way you held him by the hair. Emphasize such items as your fatigue and near exhaustion as you fought to stay afloat. Here is an example of a "thriller": "We were in swimming. I guess we'd been in about an hour. John got the cramps and yelled for help. I swam over and pulled him out. He almost took me under once, but I got him out and gave him artificial respiration. I learned that when I was a kid. Boy, I sure was scared."

   (If this were your speech, ask yourself: Was this an interesting story of an experience? Could it have been told with more vividness and description?)

   C. Do you have a curiosity-arousing introduction, one that catches the attention? Check this point carefully.

   D. Do you have a conclusion? A speech is never finished without one.

HOW TO PRESENT A SPEECH OF PERSONAL EXPERIENCE

Your attitude regarding yourself and your audience will exert a singular influence upon you and your listeners. You should have a sincere desire to entertain or inform. If it is information that you earnestly desire to give, then you must try to make your audience understand what you are telling. If it is entertainment you want to provide, then you must strive to give enjoyment by amusing the audience and causing smiles and perhaps some laughter. You should not feel that what you have to say is simply not interesting and never was, which is the attitude of some students. Consider for a moment the child who runs to you eagerly, grasps your hand, and excitedly tells you about a big dog two doors down the street. The story no doubt captivates your interest; yet there is nothing inherently interesting about a big dog you have seen many times. Why then are you interested? The answer lies largely in the extreme desire of the child to tell you something. *A child wants you to understand and is excited about the event*, and therein lies the basic secret of giving information to which people will listen attentively. You must have a desire to make your audience understand you or enjoy what you are saying.

As for your body language, demonstrate those points which you can. Let your arms and hands gesture whenever you need to physically add to what you are saying. Otherwise, your hands may hang comfortably at your sides or rest easily on a speaker's stand or chair back. Be calm about putting your hands anywhere. Change your stage position by moving laterally a few feet. This will cause attention to be drawn to your presentation.

Use your voice normally and conversationally. Talk earnestly and loudly enough to be heard by everyone present. If you are truly interested in your audience's understanding you, your vocal variety and force will take care of themselves very well.

If you use speaking notes, observe the word maximum limit. Have these written in large handwriting so that they may be easily read. Use note cards at least three by five inches in size. Do not fiddle with the card or roll it into a tube. Hold the notes calmly between your thumb and forefinger in either hand. When referring to your notes, *raise them* to a level that permits you to glance at them without bowing your head. Do not try to hide them, nor act ashamed of using them. They are your map. Treat them as casually as you would a road map were you taking a trip.

THE EARTH TREMBLED
A Personal Experience Speech by Gail Anderson

"And Jesus uttered a loud cry, and breathed his last. And the curtain of the temple was torn in two, from top to bottom." Mark 15:37-38. For Christians, Good Friday holds a point in destiny unequaled since the dawning of all mankind. March 27, 1964, Good Friday alike, holds an eminent position in the stream of my life as the day of the Alaska earthquake.

I was thirteen at the time, living in Anchorage, Alaska. The fact was that a "Good Friday suppertime" sort of atmosphere was beginning to creep into the minds of each of the members of my family. We might even have been bored had it not been for the anticipation of the evening meal that was near completion.

The day was calm. My father was typically absorbed in the newspaper. "Kitchen-puttering" occupied my mother. My brother was both engaged and absorbed in some nonsensical whiling away of time. Snow was falling in a soft and gentle manner, combating boredom with me. The subtle and peaceful cloaking it lent the earth, could only be viewed as ironic now, in the face of what was to come.

The snow was still falling when the hanging light fixtures began to swing and the rattle of furniture could be heard on the tile floor. At first, our reaction could only have been termed amusement. But our amusement soon became terror. As we stumbled down stairs and through doors, trying to avoid tumbling objects, we heard and felt the rumble of our earth mount. As the front door forcibly flung us into the mounds of snow in the front yard, the earth continued to roll and groan. And then sprawled on the sidewalk, the ground ceased to tease us with its laughing rumbles. Now it was cracking. Around me the snow was forming rifts as great expanses of the frozen earth were separating.

The noises somehow were strangely deafening. Hysterical cries of neighbors blended with the laughing of the earth and the creaking of the houses to produce a wicked sound system matched only the horror of its backdrop.

Our station wagon bounced like a rubber ball. Trees on high-crumbling mountains in the distance were waving like a wheat field in a breeze.

Finally the earth became dormant once again. Now it was still. And as the curtain of night shrouded our stricken Alaska, we were left to our contemplation. The hesitancy of the only partially existent radio gave our woes a universality. Only then did we realize the encompassing scope of this earthquake. Sitting in my rocking chair (attempting to camouflage any further shaking), I heard of this demon which had left me alive and glad with my saved family, and spared home, but had taken the lives and homes of so many others.

In Anchorage, homes, schools, and businesses lay in ruin, paradoxically powdered with snow. But the people were together, helping one another. The homes left standing were crowded, but a unity of cause made these conditions endurable.

Immediately work began to rebuild, to restore. Radio announcers neglected their families to keep the people informed, as televisions and newspapers were not to be lines of communication for some time. People were living without heat, water, mail service, and many other things. Essentials were the essence of a united survival.

I wish that I could have understood the agonizing pleas for survival, for salvation. But only now, as my mind becomes a victim of time, do I have any understanding of the emotional or intellectual influence a natural disaster exercises on life and the perception of it.

And so, as on the original Good Friday, humans were recipients of one of the most vividly educational experiences in a lifetime. As the tragedy of the crucifixion and resurrection of Jesus Christ, the tragedy of the earthquake was to bring us closer to God, more desirous of salvation, and more understanding of both God and ourselves.

A Microphone? How Do I Work With a Microphone

1. Speak clearly and distinctly. Avoid slurring words. Articulate words and sounds.
2. Speak in a normal tone of voice. A microphone amplifies your voice; there is no need to be exceptionally louder.
3. Avoid speaking too rapidly. This may cause words and sounds to run together.
4. Practice with a microphone before giving a final performance.
5. Stay at a constant distance from the microphone. Place four fingers of one hand together and put your index finger lengthwise next to your lips. This is a rough estimate as to how far away you should be from the microphone.

CHAPTER
3

SPEECH ON COMMUNICATION APPREHENSION

Time limits: None.

Speaking notes: 25-50 words for the interview report.

Sources of information: The person or persons interviewed.

Outline of speech: Prepare a 75-150 word complete sentence outline.

Question: How can you speak to a group that is older than yourself on equal grounds?

Answer: Know more about your subject than they. Older persons respect well informed students.

Key Word:
Communication apprehension

Student Expectations: In completing this assignment each student will:
- ➤ *Identify common feelings associated with performance anxiety*
- ➤ *Interview a seasoned public speaker about experiences of "stage fright"*
- ➤ *Organize and present speech material that may be associated with some of the speaker's own anxieties*

PURPOSE OF THIS ASSIGNMENT

The speech on **communication apprehension** is designed to help you identify and confront the "stage fright" that may be experienced in the speaking experience in general. You will see that practically all speakers suffer some similar fears and physical reactions, including apathy, speechlessness, shortness of breath, dry mouth, weak knees, pain in the stomach, or nervous trembling. This speech, however, is unique and not designed to be presented in a public setting beyond the classroom.

EXPLANATION OF THE SPEECH ON COMMUNICATION APPREHENSION

This speech requires you to interview one to three persons who have had a variety of speaking experiences. You should briefly interview persons you know who have done a great deal of public speaking (for example, teachers, or business professionals) and perhaps someone who has had a more limited experience in public address (for example, a nonprofessional, student leader, or classmate).

Questions to ask your interviewees should include:

How often do you speak in public?
Do you get nervous? If so, what are the symptoms you feel?
How do you deal with stage fright?
What would you recommend to a beginning speaker for dealing with stage fright?
(For the experienced speakers:) Has your nervousness changed with more experiences in speaking before others? If so, how?

Be sure you ask them to explain any ideas further that you do not fully understand. This will be your only opportunity to clarify their meanings and to understand their experiences before you present your speech. Take careful notes as they speak. If you wish to record the interview on audiocassette, be sure to ask the person for permission to be taped before you begin.

After the interview, compare the experiences of those you interviewed with your own feelings of anticipating giving a public speech. Identify the intensity of your feelings and any symptoms you may have, writing them down as you do. Review the suggestions made by those you interview, and see if there are any you would be willing to try to use for yourself. Ask your teacher about other methods of addressing communication apprehension that you may not have encountered in your interviews. Review those possibilities for yourself as well. Select one or two ideas to try before presenting this speech.

HOW TO PREPARE A SPEECH ON COMMUNICATION APPREHENSION

The order of this speech should begin with a story of someone's experience of stage fright. If you have heard a humorous story from your interviewees, or have one of your own, plan to open the speech with that. Next, tell about the people you interviewed and their experiences and advice about dealing with communication apprehension. Your speaking notes should cover each interviewee separately, but you may draw some common conclusions about all of them together after you have described each one separately. Your final main point should tell about your own anticipation of speaking anxiety, and about the one or two suggestions you tried before presenting the speech. Conclude your speech with a reference back to your opening story, perhaps imagining how one of the suggestions you tried could have changed the outcome of the opening story.

HOW TO PRESENT A SPEECH ON COMMUNICATION APPREHENSION

This should be the simplest, most non-dramatic and sincere discussion you have made. It should come straight from the heart from start to finish. Your style should be that of talking with a group of friends who will reciprocate. When you have completed the speech presentation simply return to your chair.

Just as fear of snakes is natural, so is nervousness about public speaking.

THE PET PEEVE OR OPINION SPEECH

Time limits: None.

Speaking notes: Do as you like—you will probably be more effective without them.

Source of information: Yourself.

Outline of speech: None is required.

Question: Is it all right to ask questions when giving a speech?

Answer: Yes. Rhetorical questions are effective. These questions should be directed to the entire audience; however, no answer is expected or required.

Key Words:
Dynamic
Eye contact
Pet peeve

Student Expectations: In completing this assignment, each student will:

➤ *Concentrate on establishing and maintaining eye contact with the audience while presenting a speech*
➤ *Identify the student's point of view on a topic of importance*
➤ *Experience body movements, feelings, and vocal qualities associated with dynamic speech delivery*

PURPOSE OF THIS ASSIGNMENT

Thus far in your speeches you have probably felt varying degrees of nervousness and tension. As a result, you may have taken the stage fearfully, spoken in hushed and weak tones, used little or no bodily action, and scarcely any gestures. Perhaps you have not looked your audience in the eye (called **eye contact**), or you may have lacked sufficient enthusiasm. Such behavior on your part is probably caused by thinking of yourself and how you are doing.

One way to overcome tensions and nervousness is by talking of something about which you are intensely interested. This speech is designed to give you the feeling of real, live speaking in which you cast aside all inhibitions, fears, and thoughts of yourself. See what you can do with it.

EXPLANATION OF THE PET PEEVE OR OPINION SPEECH

Your talk should be about your **pet peeve** or your opinion about something. It should concern your innermost personal feelings on that peeve which causes you greater disturbance and anger or stronger feeling than anything else. It should make your blood boil just to think about it. It may be about something of recent occurrence or it may concern an event that happened some time ago. It must, however, be about an incident that is vivid in your memory. Probably it should be of recent date; otherwise, you may have cooled off too much to make a strong speech about it.

HOW TO CHOOSE A TOPIC FOR A PET PEEVE SPEECH

A pet peeve—or anything else that stirs you up can be a good topic for this assignment. Think about the last time you were irritated about something and remember why.

SOME TOPIC POSSIBILITIES

Bad Drivers
Too Much Homework
Curfew
School Regulations
Politicians
Waiting in Line
Grades
Racial or Other Types of Discrimination

Graffiti is a topic that can generate a pet peeve speech.

HOW TO PREPARE A PET PEEVE OR OPINION SPEECH

Preparation for this speech is minimal. First, decide what your most annoying and irritating pet peeve is. Once you make your choice of peeve or opinion, mull over the irritating idea and make up your mind that you are going to "blow off a lot of steam" to your audience. Select a particular example for your introduction. State in one sentence what you believe about your pet peeve, and use that in your introduction as well. Think about what might be the most memorable way to end your speech, and memorize that for a conclusion. If you wish to rehearse before presentation, so much the better. However, for this specific assignment you are not asked to practice. All that you are asked to do is to make sure that you are "red hot" about a particular subject. *If you are,* your preparation is sufficient for this speech, and your delivery will be **dynamic**.

HOW TO PRESENT YOUR SPEECH

There is just one way to deliver a speech about a pet peeve or opinion. Put your whole body and soul into it. Mean every word. Use plenty of force framed in dynamic and colorful, appropriate language. Let a slow fire that has been smoldering within you suddenly explode. Pour hot verbal oil on the blaze and let it roar and burn! In other words, let yourself go as never before. Be strong and do not be afraid to let the world know it. If your arms feel like waving, let them wave. If you feel like scowling in disgust—scowl. If you feel like shouting—shout. Whatever you do, just be sure you go all out. No doubt you will be surprised at your own ability—when you really "unload."

After your speech, the instructor and class will comment orally on your effectiveness. They should be able to tell you whether or not you really meant what you said. It will be helpful to you to find out how they reacted.

SCIENCE, NON-SCIENCE AND NONSENSE
COMMUNICATING WITH THE LAY PUBLIC
by Honey Rand
Speech delivered to the American Hydrologist Association, Tampa, Florida, November 17, 1997

Adlai Stevenson, a man who ran for President, was a great speaker. Once, he'd given a talk at the United Nations which was very well received. Afterward a woman who had been in the audience rushed up to him and said, "Oh, Mr. Stevenson," she enthused, "I really enjoyed your talk; it was without exception superfluous!" Before he could answer she went on, "Will it be published?" "Yes," said Mr. Stevenson. "Posthumously." "Good," said the woman, "The sooner the better."

These two communicators shared a language and a culture. They did not share meaning. I'd venture to say that next to hydrology and other environmental disciplines, there is virtually as much research going on in communication as any other field. We can't understand why we can't talk to one another and even when we do, why things go so drastically awry. One need only check out the latest titles at your local bookstores to see where the focus is these days. Customers, Employees, Management, Internet, Lovers. Husbands, Wives, Kids...the list is endless...if men are from Mars and women are from Venus, it is not a big leap to imagine where the lay public thinks some scientists are from. Did you ever read something in the paper or see a colleague or other scientific, technical person on TV and think to yourself: What in the heck is he saying? Probably not. Because you're listening, hearing and seeing the comments through what you know, the literature of science, proper methodologies, and, most importantly, the language of science. But trust me, there are thousands of people who are reading, watching and listening, along with you and their response to the comment is, "huh?" They don't have your education, they don't have your technical skill, and they don't have the scientific background to understand what is being said. And to make matters worse, too frequently what is being said is counter-intuitive, or embedded in controversy or just plain badly put.

But those viewers, readers and listeners are the taxpayers who likely fund your research. They are the consumers who buy the products resulting from the research. They are the public who rely on you to protect their natural resources and they need to understand your work. In most cases, they want to. And I have yet to meet the technical expert who doesn't want his world to be understood, acknowledged and supported by someone. For that to happen, however, shared meaning must occur and therein, too frequently, resides the problem.

When social scientists look at science, they see a picture very different from most technical experts. And for my purposes today, I will continue to insist that social science is a science...even if our subjects lie to us, even if they refuse to answer questions, and even if they change their minds after they answer the question, and even if they intentionally misunderstand what we are trying to get at.

Given that, you might be asking yourself, why bother explaining my research...or even science, at all? After all, mostly, technical professionals consider their biggest "audience" their peers. Certainly that's true when you're getting your work reviewed for publication or presentation at a conference like this...but these days...when research dollars are tight and everyone is taking a hard look at the bottom line. When the public expects to be engaged in the public policy process, the competitive edge you need, to explain your work, is communication skill.

More importantly, as you are called upon to be expert witnesses in environmental disputes, your skill as a communicator will be just as important as your technical skill. The judge, mediator or arbiter may have an education, but likely it is not in your field so your ability to explain your findings, argue your position and defend your recommendations will be central to his understanding of "the big picture." Moreover, for those of you central to disputes over the allocation of limited resources, the public will look to you to provide them "truth." That's "truth" with a capital "T." Very few of you will be comfortable when put in a position to provide "The Truth" in absolute terms.

You see, the language of science is impersonal and technical while those interested in your work will find the results very personal and frequently emotional. And the bottom line is this, if the public or the judge can't understand you…they will reject what you say. Worse, when the public sees dueling experts at 100 paces in courts, in the news and elsewhere, it is difficult, if not impossible, for them to discern the fine points of the argument. They do not speak the language of modeling and measurement, of prediction and control, of probabilities. They just know that your work affects their lives, their livelihood and their community.

They are looking for clarity and most are not familiar with the scientific process, with shifting paradigms and technological advances. What's worse, with cynicism and distrust of major social institutions so high, those of us trying to explain complicated science within the terms of public policy find we start not behind the eight ball, but under it. When politics are overlaid on the situation…even professional communicators want to run screaming from the room. And these days, the measurement, use and protection of our natural resources is very political.

No less an expert than George Will says, "Creative semantics is the key to contemporary government: it consists of talking in strange tongues lest the public learn the inevitable, inconveniently early."

Laugh if you will, but there are those who believe this is true. I once had an elected official ask me if one of our technical staff was intentionally speaking in tongues so that the audience couldn't understand.

In this environment, the dispassionate, rational approach to explication has little hope. There is an interesting case study of this brewing right here in the Tampa Bay area. A local government wants to build a brackish water desalination plant in their community. For years, the leaders of this community have said that desal is expensive, dangerous for the environment and unnecessary. Now, they want citizens to believe that it's OK. The latest public opinion polls suggest that well over 85 percent of the population understand that desal will cost more but that it is the highest quality of water available. However, all of the public education that has been done to date has focused on the possibility of Gulf water desalination. The plant is a brackish water facility. You and I know they are two different things, but that argument is lost on the public. In a meeting last week, the technical experts had the "opportunity" to explain their theories to an angry crowd of 300 people. People are concerned about brine disposal, something they've been hearing about for some time. The technical people were there to explain, among other things, how deep well injection will take care of the disposal problem.

Unfortunately, for those technical experts, the public in Florida has been hearing evil things about deep well injection for years. Despite the relative merits of various methods of disposal, the public is responding emotionally, and loudly, because they don't yet have the information on which to base an informed decision. Tuesday, the day before the public meeting, one of the technical professionals involved in this asked me what I expected to see at the meeting. When I talked through the problem of deep well injection with him, from the public's perspective, his answer to me was, "Well, it's better than putting it in the surface waters." What they understand is "Despite the risk to me and my family and community, this thing is going to happen no matter what we say." It infuriates them.

There is very little that logic can do for you here and the textbook response for dealing with an angry person...agree with them...won't work in this arena. Reason flies out the window once beliefs are engaged as the primary site for information processing. So what's a technocrat to do?

Of course, none of this matters if there are no dollars involved, or no natural systems at risk, or you are not committed to the outcome, whatever it may be. On the other hand, if you are committed, dollars are involved or natural systems are threatened, then your ability to effectively communicate what is at risk, or why there is not risk can be deciding factor in policy, protection or production.

So how do you effectively separate what you are doing (which is presumably science) from the non-science and the nonsense that is so prevalent today?

Now, I'm going to say something you may not like. It will be your natural inclination to resist this notion. Some of you may insist that this is the social scientist's revenge on the so-called hard scientists: biologists, hydrologists, engineers and others that have insisted that what we do, as social scientists, is not science.

Here goes: Science is a rhetorical argument.

In reality, gone are the days when technical professionals could throw their findings on the table and walk away letting "the facts speak for themselves" and allowing others to make what they will of them. The public has been engaged and now they want to be included so what you must do in communicating your findings is partly explain and partly persuade the lay public. Here you are trapped between appropriately qualifying your findings as is common practice in the field, and appearing to not be committed to them in the eyes of the public. We are all responsible for the products of our labors. Being able to clearly explain what your findings mean and what alternatives are left based on those findings, ensures that your work is not misused, or if it is, you are a willing participant in it.

This is about control.

A well-cited communications scholar said, "While in general the truer and better cause has the advantage...no cause can be adequately defended without skills in the tricks of the trade."

Enter Public Relations.

Today even the scientist needs public relations. Why? Because there are those who would appropriate your work for their own purposes. Because your work is complicated and frequently communicated through a medium to a mass audience and that translation can distort your work. And accuracy is the currency of your profession. To ensure the highest probability for accuracy in translation, you need the kind of professional who speaks that language.

My colleagues in social science make the occasional raids on your literature in order to appropriate the models for their own use. Complexity, chaos, systems theory and others now punctuate the social science literature…what might the appropriation of the social science models add to your vision of our environment and our response to it? I suggest that if your science represents the left brain function and social science represents the right brain, might the combination of the two give us a better representation of the whole?

Our models in social science include two-way interaction, systems, integration, symbolic interaction, social and cultural contexts, group think theory, social networks, uncertainty and ambiguity analysis, structuration and so on. What these do is allow us to take the information that must be learned by the involved public, to make the necessary considerations as to the context and methodologies within which the learning must occur, the social networks, the prevailing attitudes and so on, so that your work has the best chance of a fair hearing. In the absence of information, people make stuff up. In the presence of information they cannot or do not understand, people ignore it and rely on their emotions to fill the gap. Once emotions are engaged, the opportunity for dialogue is frequently lost.

We do not live in a world of direct experience. We depend on those closest to something to describe it for us. Based on that description, we can determine what is "best" from our point of view. It is how we establish our opinions. The public depends on you to understand and describe the water resources and reasonable alternatives. While human beings must simplify information in order to process it, oversimplification can lead to misunderstanding. When we look at public opinion polls we are generally looking at the public's response to a partial truth. On the other hand, public opinion polls can also represent public judgment. Public judgment is when the public has looked at various sides of an issue, weighed the competing interests and accepted the consequences of their decision. This is a truly informed engagement.

Still, informed engagement and understanding does not necessarily equate to agreement. What it does is create a context in which genuine exchange of information, a dialogue, with shared meaning, can occur.

Somewhere between science representing truth with a capital "T" and public relations representing a perspective of truth, is a truth which allows us to identify the parameters of our natural resources, to use them in the best interests of most people, doing the most good without ruining them. We need public support for this to occur and that support is built on a clear and honest understanding of what it is we are trying to do. The responsibility for communicating this information is yours.

It is a tough job, but there is really no one better qualified to do it than you.

CHAPTER 5

THE SPEECH TO DEVELOP BODY LANGUAGE

Time limits: 4-5 minutes.

Speaking notes: 10-word maximum limit.

Sources of information: Two are required, preferably three. For each source give the specific magazine, book, or Internet site it was taken from, title of the article, author's full name, date of publication, and the chapter or pages telling where the material was found. If a source is a person, identify the person completely by title, position, occupation, etc. List these on the outline form. For Internet sites, include the address (URL).

Outline your speech: Prepare a 75-150 word complete sentence outline.

Question: Is it all right to lean on the speaker's stand?

Answer: No. It makes you appear tired and uninterested in your subject.

Key Words:
Bodily actions
Criticisms
Gestures
Posture

Student Expectations: In completing this assignment each student will:
➤ *Understand the use of bodily actions and gestures in public speaking*
➤ *Identify appropriate and meaningful body language for a given speech*
➤ *Determine the relationship between body language and sincere communication*
➤ *Listen to constructive criticism and determine necessary adaptations to make*

PURPOSE OF THIS ASSIGNMENT

Speaking is a bodily activity. To be really effective a person has to speak with the entire body. Use your feet and legs, hands and arms, trunk, head, and eyebrows. Many beginning speakers do not realize this, despite the fact that they themselves use total bodily expression all the time in their normal conversation. One sees such speakers standing before a class very stiff and rigid making speeches. They move only their vocal cords, their tongue and jaws. Actually, they are half speaking (communicating) because they are using only half of their communication tools. If they would put all their communication power into action, they would include bodily action and gestures. A speech as-signment of this kind is made because it will provide an experience which will demand that the speaker use bodily actions and gestures, and thus improve the speech.

EXPLANATION OF BODY LANGUAGE IN SPEECH

A speech to illustrate body language may be any kind, since bodily actions and gestures should be used in every speech with varying degrees. The purpose of your speech need not be influenced because increased body language is required. These activities will be aids in assisting you to communicate in a manner which fulfills your purpose, regardless of what it is.

Bodily actions may be defined as the movements of the body as it changes places. **Gestures** may be defined as movements of individual parts of the body, such as raising an eyebrow, shrugging the shoulders, or pointing. But all movements are body language.

It is nearly impossible to speak without *some* body language. Just because you may not be aware of all that goes on while you speak, it doesn't mean that you are not using some actions. Your nervousness and stage fright elicit certain gestures which tell the audience you are nervous. Now, if you substitute *meaningful* activity, you at once improve your communication and release many nervous tensions which accompany speaking. The point to bear in mind is that all speech communication should be accompanied by *appropriate* and *meaningful* body language which should not be interpreted to mean that you must employ constant bodily movements and incessant gestures. Such monotony of motion would be nerve-wracking to an audience. Someone once said that moderation is good to practice in all things. This is true of body language.

HOW TO CHOOSE A TOPIC FOR A SPEECH TO DEVELOP BODY LANGUAGE

Since the purpose of presenting this speech is to improve the use of body language, select a subject which can be demonstrated while talking about it. On the other hand, the purpose of the speech itself will be to inform the listeners. It will be wise then to choose a topic in which you are interested and about which you can find source materials. You must also adapt your material (your speech) to your audience; hence, it must be suitable to them as well as you.

SOME TOPIC POSSIBILITIES

Sign Language
Self-defense
Physical Therapy
Rollerblading
Referee Signals
Sporting Techniques (golf, swim, bowl, football)
CPR
Playing a Musical Instrument
Dancing

In choosing your topic think about your sports activities and your hobbies. Ask yourself what you know how to do that others may not. After your choice is made, *stick to it* even though you discover it is more difficult to prepare than you had anticipated. Do not change topics just because you misjudged the amount of effort it would take for preparation. It is important that you make your selection of a topic without delay, for this speech will require considerable planning.

HOW TO PREPARE A SPEECH TO DEVELOP BODY LANGUAGE

In the speech to develop body language, your *communicative purpose* will be to inform your listeners in such a way that they *understand* what you are talking about. You will find out all about this type of speech by reading the chapter in this text, *The Speech To Inform. Develop* your speech in the manner suggested for the informative speech.

In rehearsing this talk, practice bodily actions and gestures, as these will constitute a great part of this speech. These actions should not be memorized in detail, which would result in a mechanical performance. Instead, stand before a mirror while you practice. If possible, use a large mirror that reflects your whole body rather than just the upper half of it. A friend who will watch you and give helpful **criticisms** will provide an excellent means for improvement. Practicing with a video recorder will help also.

While you rehearse, your efforts should be exerted to create a well-organized set of spontaneous actions. As stated above, you must not memorize these actions. They must be motivated by the earnestness of your desire to make your listeners understand you. You must feel impelled to use your body and hands in expressing yourself. These actions of your body and hands need not be like those of anybody else—they are your own, the same as your walk and style of dancing are your own. All that you need to do is to observe yourself in practice in order to eliminate awkwardness, undesirable posture and foot positions, and distracting mannerisms.

The thought is that if you are willing to try and to

undergo a little self-inflicted criticism, you can develop your own style of gesture and bodily action. In doing this, it is advisable that you read several references on body language. However, do not "program" or adopt gestures that look unnatural. It is important to remember that gestures and movement should be large and deliberate enough for the audience to see. Your **posture** should be one of alertness in which you *stand tall.* Keep your weight on the balls of your feet and on the *forward* foot.

Bodily action should be free, relaxed, easy. It should have tonicity, vigor and coordination, without the appearance of extreme nervous tension, which is characterized by shuffling feet and restless tiger-like pacing. In moving to the left, lead with the left foot; to the right, with the right foot. Avoid crossing your legs in order to get started. Move quietly without "clomping" heels and scraping soles. Be sure that the movement is motivated and acts as a transition between ideas, as an emphasis, as a device for releasing bodily tension and holding attention. Use bodily action deliberately until you habitually make it a desirable part of your speech, a part that communicates meanings and ideas.

HOW TO PRESENT A SPEECH TO DEVELOP BODY LANGUAGE

When you present this speech, approach the speaker's stand with the attitude of a person determined to win. Take pride in the fact that you are going to use your entire body in speaking. With this attitude you cannot lose.

When you actually present your speech, concentrate on one point which will make the audience understand what you are informing them about. They have to understand you, or you will not be getting your ideas across (communicating). Now, while you are earnestly presenting your ideas, try to make them clearer by demonstrating what you have to say. Do this by acting out certain parts as

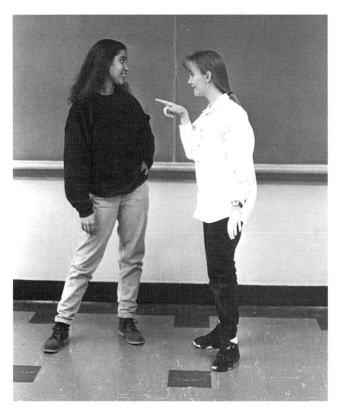

Body is as important as voice in conveying ideas to an audience.

you talk. If you tell the audience that it is best to mount a horse a certain way, show them how to do it. If you say a baseball should be thrown a certain way, demonstrate it with all the force and energy you would use were you actually pitching. If your demonstration is so vigorous that it makes you short of breath, so much the better; you will have been truly trying to show, as well as tell what you have to say. You may exhibit pictures, charts, diagrams, and write on the blackboard, . . .If you do, be sure that your equipment is ready for exhibition before you begin.

Do not be afraid to try; do your best, and you will do a good job. Plan to continue using body language in your future speeches.

(The speaker's props were canoe paddles, an armless chair, and a small rug.)

Wouldn't you like to get more fun and relaxation out of your leisure time? Those two-day weekends could be spent away from the busy, hurried city life that most of us lead. Just put a canoe on top of your car and head for water. A canoe can float on as little as four inches of water. A quiet lake, stream, or pond may hold more fascination than you ever imagined. A canoe could also bring the thrills of shooting rapids of a swift running river, but this is for the experienced canoe enthusiast.

I would like to give you a few rules and demonstrations to show you how to canoe in a very short time. Number one rule is getting in and out of a craft correctly. Canoeing is often thought of as being very dangerous, but the danger usually occurs when getting in or out of the canoe. To get in, you step first to the center, lengthwise, and place the other foot behind (demonstrate on rug). Then lower yourself to a kneeling position which is the correct canoeing position (demonstrate by kneeling on rug). There are braces across the canoe to lean against. Once you have established this low center of gravity the canoe has great stability. Getting out is just reverse. Keep your weight to the center as much as possible (demonstrate by getting off the rug).

These are the paddles (show paddles), they are made of fir, a soft wood which holds up well in water and is lightweight. To select the paddle measure it to your height. It should come to about your chin (demonstrate). (Sit in the chair to demonstrate paddling strokes). To hold the paddle grip the end with one hand and with the other hand grasp it a little above the blade (demonstrate).

The basic stroke is called the "cruising stroke," or the "bow stroke." Extend the paddle in front of you (demonstrations follow), close to the canoe, and dip into the water, bringing it straight back to the hip by pushing with the top hand and pulling with the lower hand. Now bring the paddle back to repeat. The paddling is usually done by a two-person team called tandem paddling. In tandem paddling the person in front is the steersman who steers the boat. The person in the rear is the bowman and provides the power. The bowman uses the bow stroke most of the time (demonstrations follow). The steersman uses the bow stroke also, but often makes a hook outward on the end of the stroke to keep the canoe on course. This version of the bow stroke is called the "J-Stroke." The steersman also uses the "sweep stroke" for turning. It is a wide, sweeping, arc-like stroke made close to the water surface (demonstrate). To stop or go backwards the "backwater stroke" is used. Simply place the paddle into the water at right angles to the canoe and hold it firmly to stop (demonstrate). To go backwards reverse the "bow-stroke (demonstrate). (Rise to a standing position with paddles in hand.)

This is by no means all there is to know about canoeing, but if you can accomplish these things you will be able to have fun. So to enjoy the outdoors and take a break from a humdrum routine. I hope you will try canoeing.

CHAPTER 6

THE DEMONSTRATION SPEECH

Time limits: 4-5 minutes.

Speaking notes: 10-word maximum limit.

Sources of information: Two are required, preferably three. For each source give the specific magazine, book, or Internet site it was taken from, title of the article, author's full name, date of publication, and the chapter or pages telling where the material was found. If a source is a person, identify the person completely by title, position, occupation, etc. List these on the outline form. For Internet sites list the address (URL).

Outline your speech: Prepare a 75 - 150 word complete sentence outline.

Question: What is posture?

Answer: It is the speaker's bodily position whether standing or sitting.

Key Words:
Chronological
Demonstration
Visual Aids

Student Expectations: In completing this assignment each student will:
  ➢ *Identify essential steps in a topic to be demonstrated*
  ➢ *Organize a speech chronologically*
  ➢ *Explain a process to others in a clear manner*
  ➢ *Prepare and use visual aids*
  ➢ *Identify the best means of fitting available material into a limited time frame*

PURPOSE OF THIS ASSIGNMENT

Sooner or later, each of us is asked to explain how to do something that has a series of distinctive steps to be accomplished. It is important on such occasions to remember that we may be demonstrating and explaining the topic to someone who has never done this before. Therefore, we must be sure to begin at the beginning of the process, and to include every essential step. This assignment is designed to familiarize you with creating a speech that includes all essential steps for successfully completing a process, though you may know the topic so well that you could do the process yourself without thinking too specifically about each step.

EXPLANATION OF THE DEMONSTRATION SPEECH

A **demonstration** speech is a type of informative speech, and in that regard should provide the audience with new information. The purpose of this speech is to teach the audience the essential steps to complete a task of importance to them. Because it is a demonstration speech, it will almost certainly require **visual aids** of some kind.

HOW TO CHOOSE A TOPIC FOR THE DEMONSTRATION SPEECH

Because your purpose is to inform your audience, you will want to select a topic that presents new information to them while at the same time providing you with an opportunity to demonstrate it. This means you want to avoid obvious or trivial topics such as how to make a sandwich.

Consider what types of things you can demonstrate in the room in which you will be making your presentation. This may require that you narrow your topic. For example, instead of demonstrating how to play tennis, the classroom you are to speak in may require you to narrow your topic to a demonstration of different positions for holding the racket, different swings, or different stances to take when facing an opponent. Be sure you can demonstrate the topic in such a way that all audience members will be able to see you. Additionally, you will want to narrow your topic to fit the particular time limits given by your instructor.

SOME TOPIC POSSIBILITIES
How to program a videocassette recorder (VCR)
How to take good photographs
How to play the flute
How to organize a party
How to do calligraphy
How to play soccer
How to organize a neighborhood watch program
How to give CPR or first aid
How to drive defensively

HOW TO PREPARE THE DEMONSTRATION SPEECH
Since the demonstration speech must provide each step of the process in the order in which it occurs, the most frequently used method of organization for these speeches is the **chronological** pattern. Begin by jotting down each of the steps in the process as you recall it. If possible, test the ability of a friend to complete the process according to the steps you have identified, to see if they can do it successfully, or if you may need to include other steps.

When you are satisfied you have included all the necessary steps for the topic you have selected, develop each of the steps into a full main idea, explaining any necessary ingredients and processes for each one. Identify any visual aids you will need for each step in order to make your point as clearly understood as possible. Practice completing the full demonstration with the necessary

visual aids several times before you are to present it to your audience. This will help you become aware of any problems that may arise with the use of space, the visual aids selected, or the ability of audience members to see as you demonstrate.

HOW TO PRESENT THE DEMONSTRATION SPEECH
When you present this speech, begin by taking the time to set up your necessary visual aids. You will want to have practiced the set up as well, so that you may do so with the minimum amount of time possible. Place your notes strategically so that you can see them without lowering your voice to the ground, yet they do not interfere with your visual aids.

Present the speech with the full confidence of one who knows the material very well. Remember, you have selected a topic that is new information to the audience, but is familiar to you; therefore, you are the expert here. Complete each step as you have prepared it, referring to your notes in order to assure you do not skip any necessary steps. Once you have completed your demonstration, conclude your speech with a brief review, then remove all visual aids as quickly, efficiently, and quietly as possible.

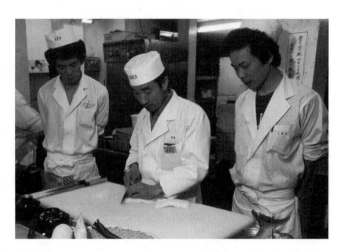

Cooking instruction is a type of demonstration speech.

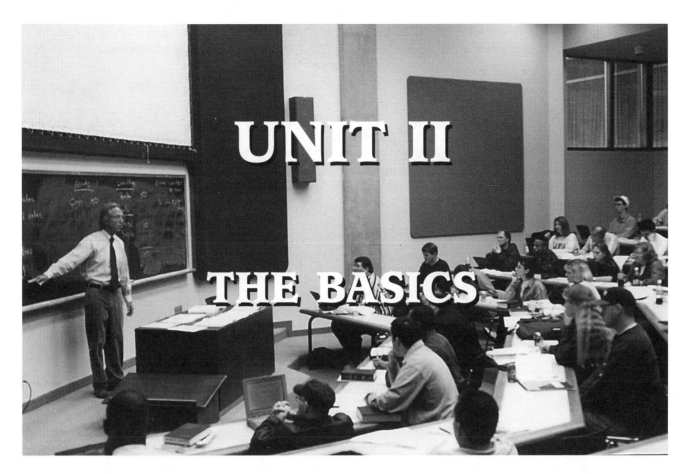

UNIT II

THE BASICS

Because speaking in public is more formal than everyday conversation, the preparation of the speech must always begin with a clear understanding of the purpose that is to be accomplished. In general, public addresses may have as their primary purposes an intent to inform, to persuade, or to entertain. Then, each speech will have a more specific purpose for the particular occasion for which it is designed.

An example of a specific purpose for an informative speech would be, "To inform my audience of the causes and treatments of 'tennis elbow.'" This speech would then be built around the two main ideas indicated in the specific purpose statement: what causes "tennis elbow," and how is it medically treated. An informative speech must always strive to present *new* information to the audience. It is important for the speaker to analyze the intended audience as thoroughly as possible in order to avoid presenting material they already know. If a speaker does not take such care in planning, at best the listeners will be bored, and at worst they will be angry that their listening energies have been wasted on "old news." *The Speech To Inform* is designed to teach the student to address this most basic of speaking purposes.

A second general speaking purpose is to persuade. Try to count how many times a day someone tries to persuade you to do something, or believe something, or change something! Persuasion happens nearly every time we communicate with others. It is a particularly important purpose for public address in a democratic society since we all strive to work together for the protection and advancement of our communities and nation. An example of a specific purpose for a persuasive speech would be, "To persuade my audience the federal government should allocate more funds for space exploration and research." While this speech could be constructed in a variety of ways, the specific purpose indicates that the speech will give the audience several reasons and plenty of evidence supporting the increased use of public money to explore and study space beyond the Earth's atmosphere. The challenge for the speaker will be to build those reasons and evidence into arguments that will compel listeners to agree or even act on their convictions in support of the speaker's position. *The Speech To Persuade* is an assignment designed to introduce the student to this public speaking purpose.

Motivation of listeners is closely related to persuading them, with particular attention to getting the listeners to take a desired action. An example of a specific purpose statement for a motivational speech would be, "To motivate my audience to begin a regular program of weight training exercise." This speech would provide sincere and dynamic enthusiasm for the proposal in addition to solid reasons and evidence. *The Speech To Motivate* provides the student with the opportunity to learn how to inspire a particular response in others.

Whenever we seek to persuade a group of people, there is always the possibility that what we wish to propose is not what they are originally inclined to support. Still, when the topic is one about which we feel strongly, we may find ourselves in need of preparing *A Speech To Gain Goodwill With A Disagreeing Audience*. This chapter helps the student learn to find the best ways to build support for an idea when audience analysis shows that they are unlikely to do so before the speech is given. In many such cases, building goodwill between the speaker and audience is the most important first step. If an audience feels strongly enough against the speaker's proposal, building goodwill may be the sole purpose of the speaker's first attempt to address the group, in hopes that another chance to address them further on the issue will be possible. This chapter provides the student with the chance to prepare for such an occasion.

The last general purpose for public speaking is both the most fun and, in some ways, the most challenging. Everyone likes to be entertained. But individuals may have differing ideas about what, exactly, is entertaining. For the speaker who seeks to amuse or delight the audience, there are several strategies to explore. *The Speech To Entertain* is an assignment designed to help the student explore the ways humor can be applied to a message of some practical value in order to make the delivery of new information or of persuasive arguments more appealing and fun for the listeners. An example of a specific purpose statement for a speech to entertain would be, "To entertain my audience by showing them the lighter side of technology." This speech would introduce the audience to the latest in technological advances, but provide them with humorous examples of how that technology came to be, or how it may be used in the future.

Finally, in this unit we turn to a particular style of speech delivery that most of us are confronted with quite often: speaking on the spur of the moment with little or no preparation time. Whenever we are called upon to speak in class or in a meeting, we are essentially speaking in an impromptu style. While many people use the opportunity to say whatever comes into their minds, we know that that is not always the most appropriate way to respond to the situation. In fact, it can be rather disastrous, especially if *nothing* comes into our minds! Therefore, this unit includes *Impromptu Speaking* to help the student understand how to make the most of an on-the-spot situation.

This unit concentrates on introducing the student to the basic general purposes of public speaking. Each chapter is designed to provide another opportunity for approaching the main speaking purposes from different points of view, thereby building the experiences the student may have with each. It is also designed to reinforce the idea that good speaking practices begin with clearly articulated purpose statements.

CHAPTER

7

THE SPEECH TO INFORM

Time Limits: 4-5 minutes.

Speaking notes: 10-word maximum limit.

Sources of information: Two are required, preferably three. For each source give the specific magazine, book, or Internet site it was taken from, title of the article, author's full name, date of publication, and the chapter or pages telling where the material was found. If a source is a person, identify the source completely by title, position, occupation, etc. List these on the outline form. For Internet sites list the address (URL).

Outline your speech: Prepare a 75-150 word complete sentence outline.

Question: Should a person use eloquent phrases when appropriate?

Answer: Yes, if you remember eloquent phrases are usually couched in simple language.

Key Words:
Analysis of the audience
Fundamentals of preparation
Outlining
Sources of information

Student Expectations: In completing this assignment each student will:

➤ *Demonstrate knowledge of material largely unfamiliar to others*
➤ *Analyze an audience's interest in, and knowledge of, a particular topic*
➤ *Relate new material directly to a particular audience*
➤ *Understand the basic fundamentals of speech preparation*
➤ *Create a full sentence outline of the speech material*

PURPOSE OF THIS ASSIGNMENT

No one knows how many speeches are given each year. Neither does anyone know exactly what kinds of speeches are presented. We do know, however, that of the millions and millions of talks, many of them are made specifically to inform people—to tell them something they will find beneficial to include in their knowledge. While no one can foretell accurately what kind of speeches you may be called upon to present in the future, it is a safe bet that you will speak many times to inform people. Because so many speeches are informative in nature, you are offered here the opportunity to become acquainted with the informative speech.

EXPLANATION OF THE SPEECH TO INFORM

The speech to inform provides a clear understanding of the speaker's ideas upon a subject. It also arouses interest in the subject because the material which is presented is relevant to the lives of those who hear it. It is incumbent upon the speaker to provide this relevant material with its accompanying interest in order to inform intelligently. To accomplish the ends of informative speaking, one is obliged to select a subject of interest to the speaker and the listener. This can be done by an apt **analysis of the audience**—in this case your classmates. You, as the speaker, are charged further with the serious responsibility of knowing what you are talking about, knowing more about it, in fact, than anyone in your audience does. For this reason, your talk demands that you study not one but several (no less than two) **sources of information**. Under no consideration should you be satisfied to glance hurriedly through an article in a popular magazine, jot down a few notes, toss the periodical aside, and rush off, content with the world and a "sloppy" job of acquiring knowledge. This kind of preparation does not even begin to enable you to give an informative discourse.

Occasions for the informative speech are many. They occur on the lecture platform, in the pulpit, in the classroom, at business meetings; in fact, wherever you find reports being made, instructions given, or other ideas being presented by means of lectures and discussions. The point to bear in mind is that any time information is disseminated, an occasion for an informative speech arises.

HOW TO CHOOSE AN INFORMATIVE TOPIC
Select something that interests you and that is appropriate to the audience you are to address or select a topic that you are curious about. Think of something that you read about or heard about on television that left you wanting to know more. Be sure that you can find information about the topic you select. Do not put off choosing a topic. Study the list below.

SOME TOPIC POSSIBILITIES
Jobs of the Future
Space Exploration
Major World Religions
Costs of College Education
Robots
Movie Special Effects
Baseball Card Collecting
Juvenile Crime
Homelessness
Best Vacation Spots in the World
Living Wills

HOW TO PREPARE A SPEECH TO INFORM
To prepare for this speech, or any speech, you must know and follow certain **fundamentals of preparation**. These consist of the following steps: (1) choose your subject; (2) analyze the occasion; (3) analyze the audience; (4) gather your material; (5) organize and support your main points with evidence; (6) word your speech by writing it out in full, in part, or by rehearsing it from an outline; (7) practice aloud.

If you wish to organize your thoughts logically, you should decide early what objective you hope to attain and what reaction you want from this particular audience. Next, if you wish, you may divide your speech into three conventional parts: an introduction, the body, and the conclusion. To be more effective, some speakers break down their talks by using various combinations of the following steps: (1) gain attention; (2) make your audience want to hear your ideas; (3) present your ideas; (4) tell why this material is important to your listeners and how it affects them; (5) ask your audience to study the topic further or to take some action on it. The time required for any one division of a speech varies greatly; however, more time is given to the presentation of ideas than any other division of the speech.

The wording of your talk may be accomplished either by writing it out in full from the outline, or by considerable practice. In any event, rehearse before a mirror or with a tape recorder as many times as necessary (usually about four) to fix the proper steps and the order of their content, along with desirable stage appearance and bodily action. Give the speech for a friend or family member and get reactions. Do not memorize the words.

How to use notes is somewhat a matter of opinion. If you are adequately prepared, you will not need notes. You will talk extemporaneously, which is the most commanding method known. If you must refer to notes, they should be either short sentences, phrases, or single words which have a particular meaning to you. The notes you hold in your hands should be brief, concise, meaningful, and entirely familiar. A glance at your notes should be sufficient for you to gather their full meaning so that you may speak fluently yet logically. The notes should be on index cards.

One other point is important. The information you present must be accurate. For accuracy of information, acceptable sources of information written by reliable and competent authorities must be consulted. Your audience should know where you got your material. What is more, you are the person to identify these sources and authorities. You are expected to go even further in this matter of giving information: you are expected to offer your conclusions and views and evaluations of your information. All this entails the neat assimilation of all you have pulled together—that is, your entire speech.

Former President Jimmy Carter informs listeners of his post-presidential activities.

A few hints might well be offered at this point. First, have only two or three main points to your speech. Support these well with examples, illustrations, analogies, and facts. Second, do not be afraid to inject humor and anecdotes into your thoughts to add interest. Be sure these additions are suited to your subject and audience. Third, be sure your speech moves ahead. Do not allow the speech to drag or become stalemated. Last, give plenty of effort toward an interesting introduction and an equally effective conclusion.

OUTLINE YOUR SPEECH

Outlining your speech is necessary if you wish to secure organization, logical order of material, coherence, and unity. Without these rhetorical qualities, your thoughts will be a jumbled mass of words with little direction or a definite goal. An outline is to the speaker what a map is to a person taking a trip; it shows you where you are going and how to get there.

After neatly constructing a 75-150 word sentence outline, be prepared to hand the outline to your instructor when you rise to speak. Your instructor will undoubtedly wish to follow this while listening to your speech and may write suggestions on it for improvement. Remember that this outline is not to be used while you are speaking. State two or three sources of information within the speech presentation.

Read at least two references on outlining. Ask your instructor for assistance.

HOW TO PRESENT A SPEECH TO INFORM

Use an easy, energetic presentation. Be enthusiastic and original in what you have to say. Use your hands to demonstrate how to do things. Draw pictures, exhibit charts, in fact, do whatever is necessary to make your ideas understood and interesting. Take stage properly, utilize expressive bodily action, maintain direct eye contact, observe time limits, and stop when your speech is finished. Your conclusion should be as strong and appropriate and as well prepared as your beginning remarks.

For most people worried about heart attacks, the salad bar is an island of serenity. Nearly every choice makes the heart rest easy; low fat, low cholesterol, low calories. But without one stunning safety feature, the salad bar could make your heart stop: the sneeze guard.

It could protect you from the heart attack bug: chlamydia pneumoniae. This tiny bacteria, according to the June 7, 1997 *New Scientist* "is now 'overwhelmingly'" linked to heart disease. The August, 1997 *World Press Review* estimates that over half of the population is infected, and probably has no idea of it, or the damage it can do.

Thanks to the discovery of the heart attack bug, however, the April 28, 1997 *Newsweek* says "cardiology is in for a revolution." This is one revolution we can't afford to miss. Therefore, we will first unravel the mystery of the heart attack; second, become familiar with the new bug's place in it; and finally, discuss some implications that this finding has for the future of hearts everywhere.

First, let's unravel some of the mysteries of heart attacks. Any red-blooded American knows that high cholesterol leads to heart problems. Doctors thought so, too, until evidence pointed to the contrary. As *Science News* of June 4, 1997 points out, most victims have normal cholesterol counts.

This is not to say that people with high cholesterol never get heart attacks. But many of us will testify that our sinful Uncle Jerry, who's smoked a pack a day and eaten red meat for dessert on a regular basis, is alive and kicking at 80. Meanwhile, some of the healthiest among us suffer from heart disease.

As the *World Press Review* explains, this last incongruity intrigued scientists in Sweden nine years ago. While training, eight athletes suddenly died of cardiac arrest. All were on low fat diets, were non-smokers, and had the heart attack bug.

But how could a bacteria causing simple flu-like symptoms shut down something as resilient as the human heart? Obviously, doctors needed a better explanation of the heart attack.

The major cause of heart attacks, if you paid attention in health class, is atherosclerosis, or clogging of the arteries. When we eat a diet high in fat and cholesterol, it accumulates in our heart's vessels, plugging the flow of blood. Without blood, the heart stops.

However, as Michael Gimbrone, Harvard Medical School pathologist, tells the April 3, 1997 *Washington Post*, atherosclerosis is much more than a simple "clogged pipe." Atherosclerosis is now thought to be a result of inflammation.

Science News explains. First, the vessel wall becomes injured and inflamed. Picture when you cut your finger. Remember the swelling and excess heat on the injury? That's inflammation, like in the blood vessel.

Now instead of a clogged pipe, imagine a car crash. White blood cells are the first set of emergency crew on the scene, doing protective duty for your body. But, as in a real life accident, curious on-lookers soon pile up on the scene. In your heart's case, these are more fat molecules.

Soon, the body sends a police crew to stop damage done by this fat accumulation. These smooth muscle cells cover the layers of cells and fat. With so many bodies in the street, traffic comes to a standstill. Though the process is much, much slower in your arteries, the same principles apply. Your body's own defenses actually clog its vessels.

But how does a common bug fit into this picture? Now that we've unraveled the mysteries of the heart attack with the inflammation hypothesis, let's see how the heart attack bug relates.

As *Newsweek* explains, chlamydia pneumoniae, known as CP, is a bacteria that spreads as a microdrop infection to the lungs. Coughs and sneezes spread the bug, leading to flu-like symptoms that can escalate into pneumonia.

Scientists in Europe linked this infection to the inflammation hypothesis by American doctors. The June 21, 1997 *British Medical Journal* explains that British doctors found CP in 79% of coronary artery samples from patients with atherosclerosis; but only 4% of non-atherosclerotic samples contained the bacteria.

Frankfurt professor of infectious diseases, Wulfgang Stille, tells *Der Spiegel* of April 21, 1997, 60-80% of atherosclerosis cases "are evidently caused by an infection with the CP bacterium."

That's right, CP is as serious as a heart attack. The *New York Times* of July 15, 1997 reports that high CP levels created a four times greater risk for cardiac arrest. Scientists are even more convinced, because antibiotic treatment practically eliminated chance for another heart attack.

The July 15, 1997 American Heart Association journal, *Circulation*, explains the theory. Remember our first white blood cells, or monocytes, on the scene of the injury of the vessel? According to vessel inflammation expert, Valentin Fuster, these cells are also designed to "root out blood-borne infection at early stages." CP has found out how to cheat our hearts, as *Circulation* states, by turning "a monocyte into live 'ammunition' for clot formation."

The helpful white blood cell becomes a Trojan Horse. It arrives at the damage with CP as an unwanted passenger, which deposits itself along with the monocyte. The body senses more trauma from the bacteria's presence. So, it sends more monocytes to help. The cells build up, plugging the flow of blood over time, leading to a heart attack.

As R. Wayne Alexander, chief cardiologist at Emory University told the *Washington Post*, "It's really a major shift in the way we think about heart attacks." Thanks to the link of the heart attack bug, we can now understand how a marathon runner can die of a couch potato disease.

Finally, let's view some of the implications this finding has for the future of hearts everywhere. We will see that the discovery will help in early detection and treatment, but we will also note that there is still more to be done in the war against heart disease.

Initially, the CP/heart attack relationship will help doctors detect the possibility of a heart attack, sometimes years in advance. As the *Doctor's Guide* website reports on December 10, 1996, a new test with "over 90 % reliability" in diagnosing CP is being marketed. This is especially important, according to the August 11, 1997 *Newsweek*, because "arterial disease may kill you in a minute, but it usually develops over a lifetime."

Because it is a bacteria, early treatment with antibiotics after early detection could reduce the risk of a heart attack. However, as one doctor told the *World Press Review*, "nothing could be more dangerous than... handing out antibiotics blindly." An antibiotic-resistant strain of CP could have worse consequences than more heart attacks. Because the bug also causes respiratory problems, scientists need to be especially careful in antibiotic treatment.

The key, then, may be an anti-inflammation drug instead: perhaps one which doctors already have—aspirin. As the *Wall Street Journal* of April 3, 1997, explains, anti-inflammatory drugs more fine-tuned and powerful than aspirin may be developed to stop inflammation caused by CP. If we know the bacteria's there, we can work to stop our body's reaction to it.

Another thing to keep in mind, though, as heart researcher, Dr. Sandeep Gupta, admits in *Heart* of January, 1997, "the atherosclerosis link between chlamydia and heart disease has yet to be verified." To do so, Gupta recommends "prospective vaccination and antibiotic" trials. Sometimes, these trials take considerable time.

So, if you think that protecting yourself from sneezes is all you need for a healthy heart, think again. CP may be a risk factor, like smoking or a sedentary lifestyle. But risk factors are extremely complex and intertwined. As *Newsweek* of August 11, 1997, suggests, we all need to limit fat, cholesterol, smoking, and become more physically active.

Heart disease is like a dangerous lottery—we don't know the combination that will guarantee the deadly prize. However, with the information we have gained today, we can take our health into our own hands. We have unraveled the mysteries of heart attacks, became more familiar with the heart attack bug and its place in the heart attack, and discussed some implications this finding has for the future of hearts everywhere.

Many people valiantly graze through the twigs and grass of the salad bar for its health benefits, no matter how it tastes. But with the awareness of chlamydia pneumoniae and its relation to heart attacks, we know there's really only one good reason to avoid the low fat oasis—if it doesn't have a sneeze guard.

CHAPTER 8

THE SPEECH TO PERSUADE

Time limits: 5-6 minutes.

Speaking notes: 75-word maximum limit.

Sources of information: Two are required, preferably three. For each source give the specific magazine, book, or Internet site it was taken from, title of the article, author's full name, date of publication, and the chapter or pages telling where the material was found. If a source is a person, identify the source completely by title, position, occupation, etc. List these on the outline form. For Internet sites give the address (URL).

Outline your speech: Prepare a 75-150 word complete sentence outline.

Question: Should a speaker talk down to an audience?

Answer: Never. Use understandable, non-technical language. Audiences are intelligent.

Key Words:
Debatable proposition
Emotion
Evidence
Logic

Student Expectations: In completing this assignment each student will:
> *Identify a debatable proposition and adopt a position on it*
> *Understand the use of evidence, reasoning, and emotion to convince another*
> *Organize arguments for clarity and maximum impact on listeners*

PURPOSE OF THIS ASSIGNMENT

A speech to persuade is used so widely that we are probably unaware of its frequency. Actually, very few persons do what someone else suggests unless they are convinced. The most common method used in convincing someone is a system of talking. The pattern of ideas employed is not always known to the person who uses it, but generally, the speaker uses certain techniques to gain conviction.

It is probable that you will be asked to present ideas and arguments at some future date. When this time arrives, you will find it a much easier task once you have practice in the art of convincing an audience.

EXPLANATION OF THE SPEECH TO PERSUADE

The speech to persuade is one which causes the audience to change, adopt, modify, or continue a belief or action. You must present sufficient logic and evidence to swing the audience to your position on a **debatable proposition**. This usually means that you will also ask them to take the action which you suggest. It is usually wise and necessary to appeal to emotions that accompany attitudes and decisions which you desire from your audience. These basic emotions may be reached by certain basic appeals to needs and desires such as, wealth, love of country, self-preservation, desire for recognition, desire for new adventure, loyalty, political beliefs, religion, and the like. This necessitates a thorough analysis of your audience so that you may base your appeal on their beliefs and attitudes. It also means that you must present your logic and evidence in such a way that it directs the audience's thinking through channels they readily follow.

The speech to convince is utilized on many kinds of occasions. At most popular gatherings, such as political meetings, lecture forums, charity drives, community drives, church services, and other civic gatherings, an effort is made to convince. Business meetings involve conviction any time differences of opinion prevail. Decisions are reached by persuading someone. Any time that a debate is in progress, be it a formal argument between two rival schools, within a legislative body, among three friends, or in court proceedings—the statements of the speakers involve persuasion through **logic**, **evidence**, and **emotion**. (Could it be that the last time you asked your parents for a special type of clothes you gave a most convincing argument containing much logic, considerable evidence, and some emotion by stating why you should have it?)

HOW TO CHOOSE A PERSUASIVE TOPIC

Examine the topics on this page. If you do not select one of them, be extremely careful in the choice of a topic of your own. The points to watch are the ways you word your topic and what you propose to persuade your audience to believe. In wording your topic *be sure* you propose to your audience that they *should* adopt a certain debatable proposition. For example, if you decide to convince your listeners that "All school books should be free," notice the word "should." It implies "ought to be." So your purpose is to persuade your audience *to believe* this is a sound idea and it will be beneficial *if carried out*. You are not asking them to carry it out by standing behind a book counter and handing out free textbooks.

A *sales talk* is not appropriate for this assignment because its purpose is to make your listeners reach down in their pocket, pull out money, and give it to you. This *requires* them to do something. Naturally a certain amount of convincing will precede your request for money, but the *actual purpose* is to cause them to hand you the dollars. This type of speech is discussed in Chapter 13. We may conclude then that a speech *to convince* is not a sales talk, it is not primarily to motivate to action, but it is one in which your purpose is to *change a person's mind* about something on which there is definite disagreement.

Your topic must be a proposition which is specific and which offers a debatable solution to a controversial problem. It is not adequate to propose the subject "We should all drive more carefully." We agree on this already. If you wish to do something to make us more *careful drivers*, suggest a definite and debatable *solution*, such as: "The legislature should pass a law limiting speed on the highways to sixty miles per hour," or "All persons who are convicted of traffic violations should be compelled to attend a driver's school for two weeks." These are proposals about which people disagree. We can readily say *yes* or *no* to them. We can *debate* them, but we cannot debate the subject that "We should all drive more carefully," since we agree on it. Examine your topic closely to be certain you have a correct topic on which to base your speech to convince. If you are in doubt, consult your instructor.

SOME TOPIC POSSIBILITIES

Raising Teenage Driving Age
Rock Lyrics
Juvenile Crime
Affirmative Action
Drug Education
American Values
Vegetarianism
Campaign Finance Reform
Immigration Laws
TV and Movie Violence
Population Control
AIDS Education
Multilingual Education

HOW TO PREPARE A SPEECH TO PERSUADE

In preparing the speech to persuade remember that your purpose is to swing people over to your beliefs. This is obviously not an easy task; however, it is not at all impossible.

To achieve the "convincing effect," you need to look carefully into the organization of your speech. Briefly, it may be as follows:

1. *Present a history of the problem.* Discuss the events leading up to the present time that make the topic important. Tell why it is significant that the audience hear the discussion you are about to present. (Do not spend too much time on the history—you have other points to cover.)

2. *Discuss the present day effects of the problem.* Give *examples, illustrations, facts,* and *views of authorities* that clearly demonstrate the situation you are talking about. These are *musts* if you wish to be convincing.

3. *Discuss the causes that brought about the effects you listed in point 2.* Here again you must present *examples*, illustrations, facts, and views of authorities to prove your points. Be sure you show how the causes have and are bringing about the effects you mentioned. For example, if you say your car died (effect) because of a blowout (cause) you must definitely establish this *cause* rather than permit your audience to believe that the car *may* have died because the steering mechanism on the car suddenly broke.

4. *List possible solutions to the problem.* Discuss briefly the various alternatives that could be followed but show they are not effective enough to solve your problem. *Give evidence for your statements: examples, illustrations, authorities' views, facts, and analogies.*

5. *Give your solution to the problem.* Show why your solution is the best answer to the proposition you are discussing. *Present your evidence and the reason for believing as you do.* This must not be simply your opinions. It must be logical reasoning backed up by evidence.

6. *Show how your proposal will benefit your audience.* This is the real meat of your entire speech if you have thoroughly fulfilled each preceding step up to this point. Here is that part of your speech where you must convince. You definitely have to show your listeners how they will benefit from your proposals. For example: How they will make more

money, how they will be safer from an enemy, how they will live longer, how they will be happier, how

Environmental issues such as recycling are popular topics for persuasive speeches.

they will get better roads, better schools, lower taxes, cheaper groceries. . . In other words, your listener must see clearly and vividly that your proposal will help *them*.

If you do not care to follow the preceding organization of a speech to convince, here is one which accomplishes the same end but is described differently:

1. State your proposition in the introduction.

2. Present a history of the problem which brought up the proposal you are asking for adoption.

3. Show that your proposal is *needed*. Offer evidence which establishes a *need* for *your* proposal. No other proposal (solution) will do.

4. Show that your proposition is *practical*. Give evidence to prove that it will do what you say it will do. In other words, show that it will work.

5. Show that your proposition is *desirable*. This means to give evidence showing that what it will do will be *beneficial* rather than harmful. For example: Concerning the desirability of gun control legislation say, "Even though the Constitution guarantees citizens the right to bear arms, children must be protected from having easy access to weapons because too many innocent lives have been lost."

6. Conclude your speech with a final statement in support of your proposal.

Note: If you are opposed to a certain proposal, you may establish your point of view by offering arguments which show any one of the following to be true:

1. The proposition is not needed. (Give evidence.)
2. The proposition is not practical. (Give evidence.)
3. The proposition is not desirable. (Give evidence.)

Of course, if you can establish all three of these points, you will be more convincing than if you prove only one.

You should be warned that you will face untold difficulty from your audience if you fail to have the body of your speech properly organized and all your points supported by evidence. The best guarantee of success is careful preparation. In addition to a well-organized speech with its points supported by evidence, you must have a well-constructed introduction and a powerful conclusion. Besides these considerations in relation to the materials of the speech itself, your oral practice will determine whether or not you are actually prepared to present a convincing speech. Even though you possess volumes of evidence, clear-cut organization, and vivid language, *you must deliver the speech confidently and well*, without excessive use of notes if anyone is to be convinced that you yourself are convinced of your own proposal.

Materials for preparing your subject can be secured from your library. Encyclopedias, reader's guides, magazine and newspaper guides all offer excellent sources. Check with your instructor and librarian for assistance.

HOW TO PRESENT A SPEECH TO PERSUADE

In general a frank, enthusiastic, and energetic presentation is desirable. A reasonable amount of emotion should be evident; however, it should not be overdone. Your bodily action should suit the words you utter and be such an integral part of your overall presentation that no attention is directed toward it. Vigor and intensity should characterize your bodily action. You must show by your actions that *you* are convinced. Your voice should reflect a sincere belief in your views, and through inflections and modulations, carry the ring of truth and *personal conviction*. Sufficient force should be utilized to convey sound and meaning to all who listen.

Naturally, your presentation must vary according to your audience, the occasion, the size of the room, its acoustics, and the type of meeting before which you present your speech. You would not speak to a small group of business people in the same manner that you would address a large political gathering.

If you use notes, know them thoroughly. Do not try to hide them. Hold them high enough when looking at them that your head is not bowed or place them on the podium. After the conclusion of your talk, remain standing at least two to three seconds before you return to your seat. Check with your instructor to see if there will be time to take questions.

How Can I Organize a Persuasive Speech?

Persuasive speeches may be logically ordered in any of the following ways:

1. Problem – Solution
2. Reasons to Support the Proposition
3. Cause – Effect(s)
4. Motivated Sequence (See Chapter 9 for details on this.)

WE NEED A BEREAVEMENT CENTER
A speech to persuade by Meghan Ortego

Dan McFeeley, writing for the *Indianapolis Business Journal* stated, "Thousands of kids across the country are forced every year to deal with the untimely death of a father, mother, sister, or even a close friend."

At Baker University, many students and faculty members have lost a loved one and have had nowhere to turn for comfort. A support group is very much needed to help individuals cope with loss. With the implementation of a bereavement program, faculty members and students would have a support system that they can turn to.

Less than three months ago, my father unexpectedly passed away, and I am currently enrolled in a bereavement program called the Solace House. Today I am going to show you the need for a bereavement program at Baker and a proposed solution.

First of all, how many of you know the definition of "bereavement"? I have said this word many times and yet many people don't know what it is. Bereavement is suffering the loss of a loved one, whether it is through divorce or death.

While being at college and away from your family which is your ultimate support system, it is harder for students to cope with problems such as death. Having a campus support system would give students and faculty a place to turn to.

You would not believe how many of us are affected by death: My father recently passed away. Another student, Nicole, also had her father pass away a few weeks ago. Dr. Emel told us today that she has a funeral to attend after this class. And I'm sure all of you remember Bree who passed away this last fall. In some way we are all affected by death.

I contacted Head Quarters, which is a twenty-four hour crisis hot line, to see where the closest bereavement center is. The closest center is twenty minutes away in Lawrence. I strongly feel the need for a facility here in Baldwin where students will have easier access.

Bereavement is a positive process; it is not meant to be bad. Bereavement is meant to help the individual cope with death, accept death and keep on living. It is a healing process.

If the bereavement process is not supported, the individual becomes depressed. In the *Solace House Quarterly* newsletter it is stated that when individuals don't have a source of support, they turn toward "self-destructive forms of expressing their grief, which lead to depression, anti-social behaviors, physical complications and lack of family communication." In other words, they shut themselves off and become dysfunctional to society.

Now that I've told you how important this need is, let's look at a solution to the problem. My idea of a bereavement center here at Baker is modeled after the Solace House. Meetings would be one day every other week, and trained volunteers would help individuals in a group setting. They are not there to tell individuals what to do, and how to do it, but to guide and listen.

When you have lost someone, the most comforting thing is just to have someone listen to you. Volunteers at the bereavement center help you go through problems you are experiencing now, and prepare you for future obstacles that individuals will have to face. They help you accept death and not to be angry and deny it.

Speaking with students on campus, I have found that many see the need for a bereavement program. Reghan, who was a cheerleader with Bree stated that, "Finding support and having someone understand what you are going through always makes it easier to cope and share feelings." I believe that it is very important for the individual to feel comfortable.

You may be wondering why a bereavement program is needed when our campus already makes a counselor available to us. I honestly would not get the same benefits from one-on-one counseling as I would from group counseling. With group sessions an individual is able to inter-act with others who have had the same experiences. It allows the individual to see that they are not the only one going through this, but that other people are going through it, too.

(Show a picture of Bree, a Baker student who passed away, and a picture of my siblings.) In closing, I want to note that Bree used to watch my siblings over the summer. Mallory, my younger sister, was really attached to her. So not only did she lose her favorite baby-sitter, but a father (Show picture of Dad). I want to share with you an excerpt from a story my younger sister wrote shortly after my father's death, entitled, "My Father's Ending":

"When we were at the hospital all I was thinking was is he going to die? Is he to be hooked up to machines all the rest of his life? Will he still be athletic? Those were all of the questions that were running through my head all at once. Later during the night around 8:50 my sister and I went to go see my dad. We were almost to the door and then all of a sudden over the intercom we hear CODE BLUE which means someone's heart has stopped. When we heard that, me and my sister started crying so hard and hugging my mom and crying on her shoulder. They told us to wait. So we did. We waited about 20 minutes and then one of the doctors came in and said, 'Well, Terri, I'm sorry, but he died.' We all started crying because everyone in that room loved him in a different way."

Losing a loved one is unavoidable, but how we treat the bereavement process can be changed. A support group is very much needed to help individuals cope with loss. After speaking to individuals on campus who have lost loved ones, the majority agreed that a support group is needed. Faculty, such as Rev. Ira DeSpain, would be "pleased to facilitate" such a group.

The first step would be an initial meeting with Student Senate to present a petition requesting the program. Your support would be greatly appreciated in signing the petition and attending such a meeting with the Student Senate. Thank you.

9

THE SPEECH TO MOTIVATE

Time limits: 4-5 minutes.

Speaking notes: 50-word maximum limit.

Sources of information: Two are required, preferably three. For each source give the specific magazine, book, or Internet site it was taken from, title of the article, author's full name, date of publication, and the chapter or pages telling where the material was found. If a source is a person, identify the source completely by title, position, occupation, etc. List these on the outline form. For Internet sites give the address (URL).

Outline your speech: Prepare a 75-150 word complete sentence outline.

Question: Should a speech be long or short?

Answer: Speeches today seem to be growing shorter. Leave an audience wanting more rather than having had too much.

Key Words:
Action
Attention
Need
Satisfaction
Visualization

Student Expectations: In completing this assignment each student will:
> ➤ *Identify speaking strategies that stimulate listeners to action*
> ➤ *Understand the role of emotional appeals in motivation*
> ➤ *Select appropriate language for vividness to motivate the audience*
> ➤ *Organize ideas in a manner that builds enthusiasm in listeners*

PURPOSE OF THIS ASSIGNMENT

It is an accepted truth that people need to be stimulated or aroused if they are to be concerned about a proposition or problem that is laid before them. Often a speaker appeals to the audience to do something, to change their minds, to give consideration to an idea, but does not stir them sufficiently to make them willing to be more than mildly interested. As a speaker it is to your advantage to learn the methods and approaches that cause audiences to be stimulated by speech. This assignment will provide an experience for the speech to motivate so that you will be fully aware of the importance of this type of speech.

EXPLANATION OF THE SPEECH TO MOTIVATE

The speech to motivate an audience is one that does just that—it stimulates some action. It makes people want to do something, perhaps generalized, to correct a problem, although a specific action may not be in mind. If its purpose is fulfilled, it touches the emotions and influences the intellect of the audience sufficiently that they feel impelled to adopt new attitudes and/or take action suggested by the speaker. The basic features of this speech are these: use of vivid language, obvious sincerity and enthusiasm on the part of the speaker, and appeals to basic drives that all persons possess. Much of the persuasion is achieved by utilizing catchy slogans, concreteness, specific examples, illustrations, and facts. Contrast is stressed by playing the big against the little, the bad against the good, the money that can be earned against that which will not be earned, the sick against the well.

Best known occasions for the speech to motivate are anniversary memorials, dedications, commencement exercises, religious gatherings, conventions, rallies, pep meetings, sales promotions, and between-halves situations in which a coach arouses the team to a high pitch of fury accompanied by a will to win.

The speech demands that the speaker be aroused and vigorous. It calls for enthusiasm, energy, force, power, and spirit—the quantity and quality depending upon the response sought from the audience. But most of all it requires that the speaker be sincere.

HOW TO CHOOSE A TOPIC TO MOTIVATE AN AUDIENCE

Regardless of what kind of speech you present, it should always possess *sincerity*. Of all the many kinds of speeches there is none that demands sincerity from the speaker more than the speech that is intended to motivate. Therefore, in choosing a topic from the above list or in formulating your own topic, place sincerity foremost in your thinking. Do not try to find a subject that is suitable for the national congress or for presentation over a national radio network. Find a discussion suitable for your audience, in this case, your classmates. It

Coaches use many principles of motivational speaking.

does not have to be something big, something startling or overwhelming. The occasion does not call for such a speech. It does call for a speech appropriate to your situation, your audience, one within the scope of your experiences, and, above all, one in which you are sincere.

SOME TOPIC POSSIBILITIES
Volunteer Your Time
Time Management
Join a School Club
Show Respect to Your Classmates
Change Your Eating Habits
Stop Procrastinating
Cut Back on TV Viewing
Stop Smoking
Exercise to Be Healthy
Be Responsible Behind the Wheel
Learn a Foreign Language

HOW TO PREPARE A SPEECH TO MOTIVATE
Basically, you will prepare this speech according to the steps followed in preparing any speech. It is essential that you give more than passing attention to your purpose to stimulate or arouse. This purpose will be behind every statement you utter. It will be superimposed over your entire construction; hence, it will receive first consideration.

Having made yourself keenly aware of your purpose, you will next set about achieving this purpose. Naturally, your attention turns to organization. We will assume that you have gathered your materials and are ready to arrange them in a logical way that makes it easy for your audience to follow your thoughts. In *The Speech to Motivate*, a key five-point strategy of organization developed by Alan Monroe is a popular format for these purposes. First, look through your materials for an attention-grabbing story or statistic and use this to create an introduction that gets your audience's **attention** as well as reveals the topic.

Second, develop the sense of **need** by explaining why there is a problem or why something needs to be done. Be sure to use plenty of illustrations to help your audience understand the full scope of the problem at hand.

Third, provide **satisfaction** for the problem by offering a solution that will eliminate the need you have just explained. Give enough details about the solution so that the audience can thoroughly see how it will be applied and how it will stop the problem.

Fourth, help the audience envision what it would be like if they did what you ask. **Visualization** is the art of painting a verbal picture in the audience's mind showing how things will be better if they take the action you recommend, or how things will be much worse if they do not.

Finally, explain to the audience what specific **action** they can take to solve the problem. Be as specific as possible and give your audience any information you have that will make it easier for them to take the action requested. Conclude by reviewing the problem and the solution and directly calling upon the audience to take the requested action. Psychological unity is provided if you can tie your closing lines to the attention-getter used in the introduction.

You will also be concrete and specific by naming certain persons and definite places that the speech calls for. You will avoid the abstract and intangible when giving examples, illustrations, and facts. This does not mean that you are to employ needless detail, but it does mean that your ideas must be aimed to hit their mark and make a strong impact. If you do not do this, it will be like trying to drive a spike with a tack hammer. And last, you will stimulate your audience, because throughout your entire speech you will have appealed to the basic drives in people— security from enemies, saving or making money, keeping their homes intact, gaining recognition, enjoying social prominence, having a cleaner city or town, an dknowing new experiences. You will have touched your listeners' pride, their pocketbooks and bank accounts, their sympathies, their families—yes, even their fighting spirit. Once you have stimulated your audience, be sure to tell them what action to take whether it be to think or to perform. If you do not do this, you will have generated power, but failed to use it.

The last step in preparing this speech will be rehearsal. Be sure you rehearse enough that you know from memory the sequence of ideas, not words, that you plan to present. Practice before a mirror and/or friends until you feel competent to stand before an audience.

HOW TO PRESENT A SPEECH TO MOTIVATE

A forceful, dynamic, and energetic presentation should be used unless you are speaking on a solemn occasion involving reverence, devotion or deep feeling. In such cases your voice and manner should be animated and sincere with projection of your ideas accompanied by appropriate bodily action and gestures. On other occasions, indications should show that you are alive with your subject, full of it, and eager for others to share it. Above all, you must be sincere and earnest. Remember that your audience will reflect your activity and eloquence. They will be just as lively or solemn as you stimulate them to be. The use of appropriate diagrams, charts, and demonstrations can add much to your speech.

AN EXPLOSIVE NIGHTMARE
by Robyn Long

Crezencia Antonio is the oldest of twelve children living in Southern Angola. In 1994, just yards from her home, Crezencia lost her leg, a portion of her face, and her hope—to a landmine. Landmines are small, indiscriminate weapons triggered to explode and maim people and machinery.

President Clinton is gravely mistaken in refusing to sign the Anti-Personnel Landmine Treaty, and it is the responsibility of Americans to encourage him to reconsider his position.

Throughout my research, I have encountered story after story about children who lose their lives and their futures, and countries ripped apart by the indiscriminate landmine. As we become more of a globalized society, each of us is realizing the impact of what happens around the world on our own lives. Likewise, it is in our best interests as humanitarians to encourage President Clinton to sign the treaty banning landmines.

In the next few minutes, I hope to warn each of you of the dangers of landmines, their devastating impact on our world, and encourage you to take action to convince President Clinton that his reasoning is incorrect in his refusal to sign the treaty.

First, landmines present many unintended dangers. They are cheap and dirty weapons, hidden to be effective, and are responsible for the end of innocent, civilian lives after the war is over. According to the International Committee of the Red Cross, since 1939, over four hundred million landmines have been placed in over sixty countries in the world.

Similarly, the United Nations reports that over one hundred million of these landmines are still active, the majority of which are in heavily populated areas. Nine out of ten mine victims are civilians, the majority injured or killed after the war is over.

In our President's own words, twenty-five thousand people are killed each year by landmines, one every fifteen minutes. For a weapon designed to protect lives, it is apparent that the mines have failed miserably.

Second, landmines have a frighteningly negative impact on our world, both directly and indirectly.

Many landmines are planted in farm fields, which makes is difficult if not impossible to cultivate the fields for food. This creates malnutrition and hunger in nearby villages. In Afghanistan and Cambodia, thirty-five percent of the land is unusable due to landmines.

Also related, and apologies to those I offend, many people in these areas have traditionally used these fields for their toilets. Now, due to the threat on their lives, they stay close to homes and waste builds up, harboring many diseases, such as bacterial diarrhea. Thus, water is contaminated and even firewood is a threat.

Additionally, because landmine injuries are so devastating, blood transfusions are often necessary. Countries infested with landmines rarely have adequate medical resources to treat patients, and blood cleanliness is the last of their concerns. In turn, HIV and other blood diseases spread quickly. Further, roads coming into these devastated areas are mined, so famine relief teams and immunization and health care groups cannot risk their own lives to get in.

Finally and most importantly, landmines have not been adequately considered since their conception. As I previously mentioned, they are a "cheap" weapon when you consider their original cost, roughly three dollars per mine. However, the cost to remove a mine is three thousand dollars. Clearly, in the long term, they are not the most cost-effective weapon.

In spite of these facts, President Clinton has not sided with the one hundred and twenty-five other countries who have agreed to sign this treaty. It was this past Wednesday, December 3, that these countries met to sign a treaty that aims to destroy stockpiles of mines within the next four years and to remove deployed mines within the next decade.

It is my hope that I have convinced you to take action by showing the effects, devastation, and senselessness of landmines. There are dozens of organizations that could use your support such as the Red Cross and the Humanitarian Foundation of People Against Landmines. Also, please contact your Senators and Representatives. To quote Shabban Yakkoot, and eleven-year-old girl orphaned by landmines, "I hate landmines; they are ripping our world apart."

10

A SPEECH TO GAIN GOODWILL WITH A DISAGREEING AUDIENCE

Time limits: 6-7 minutes.

Speaking notes: Key words only.

Sources of information: To build and maintain credibility you must use as many outside sources as possible, while still presenting your perspective on the issue. For each source give the specific magazine, book, or Internet site it was taken from, title of the article, author's full name, date of publication, and the chapter or pages telling where the material was found. If the source is a person, identify the source completely by full name, title or position, occupation, etc. List these on the outline form. For Internet sites give the address (URL).

Outline your speech: Prepare a 75-150 word complete

Question: How long does it take to prepare a good five-minute speech?

Answer: Three to five hours would not be too much. Short speeches require proportionately more preparation time than long speeches because they must be more succinct.

Key Words:
Common values
Counterarguments
Goodwill

Student Expectations: In completing this assignment each student will:
➢ *Present ideas to a disagreeing audience in a clear manner*
➢ *Understand the role of shared values in developing goodwill with an audience*
➢ *Anticipate and refute counterarguments*
➢ *Determine a respectful approach to speaking to disagreeing audiences*

PURPOSE OF THIS ASSIGNMENT

Facing an audience that does not agree with your position on a particular issue may seem a daunting task, but there are several things you can do to present your ideas to such a group in order to get as fair a hearing as possible. A second objective in giving such a speech is to establish and build a relationship of goodwill in order to leave open future possibilities for addressing this audience on this or other topics of concern to you. This assignment is designed to give you an opportunity to try your hand at such a challenge.

EXPLANATION OF A SPEECH TO GAIN GOODWILL WITH A DISAGREEING AUDIENCE

A speech to gain **goodwill** is one in which the purpose is to secure a favorable attitude toward the speaker (and the topic, if possible). Normally this would be a persuasive speech if presented to an agreeing or neutral audience. However, with a disagreeing audience, too much persuasiveness can serve only to strengthen the listeners' defensive tendencies and would be counterproductive to your cause. Therefore, the speech to gain goodwill with a disagreeing audience should be approached from the perspective of the informative speech, as you will want to inform the disagreeing audience of values you share with them as well as an explanation of how you have drawn a conclusion on the issue that is different from theirs.

HOW TO CHOOSE A TOPIC FOR A SPEECH TO GAIN GOODWILL WITH A DISAGREEING AUDIENCE

For this assignment you will need to select a topic that you feel strongly about, but find others frequently disagreeing with you when you bring it up. You may wish to do an informal, verbal survey of classmates to determine their perspectives on particular issues of interest to you. Or you may wish to select a topic with a particular disagreeing audience in mind, such as a topic on which you disagree with parents, teachers, or other groups you know. Consult with your instructor before finally choosing the topic you will work with for this assignment.

Some examples of topics for this speech might include: speaking to parents about the disadvantages of curfews; speaking to teachers about the disadvantages of assigning grades; speaking to lawmakers about legalizing marijuana for medical purposes; or, taking one side or the other in the debate over physician-assisted suicide.

HOW TO PREPARE A SPEECH TO GAIN GOODWILL WITH A DISAGREEING AUDIENCE

First of all, remember that your purpose is to gain goodwill and that you will want to do this primarily through an informational approach to the speech. As soon as you have selected your topic, you will need to begin to gather materials of support for your position on the issue. These supporting materials must come from sources your disagreeing audience will respect—usually persons who are widely known as experts in the field, institutions that do not have a financial interest in the issue one way or the other, and news outlets that are known for their objectivity.

After you have gathered your materials, carefully select the information that will support your point of view, and provide basic information on the topic to the audience in a clear manner. Look for particularly vivid examples, stories, or statistics that illustrate your points. Narrow the issue down to the two or three main points you most want to make to your audience. Organize them logically so that the audience can easily anticipate the flow of your ideas in much the same way that you would for any informative speech.

Plan to begin the speech by finding something everyone can agree on. By establishing **common values** with your listeners, you can gain their sympathies because they can easily support *your* holding values *they* already hold. In this way you will begin the speech in good accord with your listeners and it will set a nice tone for them to follow you further through the rest of the ideas as you present them. However, you should be cautioned that this strategy will not have any effectiveness at all if the audience believes you are insincere in any way. In fact, an insincere attempt may cost you the bulk of your credibility with them.

A disagreeing audience is likely to be pondering **counterarguments** to your position as you speak. If their objections are well known and available in advance, it may be prudent to acknowledge them in your speech and take the opportunity to refute them or tell why you do not hold that position. However, if you have not thought through and researched them in advance, it can be unwise to toss them in at the last minute. If you do choose to address the counterarguments you are aware of, support them with outside sources as much as

U.S. Presidents are often faced with the need to gain goodwill.

possible to indicate that you are not the only one holding this position.

Conclude your speech with a review of the values you share with them and a brief statement of your position. Show your audience how those shared values can be most fully realized through the position you have taken.

HOW TO PRESENT A SPEECH TO GAIN GOODWILL WITH A DISAGREEING AUDIENCE

Do not expect to completely convert your audience. Set your goals toward establishing goodwill so that the dialogue on this topic may continue in any avenue possible. Above all, your audience must have the feeling that you are sincere and that you ultimately have their best interest at heart. Creating a sense of goodwill means that you seek a friendly, positive relationship with them even if you continue to disagree on this particular topic.

Deliver your speech with confidence, friendliness, good humor, and some amount of modesty. Do not take on an air of superiority in any way. Your audience must believe you will respect their views even if they are not willing to shift their position on the issue.

Dress respectfully for the occasion. Give attention to your posture. Be alert and eager to communicate. Avoid unnecessary formality. Speak clearly and loudly enough for all to hear. Body language and gestures are, as always, in order if used properly.

The Queen Elizabeth spoke to the nation live at 6.00 p.m. on Friday, 5 September, 1997 from the Chinese Dining Room at Buckingham Palace.

Since last Sunday's dreadful news we have seen, throughout Britain and around the world, an overwhelming expression of sadness at Diana's death.

We have all been trying in our different ways to cope. It is not easy to express a sense of loss, since the initial shock is often succeeded by a mixture of other feelings: disbelief, incomprehension, anger—and concern for those who remain. We have all felt those emotions in these last few days. So what I say to you now, as your Queen and as a grandmother, I say from my heart.

First, I want to pay tribute to Diana myself. She was an exceptional and gifted human being. In good times and bad, she never lost her capacity to smile and laugh, nor to inspire others with her warmth and kindness. I admired and respected her—for her energy and commitment to others, and especially for her devotion to her two boys. This week at Balmoral, we have all been trying to help William and Harry come to terms with the devastating loss that they and the rest of us have suffered.

No one who knew Diana will ever forget her. Millions of others who never met her, but felt they knew her, will remember her. I for one believe there are lessons to be drawn from her life and from the extraordinary and moving reaction to her death. I share in your determination to cherish her memory.

This is also an opportunity for me, on behalf of my family, and especially Prince Charles and William and Harry, to thank all of you who have brought flowers, sent messages and paid your respects in so many ways to a remarkable person. These acts of kindness have been a huge source of help and comfort.

Our thoughts are also with Diana's family and the families of those who died with her. I know that they too have drawn strength from what has happened since last weekend, as they seek to heal their sorrow and then to face the future without a loved one.

I hope that tomorrow we can all, wherever we are, join in expressing our grief at Diana's loss, and gratitude for her all-too-short life. It is a chance to show to the whole world the British nation united in grief and respect.

May those who died rest in peace and may we, each and every one of us, thank God for someone who made many, many people happy.

Text taken from www.royal.gov.uk/main/message.htm.

THE SPEECH TO ENTERTAIN

Time limits: 5-6 minutes.

Speaking notes: 10-15 word maximum limit.

Sources of information: Two are required, preferably three. For each source give the specific magazine, book, or Internet site it was taken from, title of the article, author's full name, date of publication, and the chapter or pages telling where the material was found. If a source is a person, identify the source completely by title, position, occupation, etc. List these on the outline form. For Internet sites give the address (URL).

Outline your speech: Prepare a 75-150 word complete sentence outline.

Question: Should a person learn to tell good jokes?

Answer: Yes. You will enjoy it and so will others.

Key Word:
Humor

Student Expectations: In completing this assignment each student will:
➢ *Understand the complexity of using humor in a speech*
➢ *Identify several strategies for making a speech humorous*
➢ *Plan and deliver a speech that both entertains and enlightens an audience*

PURPOSE OF THIS ASSIGNMENT

Many persons try to be entertaining when giving speeches. Some succeed and some do not. There is a common misconception about the difficulty of presenting a speech to entertain. The idea is current that the speech to entertain is a "breeze," that nothing is difficult about it, and that a series of risqué stories or jokes meet the requirements for a speech to entertain. This is far from the truth. A humorous speech is one of the most difficult to present effectively. Because of this difficulty and for the reason that you may be called at a future date to deliver a humorous speech, this assignment is presented.

EXPLANATION OF THE SPEECH TO ENTERTAIN

A speech to entertain utilizes **humor**. It may rely on words, anecdotes, bodily actions, gestures, voice, speech construction, special devices, demonstrations, unusual situations, pantomimes or a combination of any or all of these.

Its purpose varies both in relation to the amount and type of humorous response the speech is planned to elicit from the audience. Some speeches make listeners laugh gaily and loudly; others produce only chuckles and snickers; and others bring forth only grins and smiles of amusement. It is important for a student to understand that a humorous speech does not need to be uproariously funny to entertain. We might be better understood if we were to call this speech a speech to amuse.

The special feature of a humorous speech is that it does not demand that a speaker do more than catch the attention and interest of an audience and then hold these by developing a *trend of thought* or *an idea*. The speaker is not required to make the audience feel that they are closely related to the subject and that they must derive a moral or new philosophy from the remarks. Nor does the speaker have to ask them to take any action. It should be understood at this point, however, that a humorous speech *may* do more than simply entertain. There is nothing to prevent its being informative, stimulating, or convincing, provided none of these goals becomes the chief aim of the speaker. The chief aim of the speech is to entertain. The thought or ideas presented are the core of the speech around which humor is built. The overall effect is one in which the audience finds a definite trend of thought and philosophy presented delightfully and entertainingly.

Occasions for humorous speeches are found ordinarily at dinners, club meetings, special assemblies, parties, and gatherings at which weighty discussions are inappropriate and out of harmony with the mood of the occasion.

HOW TO CHOOSE A TOPIC FOR A SPEECH TO ENTERTAIN
In selecting a topic for a humorous speech, keep in mind the five necessary considerations that govern the selection of any speech topic. They are the audience, the occasion, the speaker, the speech itself, and the surroundings in which the speech will be given. Your choice of a topic must be keyed to controlling factors. It is important to note that you may have a mixed audience with a widespread interest or taste. You must consider the probable speaking environment. Of course, since you will be the speaker, the subject that you choose must be one which you can present acceptably.

The topic should be viewed from the standpoint of the time allowed for preparation, the availability of materials from which to build the speech, your own personality, your position in the community,

your ability to present certain kinds of material and ideas, and your type of presentation. You should make your choice of topic with all of these considerations in mind. The following topic ideas should stimulate your thinking.

SOME TOPIC POSSIBILITIES
Eavesdropping
Embarrassing Moment
School
Learning to Cook
Getting a Pet to the Vet
Finding an Old Diary
Parents
I Predict ...

HOW TO PREPARE A SPEECH TO ENTERTAIN
As in the preparation of any good speech, particular attention much be paid to organization of points, the arrangement of materials, and the rehearsal of the speech. The purpose, to entertain, should be clearly in mind; the purpose is assisted by a thorough understanding of the methods to be used for fulfilling this purpose (See list below.)

This type of speech requires a considerable study of references and some consultation with your instructor. In addition to the factors of good speech preparation previously studied, ample rehearsal is positively necessary. It is difficult to imagine anything more grotesque than a speaker's attempt to present a humorous speech and constantly referring to notes, because of inadequate preparation of the speech. Timing is important in securing a humorous response, and practice improves timing.

The humorous speech should not degenerate into a series of unrelated funny stories, nor should it merely consist of the telling of one story. Exaggerations or episodes used as illustrations must apply to the theme of the speech or in some way assist the speaker in making the point. Only careful preparation and rehearsal will assure one that they are using illustrations properly.

A few methods used to achieve humor are the following:

1. Telling a joke on oneself.
2. Telling a joke on someone in the group or some well-known person.
3. Making reference to the speech situation, local,

state, or national situation.

4. Making reference to the occasion or other occasions.
5. Associating a speech with past incidents.
6. "Panning" members of the group, local, state, national, or world figures.
7. Exaggeration.
8. Deliberate underestimation.
9. Sudden change of thought.
10. Surprise thoughts.
11. After-thoughts tacked to the end of an otherwise serious statement.
12. Twisting ideas (do not overdo this).
13. Misinterpreting facts or figures (be clever about this).
14. Intentionally making errors (this must be skillfully done).
15. Intentionally placing oneself in a humorous situation.
16. Misquoting someone present or a well-known authority (be discreet).
17. Restating a well-known quotation to give it a humorous twist.
18. Pantomime.
19. Gestures poorly timed or timed too late.
20. Facial grimaces.
21. Using anecdotes.
22. Giving examples that are entertaining or that make an amusing point.
23. Impersonating a character that is used as an illustration (do not make your whole speech an impersonation).
24. Demonstrating or dramatizing a point (do this for purpose of illustrating to achieve humor).
25. Clever wording (concoct new words, apply certain words to new situations or give them new meanings, join two or more words together with hyphens then apply them to your speech).
26. Be quick to adapt your opening remarks to slips of the tongue of other speakers. Do not overwork this device or it will become tiresome and trite; be appropriate.
27. Persons in public life, international situations, recent happenings in the news... all offer excellent opportunities for entertainment. Think about the strategies talk show hosts employ in their monologues.

In actually setting up the speech to entertain you will follow the principles laid down for any speech. You will construct a clever and interesting introduction. You will develop your remarks point by point in logical order. You will bolster these points with examples, illustrations, facts, quotations from authorities, analogies, and conclusions, which you will draw from the material you present. Lastly you will have a conclusion to your speech which is appropriate to all you have said. It becomes evident that a speech to entertain simply does what every other speech does, and in addition—this is important—it utilizes materials that in themselves carry and imply humor. The selection of these humorous materials, their arrangement in the speech, and the words used to present the ideas are what achieve the effect of entertainment.

Now, you ask, "How do I know my speech will be entertaining?" The answer is that you do not. The only assurance you can get is from your preparation. Frankly this is dependent entirely on your own effort and ability. It is difficult, very difficult, to select, to organize, to word, and to rehearse a speech to entertain, but you must do these preparations, nevertheless. Your own ingenuity and your own intelligence are the only assets you can have in preparing the humorous speech for presentation. Use these inherent personal resources well and you will have little to worry about. There simply is no quick, easy way to prepare an entertaining speech—or any other for that matter. Any student looking for a short cut, would be wise to end the search and to apply the time to preparation. That is what is necessary in the end anyway, if anything more than a mediocre speech is to be prepared for presentation.

Every speaker wants an audience to react to humor with laughter.

HOW TO PRESENT A SPEECH TO ENTERTAIN

The humorous speech is characterized generally by a lively presentation. The speaker may be whimsical, facetious, lighthearted, jovial, or may present a mixture of these moods. The speaker should be pleasant, of course. Bearing and decorum should reflect visibly the feelings and tenor of the remarks.

The speech should progress with a smooth forward motion. Delays and hesitations should be avoided, excepting those employed for a special effect. If laughter is incited, the speaker should carefully refrain from resuming the talk until that moment just before all laughter has stopped. Speakers should never laugh at their own jokes or indicate that they know they are funny. It is necessary, however, that the speaker obviously enjoys the audience and occasion. One of the greatest dangers is that the inexperienced speaker will prolong anecdotes, the jokes, or the whole speech. Try to hit the punch lines when they are hot and then move on to the next ones.

There is one last word of caution: watch your posture; use appropriate bodily actions and gestures; speak loudly enough to be heard by everyone; articulate well; and use good English.

THE PLIGHT OF THE ONION
A Speech to Entertain by John E. Koch

Ordinarily, Ladies and Gentlemen, I am a very peaceful individual. It requires an event of great importance to stir my peaceful nature. Lately, such an event has come to pass. I must speak out in defense of my convictions, for silence would prove me a traitor not only to my own generation, but to generations to come. I cannot display indifference when the issue demands enthusiasm.

Just what is this issue that stirs the hearts of men to take arms against that sea of troubles and by opposing, end them? I do not feel that I am unique in being affected by this onslaught on human liberty. You, ladies and gentlemen, have also been touched by this debasement of our customs and traditions. What is this menace of which I speak that poses such a threat to all that we hold so dear? Is it a green-eyed fire-spouting monster from Mars, or a creature from the moon? No, it is not. It is one of our own kind. It is referred to as a scientist.

It will suffice to mention no names since we must judge them by their works. The intrusion of these people on our liberties has caused many to sound the call to arms; for when we are enveloped by that sea of troubles, we must fight back or swim.

The scene of attack is Idaho State University. There, a group of scientists, as they call themselves, have been secretly experimenting, unbelievable as it may seem, to deprive the onion of its cooking odor. In some secret cache are hidden away thousands of odorless onions, the first line of odor-free American vegetables.

Picture the onion without its smell, and you deprive millions of Americans of a familiar fragrance that signals the secrets of the coming meal. To remove its odor is to destroy all that is dear to it—its personality. The thought is enough to bring tears to one's eyes.

Although this is bad enough, the scientists will not stop here. They will not remain content with having removed the odor from the onion, but with their long tentacles they will reach out farther into the realm of life. What will be next—the smell of cooking cabbage, the grit of spinach, the hot of peppers, and soon the removal of color and taste? Will our diet become a mass of odorless, tasteless, colorless nourishment? It might, if we do not arise and take arms to prevent this calamity. I beg you to rally defenders to the cause of the onion.

As Americans, we must demand the onion *with* its odor, the spinach *with* its grit, the pepper *with* its hot. Let us not sit here idly any longer. Arise and carry that plea to all Americans. Keep the scientist out of the kitchen; keep the onion out of the college.

HOW SHOULD MY SPEECH BE ORGANIZED?

Speeches for purposes other than persuading or motivating may be organized in the following ways:

1. *Chronologically.* Arrange the information according to how it happened in time.
2. *Topically.* Arrange the information according to the different topics you will cover.
3. *Spatially.* Arrange the information how it physically appears in a certain space.
4. *Problem/solution.* Present the problem, then the possible solutions to the problem.
5. *Cause/effect.* Identify the cause of something, and then identify its effect.

IMPROMPTU SPEAKING

Time limits: 2-3-4 and 5 minutes. (Start with two minutes. Increase the length of speeches until a student can talk five minutes.)

Speaking notes: During the first two experiences you may use notes which designate a "method." After this, memorize your method and apply it as you speak.

Question: Is impromptu (unprepared) or extemporaneous speech (well prepared but not memorized) more effective?

Answer: The extemporaneous speech (well prepared but not memorized) is the most effective known.

Key Words:
Impromptu
Poise

Student Expectations: In completing this assignment each student will:
➤ *Experience the challenges of unprepared discourse*
➤ *Prepare a strategy for dealing with the need to speak on the spur of the moment*
➤ *Practice organizing ideas quickly for clear communication*
➤ *Develop composure for speaking in a challenging setting*

PURPOSE OF THIS ASSIGNMENT

This speech experience is for the purpose of further enlarging your speech knowledge. It is to expose you to impromptu speaking and to provide you with a basic acquaintance with the difficulties and nature of unprepared discourse. Many students assume that impromptu speaking is easy. Nothing could be further from the truth. In reality impromptu speaking is extremely difficult. It is used effectively only by experienced speakers. There are methods, however, which if properly used, will enable you to perform acceptably on the spur of the moment. This assignment will assist you in learning these methods.

EXPLANATION OF IMPROMPTU SPEAKING

Impromptu speaking is giving an unprepared talk. A person simply takes the floor, selects a subject, and begins. Various methods are used to conduct impromptu expression. A common procedure is one in which the speaker takes the floor after being asked to talk on a certain subject about which something may or may not be known. This is another method: one topic is suggested by each of several persons in the audience; a few seconds are permitted the speaker to choose a topic from the list of topics suggested; and then the speaker begins the presentation. Differences in the manner of selecting a topic are many; however, with any system, one fundamental principle is that the ideas voiced are unrehearsed and unprepared.

The purpose of presenting the speech is the same as that for any other type of speaking. The distinctive feature is the unprepared delivery and the suddenness with which a person is confronted with a speech situation. Impromptu speaking is often required at those times when a person is called upon without warning "to say a few words" at a luncheon, special meeting, social gathering, or other occasion.

SUGGESTED TOPICS FOR IMPROMPTU SPEECHES

Write three suggestions on a paper. They should be suitable to those who will be asked to use them as subjects. Avoid those such as: "What Did You Do Last Night?" or "A Trip to Yellowstone Park." Your instructor will ask you to supply a topic from time to time as needed during the class. Examples of suitable topics for impromptu speaking are: dancing, movies, what is your opinion about (1) recycling, (2) minimum wages, (3) state operated lotteries, (4) traffic laws, (5) music videos.

HOW TO CHOOSE A TOPIC FOR IMPROMPTU SPEAKING

There is one general rule to follow in selecting a topic, if you have a choice. This rule is: choose the one on which you are best prepared to speak. Consider your audience and the occasion when you are making a choice of topic.

An impromptu topic on favorite pastimes might produce a speech on bicycling.

HOW TO PREPARE FOR AN IMPROMPTU SPEECH

Naturally you cannot prepare for an unknown topic, but you can prepare a method of attack on surprise offerings from your audience. One system of doing this is to have in mind various orders by which to develop your ideas.

One order might be the *time sequence* in which events occur by the hour, day, month, or year, moving forward or backward from a certain time. This example will illustrate the principle involved: Topic—Houses: (1) Give the history of houses from a definite date; (2) Tell in which part of the country houses were first built and their subsequent westward movement with time; (3) Describe how the styles of houses changed, over time.

A *space order* would take you from east to west, top to bottom, front to rear. For example, take the topic houses, then develop the speech in space order, giving the items in this way: (1) Specify the location of houses and their types, starting in California and traveling east; (2) Locate various types of houses found in a city, starting in urban setting and moving to the suburbs, (3) Describe houses according to locations in various parts of the world.

Using causal order, you might discuss certain forces and then point out the results which follow. Using houses: (1) Eskimos lived in igloos. Why? Give reasons (causes). Or you might mention that South Pacific islanders constructed grass and mud huts. Why? Give reasons (causes). (2) Prefabricated houses are now being built. Why? Give the causes that led to their development. (3) There are many hundreds of styles of houses of different architecture. Why? Give causes for this great diversification.

A topic order is one of your own devising. For example take the same topic—houses: (1) tell how to build a house or different kind of house. (2) give the legal aspects of house construction—such as, wiring, sewage disposal plants, plumbing, type of dwelling in restricted areas, distance from street, and (3) how to contract for house construction.

Another method which may be effective is given below. It should be kept in mind that any method you elect to use requires you to apply the method and keep their composure. Utilize only those portions of the organizational device which are adaptable to the particular speech, the occasion, the audience, and your own background and knowledge. You may find it necessary to literally memorize the points which follow. If you do this and then develop the topic in the order of the various headings, you will have a logical discussion and a successful impromptu speech.

I. Why is this topic important to your audience? To you?

II. Give a history of important events which will show the background and development of your subject.

III. What are the overall effects of your topic (such as, gambling) on your audience, the state, the nation, the world?

A. What are the geographic effects?
B. What are the political effects?
C. What are the economical effects?
D. What are the social effects?
E. What are the religious effects?
F. What are the educational effects?
G. What are the moral effects?
H. What are the psychological effects?

IV. What caused these effects? (Give as many causes as you can which will explain the effects you have enumerated. You may do this by discussing an effect and then by giving the cause of it immediately after.)

V. What are the different solutions to the problems? (You have told what is happening (effects) and you have told what brought them about (causes). Naturally, you must tell now what you propose to do about the problem or problems. Thus, you will have offered several different solutions.)

VI. Discuss the advantages and disadvantages of each solution you propose.

VII. Select one or two solutions which you think are best. Tell why they are best.

VIII. How do you propose to take action on these solutions? How may you and your audience go about putting your solutions into practice? Mention one or more ways to do this.

IX. Conclude your speech.

A. You may summarize.
B. You may appeal to your audience.
C. You may ask your audience to do a specific act.

Example:
Write to your congressman or congresswoman, Vote against_____,

HOW TO PRESENT AN IMPROMPTU SPEECH

In presenting an impromptu speech your attitude is a deciding factor in determining your effectiveness. First of all, you must maintain poise. It does not matter how surprised you are or how difficult your topic is. It does not make any difference what happens when you receive your subject, while you are speaking or after you have concluded your speech. You still must maintain poise. It is impossible to over-emphasize the importance of poise. Now you ask, how do you maintain poise? Here are a number of suggestions and answers: (1) Do not fidget around at your seat before you speak, just because you know you will soon be "on the spot." (2) When you are called on to speak, rise calmly and take your place before your audience. (3) If you know your topic when you take the platform, begin your remarks calmly, without hurrying (have some vigor and force), and be sure that you have a plan in mind by which you will develop your thoughts. Do not apologize to your audience in any way, by word or action. (4) If you do not know your topic when you rise to speak but are offered several choices after obtaining the floor, simply stand calmly before the group and listen carefully to the suggestions which are made. You should ask that a topic be repeated if you do not understand it. After you have received all of the proposed subjects, either stand calmly or walk calmly back and forth a few seconds while you decide which offering you will talk about. Ten seconds should be the maximum time taken to decide.

Once your selection is made, decide immediately what method or organizational pattern you will use in developing it. Organizational patterns should have been committed to memory before you ever attended class or placed yourself in a position where you might be asked to give an impromptu speech. After you have chosen your method of development, make your introductory remarks by telling why the subject is important to your listeners. When you begin to speak, do not make any apology of any sort.

In actually delivering an impromptu talk, it is wise not to start too fast but rather to pick up speed and power as you go along. Aside from this, you should observe bodily actions and gestures which are in keeping with the speech situation. Your voice should be filled with meaning and easily heard by all. Naturally, your articulation, pronunciation, and grammar will be of a high standard.

There is little to fear from impromptu speaking if you follow a preconceived method of attack on your subject. The way to do this is to refuse to allow yourself to become panicky, to recognize that some nervousness is a good sign of readiness, and to realize that your audience will expect nothing extraordinary. They, too, will know you are speaking impromptu. Actually, they will be "pulling for you." If you go about your task with poise and determination, your chances of success are exceedingly good. A well-rounded knowledge attained from a strong reading program will assist immeasurably.

WHAT SHOULD YOU KNOW ABOUT YOUR AUDIENCE?

Ask yourself these questions and then find the answers either through actual interviews or if that isn't possible make an educated guess.

1. Who will be in your audience? Classmate? Adults? Children?
2. What are the interests and past experiences of the audience members? How do they relate to your topic?
3. What do they already know about your topic?
4. Will they have any preconceived opinions about your topic?
5. How can you adapt your speech to make it interesting to the majority of your audience?

UNIT III

BUSINESS AND CAREER SPEAKING

A quick survey of job advertisements will reveal that one of the most sought-after qualities in the job market today is the ability to communicate well. This unit is designed to highlight some of the most important speaking and listening skills needed in the workplace today. Regardless of what career path you pursue, these skills will be the ones you will draw upon most frequently.

As noted in Unit Two, we are being bombarded with persuasion everywhere we go. In business settings, it is often in the form of an appeal to us to buy. For that reason, *The Sales Talk* is designed to focus your speaking practice on this very specific objective. In this chapter you will have the opportunity to actually attempt to sell a product to your audience. It will help make you aware of the necessary components for accomplishing that goal.

Many professions require the well-organized dissemination of information. One of the most effective ways to get large amounts of information out to a group of people is through *The Lecture Forum*. In this chapter, you will have the opportunity to provide new information to listeners, and then receive and respond to any additional questions the audience may have. Fielding questions is a challenging skill to develop because the speaker must provide direct answers that are genuine and based on sufficient knowledge. At the same time, a speaker must not attempt to "skirt" the questions if unsure of the answers by either ignoring the point of the question or by belittling the questioner. To do so comes at the high cost of alienating the audience by making them feel disrespected. In this chapter you should be able to see how such tensions arise, and to attempt to respond to those tensions creatively and sincerely.

Visual aids are always a bonus when making a presentation because so many audience members may be "visual learners," meaning they remember material best when it is put in visual forms. In today's world of high technology, hand drawn posters are no longer appropriate forms for visual aids. It is now so easy to prepare and display professional-looking visuals with computer graphics and fonts that the student must learn to take advantage of this technology in modern presentations. *Computer-Enhanced Presentations* describes examples of the available software programs that provide students with help in organizing their ideas in a clear manner, and with help in developing visual aids to enhance those ideas. This chapter invites you to explore those popular programs by creating a professionally designed presentation for the audience.

The most frequently used communication skill is the ability to listen, which means understanding the meanings of what you hear. Nowhere is this skill more critical than when you are in an interview situation. Interviews occur for many reasons such as to gather important information directly from an expert source, or to select an appropriate candidate for a particular position. In each of these cases, listening is the central feature that allows the clearest exchange of the vital information being sought. The chapter on *The Interview* provides several different ways for you to practice these important listening skills. It is hoped that your instructor will be able to offer you more than one interview opportunity to increase your experiences and knowledge of the listening skills used here.

The last two chapters of this unit provide a look at the skills needed in communicating together with a small group of people. So much of business today is conducted in small group settings. Learning how to maximize your skills in such situations can greatly enhance your productivity. In *The Panel Discussion* students work with a small group of classmates to focus particularly on the communication skills necessary to solve a problem. Each panel member prepares personal thoughts and ideas on the problem in advance, then comes to the panel with a clearly outlined problem-solving process to try to work out a single solution together, making the most of each member's best thinking. In *The Symposium* members of the small group prepare public statements on differing aspects of the same topic and present their speeches in turn before opening the discussion up to the audience for questions. Each of these experiences provides the student with an opportunity to coordinate important communication skills with others.

Finally, this unit concludes with a chapter on *The Keynote Address* in which the student will learn how to open a conference or meeting with a speech that sets the tone for the entire event, perhaps challenging the listeners for the tasks ahead. A keynote address requires the speaker to generate enthusiasm and unity in the audience. This assignment offers the student the chance to practice those skills while coordinating the remarks with the conference theme or focus.

This unit is designed to frame important communication skills in the contexts most often encountered in the workplace. By doing these assignments, students will have a solid introduction to the demands of communicating competently in professional life.

THE SALES TALK

Time limits: 5-6 minutes.

Speaking notes: Do not use notes when trying to sell something to an audience.

Sources of information: Two are required, preferably three. For each source give the specific magazine, book, or Internet site it was taken from, title of the article, author's full name, date of publication, and the chapter or page telling where the material was found. If a source is a person, identify the source completely by title, position, occupation, etc. List these on the outline form. For Internet sites include the address (URL).

Outline your speech: Prepare a 75-100 word complete sentence outline.

Question: Should a person vary the rate of speaking?

Answer: Yes, but be natural. Variety is a prerequisite of good speech.

Key Word:
Sales

Student Expectations: In completing this assignment each student will:
➤ *Identify speaking strategies used to sell products to others*
➤ *Understand the competitive nature of sales talks*
➤ *Adapt arguments for the sale of a product to a particular audience*
➤ *Prepare responses to anticipated objections*

PURPOSE OF THIS ASSIGNMENT

The sales talk is something you may be called upon to present much sooner than you now expect. It involves a situation in which you usually try to trade or sell a group of persons sometimes in exchange for their money. Sometimes this is a difficult task. Many persons have had little or no experience in this particular type of speaking and selling. This one experience is not intended to make a sales expert out of anyone, but certainly it will help the person who later finds it necessary to sell something to a group.

EXPLANATION OF THE SALES TALK

A **sales** talk is a speech in which you attempt to persuade a group of people to buy a product from you now or at a later date. In some instances, you will actually take orders at the conclusion of your remarks. In other cases, you will merely stimulate an interest in your goods so that prospective customers will buy from you later. But in either case, your purpose is to sell by stimulating the customer to want what you have and to be willing to part with money to acquire the goods you have for sale.

The sales talk makes special demands on the speaker. You must be pleasing in appearance, pleasant to meet, congenial, and friendly. You must be thoroughly familiar with the product and be conversant with all matters pertaining to it, including many details.

Good communication skills are essential to a career in sales.

This will necessitate your having pen and ink, order forms, credit information, and receipts for use. Do not make buyers wait if they are ready to buy. Another point is to be prepared to greet the audience promptly. Go to the designated meeting place early. Have everything in proper and neat arrangement before your audience arrives. After you think you have every display most advantageously placed, all sales forms in order, and everything in shape, go back for a final check. If you have omitted nothing, then you are ready.

As for your speech, have it well in mind. Do not use notes. It would be foolish to attempt to sell something while referring to notes in order to discover the good points of your product.

The organization of your speech should be well thought out. One plan that can be recommended is the one that follows.

1. Give a friendly introduction, stating your pleasure in meeting the audience. Be sincere.

2. Present information about yourself and your product. Who are you? What position do you hold? How long have you been with this company? Why did you choose to work for your particular company? What is the name of the company? How old is it? Is it a nationwide organization? Is it financially sound? Is it reliable? Does it stand behind its products? Does it guarantee its products? Does it quibble over an adjustment if a customer asks for one? Does it have a larger dealer organization? Can you get parts and repairs quickly if these are needed? Does the company plan to stay in business? Does it test all of its products before placing them on the market? How large is its business? What special recommendations does the company have? Of course, it may not be necessary to answer all of these questions; however, many of them will have to be answered by giving information which establishes you as a reputable salesperson and your company as a reputable firm.

3. Now that you have laid the groundwork, you are ready to show and explain the goods or services you have for sale. The nature of what you are selling will demonstrate how you do this. Probably, the first thing you will do will be to explain the purpose of your product. That is, you will tell what it is for.

4. Next you will explain and demonstrate how it operates. In doing this, be sure to emphasize its advantages, its special features, new improvements, economy of operation, dependability, beauty, ease of handling, and the like. Give enough details to be clear but not so much that you confuse your listeners.

5. Your next step will require careful analysis of your audience. This is done to show how your product will benefit them. You must know their wants and needs and let them see vividly how your products will benefit them. If the article is a box of chocolates, the buyer will delight family and friends by serving them. If the salesperson is offering a distance learning course, the buyer will make more money, gain prestige, and secure advancements by registering for the course. Whatever the sales item, you must show the advantages and benefits of the ownership of it. Sometimes it is helpful to mention the names of other persons who have bought the product from you and are now benefiting from it.

6. And now comes the last step. How may they buy it? Where? When? Who sells it, if you carry only samples? How much does it cost? Do you sell on the installment plan? What are the interest charges? How much do you require as a down payment? How many months are allowed in paying for it? What is the amount of the monthly payments? Or is it cash? Is any discount allowed for cash? What special inducement is offered to those who buy now? How much can they save? Will future prices be higher? Do you take trade-ins? How much allowance is made on a trade-in?

Make it as easy and simple as possible to buy the goods you are selling. Be sure that your explanations are clear and exact. Do not use misleading terms or glib wrong impressions. If your sales ability will not withstand a full, complete, and candid examination, you will be wise to change your policies or change your vocation.

To be able to present the above information effectively, to demonstrate the product, to show the prospective customers how they will benefit from owning your goods, and how they may buy it, you will rehearse the demonstration and accompanying speech aloud many times. Do this until you have attained complete mastery of the entire speech.

HOW TO PRESENT A SALES TALK

Look good. Be good. In other words have a neat and pleasing appearance, plus a friendly and polite attitude. These points are extremely important. Your own good judgment will tell you what is appropriate dress. Your common sense will provide the background for the right attitude. Generally, you should begin your speech directly, if this procedure is appropriate to the mood of your listeners. Avoid being smart or using questionable stories to impress your listeners. Put the group at ease and get on with the speech.

Your manner should be conversational. Your voice should be easily heard by all but not strained. Your bodily action should be suitable for holding attention, making transitions, and demonstrating what you are selling. Your language, of course, should be simple, descriptive, vivid, and devoid of technical terms.

In using charts, pictures, diagrams, or the sales article itself, your familiarity with these should be so great that you can point out any information or refer to any part of the product while retaining a posture that permits focusing your attention on the audience. In answering questions you should be as clear as possible and sure that your questioner is satisfied with the information you give. Avoid embarrassing anyone. An alert and enthusiastic yet friendly attitude is most desirable.

SPECIAL HINTS

Do not criticize your competitors or their products. It is better to praise the competition, but show the superiority of yours. If you have any special inducements for buying your product, be sure to present them at the appropriate time.

After concluding your talk, allow your audience time to ask questions. It may be that some of them will wish to ask questions during your speech. If this is the case, be sure to answer them clearly; however, do not turn the meeting into a question and answer occasion before explaining your product.

THE JAYHAWK MUG
A Sales Talk by Margie Hapke

Good Morning... Excuse me... Just a minute... Oh man, I hate it when it happens... You know what the problem is. It's these styrofoam cups. They are so flimsy and unreliable. I'm sure it's happened to you too. It happens to everyone at some point in time or another. These styrofoam cups are just worthless. But today I've got a product here to show you that will solve the problem of the flimsy and unreliable cups forever.

It's the Jayhawk Mug. Now the Jayhawk Mug has numerous features that give it a definite advantage over styrofoam and paper cups, and produces benefits not only to you the user, but to the environment as well. Now the Jayhawk Mug is made from hard plastics that are guaranteed not to split or crack, eliminating the problem that you all just witnessed. The mug also features double wall construction that provides it with thermal insulation keeping your hot drinks hot and your cold drinks cold without changing the outside temperature of the mug. How many times have you filled a styrofoam cup with hot coffee only to find out it's so hot you can't hold on to it? And what about in the summertime when you have the styrofoam cup full of ice and Coke and the thing sweats and gets your hand all wet and drips all over your shoes? It's really a nuisance. The Jayhawk Mug's double wall construction eliminates that problem—a definite advantage.

Another benefit of the mug is a reduced charge for refills offered at all the Kansas Union concession outlets. This mug holds 32 ounces of any beverage like Coke, coffee, iced tea, and can be refilled with any beverage for just 60 cents. That same amount of product in a one-time use styrofoam cup would cost you at least a dollar.

And speaking of one-time-use-only, that's probably the biggest benefit of using the Jayhawk Mug—the benefit to the environment. Styrofoam is a hazard in our landfills because it just doesn't biodegrade. By reusing the Jayhawk Mug you can help significantly reduce the amount of non-degradable styrofoam that the KU campus sends to landfills each week.

Now, how can you get your very own Jayhawk Mug? It's easy. You just stop in at any one of KU's concession outlets. The Mug sells for two dollars and fifty cents. It's a great price. It's affordable. And a savings from just six refills pays for it. So run across the street to the Wescoe Beach and pick yourself up a Jayhawk Mug today. You'll never walk around with a wet T-shirt again.

CHAPTER 14

THE LECTURE FORUM

Time limits: 7-8 minute speech. Questioning period 5 minutes.

Speaking notes: 15-word maximum limit.

Sources of information: Three are required, preferably four. For each source give the specific magazine, book, or Internet site it was taken from, title of the article, author's full name, date of publication, and the chapter or pages telling where the material was found. If a source is a person, identify the source completely by title, position, occupation, etc. List these on the outline form. For Internet sites include the address (URL).

Outline your speech: Prepare a 75-150 word complete sentence outline.

Question: Do gestures make a speech better?

Answer: If they are appropriate to all elements of the speech situation, yes.

Key Words:
Forum
Rephrase

Student Expectations: In completing this assignment each student will:
  ➤ *Experience the need to be better informed on a topic than the audience*
  ➤ *Demonstrate the ability to answer questions from the audience*
  ➤ *Understand the procedures to follow in conducting a lecture forum with an audience*

PURPOSE OF THIS ASSIGNMENT

Persons who give speeches often do so without knowing how many unanswered questions they leave in the minds of their listeners. These questions are unanswered because the audience has no chance to ask questions. It is becoming evident daily that speakers can be more helpful to their listeners if speakers remain on stage following their lectures to answer questions which have arisen in the minds of their audience.

Most students do not receive training in answering questions about the material they present in speeches. Thus, when they are confronted with a **forum** (question period) following a speech, they are in danger of awkwardly handling themselves

and their audience. The lecture forum type of speech is designed to provide experience in speaking as well as answering questions. It should be both enlightening and challenging to you.

EXPLANATION OF THE LECTURE FORUM

The lecture forum is a speech followed by a period in which members of the audience are permitted to direct questions to the speaker. The purpose of the lecturer generally is to inform the listeners on a worthwhile subject. The speaker could present a speech intended to motivate or one to persuade; however, the persuasive speech would probably not suit the lecture forum atmosphere so well as the speech to inform. We cannot preclude the speeches to motivate and to persuade, because

Classroom lecture is a type of lecture forum.

they can well be followed by periods of questioning and often should be. However we can and do suggest that for most lecture forums the speaker should utilize the time by discussing an informative subject. If the audience wants to follow any advice therein, that is their privilege. The speaker should not urge it on them.

The lecture forum demands that the speaker be well informed; better informed than any member of the audience. It demands further that the speaker be capable of receiving and answering questions from an audience. In short, the speaker should be something of an expert and an excellent speaker.

Occasions for the lecture forum occur whenever an informative speech is in order. These speeches may be given before committees, business groups, church organizations, civic audiences, educational meetings, fraternal orders, and the like. There is scarcely a limit to the occasions for lecture forums.

HOW TO CHOOSE A TOPIC FOR A LECTURE FORUM

You will be expected to know your subject unusually well, since you will appear before your audience to inform them and be present to open the meeting to questions centered around your remarks. Thus, it is advisable to choose a topic of interest to you and your listeners, as well as a subject about which you can secure plenty of information. Do not select a subject for which there are only limited sources. An apology to an audience for ignorance on your subject is not conducive to confidence in you as a speaker. Base your choice

then, on interest, appropriateness, and the availability of source materials.

SOME TOPIC POSSIBILITIES

How Can Local Government Meet City Needs?
Community Policing Programs
Renewable Energy Sources
Alternatives to College for Career Success
Summer Employment Opportunities
Study Techniques for Better Grades
Overcoming Stage Fright
How Technology Is Changing Education
Preparing a Living Will or Organ Donor Card
Best Vacation Spots in the State or Region

HOW TO PREPARE FOR A LECTURE FORUM

Since this is an informative speech, you should read the chapter in this text entitled *The Speech To Inform*. Here you will find complete information relative to preparing this type of speech. Follow it closely.

HOW TO PRESENT A LECTURE FORUM

You should read the chapter in this text entitled *The Speech to Inform*. It will tell you how to present your speech but not how to conduct the period of questioning from your audience. A discussion of this point follows:

Immediately after the conclusion of your lecture the audience will be advised by the chair or yourself that they may question you. In making this announcement several points should be explained politely but thoroughly, such as:

1. Tell the audience to please confine their questions to the material presented in the lecture, because you are not prepared to answer questions outside this scope.

2. Request your audience to ask questions only, unless you wish to permit short speeches on the subject. Whatever policy you intend to follow— that is, strictly a questioning period or a question and short speech period—must be specifically announced and understood. Otherwise you will run into trouble with those persons who want to make short speeches. If you allow short speeches, announce a definite time limit on them. For the

classroom one minute is enough. In large public gatherings, two minutes is adequate.

3. If the audience is small and informal, permit the speakers to remain seated during the forum period; that is, do not ask them to stand while participating. If the gathering is large, require them to stand. Conduct yourself in a like manner, that is, by standing, or seating yourself.

4. Announce the exact amount of time which will be given to the period of questioning. Do not make this questioning period too long. You can always extend the time if the questions are coming briskly at the moment you are scheduled to close. On the other hand, do not continue to hold an audience for the announced time if it becomes obvious that they no longer care to ask questions. It is better to have them go away wanting more than having had too much. Always announce the last question before you take it. Don't suddenly stop.

5. Once your announcements are made, open the question and answer period by telling the audience to direct their questions to you. Also explain that you will answer the questions in the order in which they are asked. Thus, if two persons speak at once you will designate which one may ask a question first. Speakers should be urged to raise their hands rather than speak out, and then wait to be called on.

Having made the above explanations to your audience, tell them you will be glad to answer their questions as best you can. Do not promise to answer all questions, since it is likely that no one could do that. If a question is raised that you do not feel qualified to answer, tell the questioner you do not have the information necessary to give a reliable answer. Promise to find the answer and ask the questioner to see you after the speech to give you a phone number, mailing address, or e-mail address so you can forward the answer when you have it. However, if you do not know the answer because you are poorly prepared, you will quickly lose the confidence and respect of your audience—and you should.

If questions are asked which do not pertain to the subject under discussion, politely tell the questioner that the question is beyond the scope of your talk and you are not prepared to answer it. Should you by chance possess information which will enable you to answer it, state briefly that the question is somewhat afield, then give what information you do know. Make a very brief reply. Do not let this take you off your subject more than a moment. Should hecklers trouble you, handle them politely but firmly. Do nothing drastic. Always repeat the question so the audience can hear it.

If some questions are obscure and drawn out, it may be necessary for you to **rephrase** them. If you do this, inquire of the person who gave the question as to whether or not your rephrasing asks what they want to know. At other times it may be necessary for you to ask for a restatement of an inquiry. Do this anytime that you do not hear or understand the question clearly.

Observe acceptable speaking practices throughout your lecture and the period following. Retain an alert and friendly attitude. Do not become ruffled when you meet obvious disagreement or criticism. Simply explain your position firmly but politely. Do not engage in a debate or an exchange of unfriendly remarks and accusations. Dismiss the matter and move on to the next question. If some of the questions are "hot" and they will be, keep your head, add a touch of humor to cool them off if it seems advisable; then reply as capably as you can. If any person asks a question that cannot be heard by the entire audience, repeat it to the audience then give your answer. When you are ready to turn the meeting back to the chair, conclude with appropriate remarks in which you sincerely express your pleasure for having been with the audience. Also compliment them for their interest in the subject.

COMPUTER-ENHANCED PRESENTATIONS

Time limits: 4-5 minutes.

Speaking notes: None needed in addition to slides/transparencies from the software preparations.

Sources of information: Two are required, preferably three. For each source give the specific magazine, book, or Internet site it was taken from, title of the article, author's full name, date of publication, and the chapter or pages telling where the material was found. If a source is a person, identify the source completely by title, position, occupation, etc. List these on the outline form. For Internet sites give the address (URL).

Outline your speech: Follow the computer software instructions.

Question: What is meant by "adjusting to the situation"?

Answer: You should make your speech fit the assignment, the audience, the environment, your own abilities, and the occasion.

Key Word:
Proofreading

Student Expectations: In completing this assignment each student will:
> ➤ *Apply a computer presentation development program to speech preparation*
> ➤ *Create and present appropriate visual aids to illustrate the speech*
> ➤ *Practice proofreading of created materials*

PURPOSE OF THIS ASSIGNMENT

Software programs for creating modern presentations have become increasingly popular in many business settings. They have the additional feature of being able to create visual aids that allow your audience to follow your speech just as you have planned it. The software is designed to help speakers organize the materials they have researched, after the speech's purposes are determined. Because of the popularity of this particular type of program, this assignment is included here to encourage you to gain experience in its use.

EXPLANATION OF COMPUTER-ENHANCED PRESENTATIONS

Computer-enhanced presentations begin with the same purposes, topics, and research of many of the other speeches we have discussed in this text. The software simply provides guidance for organizing speech materials into standardized formats. It offers the opportunity to create "slides" or transparencies of the outline, as well charts, graphs, or illustrations; or you can prepare an assignment of presentation as a special project.

The presentation software programs are valuable tools for creating clear, visual presentations quickly and relatively easily. However, the formats are limited and should not be considered appropriate for all speaking occasions and topics.

HOW TO CHOOSE A TOPIC FOR A COMPUTER-ENHANCED PRESENTATION

In selecting a topic for a presentation, first consideration should be given to the purpose of your presentation, just as it is in the other chapters of this text. Purposes, or types, of speeches developed for example by the PowerPoint software program include Recommending a Strategy; Selling a Product, Service, or Idea; Training; Reporting Progress; Communicating Bad News; and General. Once you have determined the purpose of your presentation, you can select an appropriate topic.

Consult the topic ideas listed in related chapters of this text, such as *The Speech To Inform* (Chapter 7), *The Speech To Persuade* (Chapter 8), and *The Sales Talk* (Chapter 13) for additional ideas.

HOW TO PREPARE A COMPUTER-ENHANCED PRESENTATION

Using the PowerPoint program as an example, begin to create your presentation by having your key ideas and subpoints identified from the research you've done on your topic. Choose a title, if desired. Identify any other information you wish to include on the title slide of your presentation.

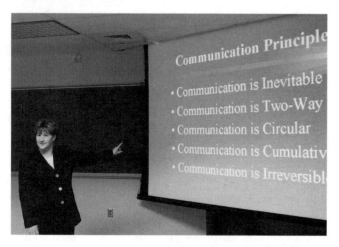

Computer-assisted presentations are common in business and professional speeches.

Select the "Auto Content Wizard" from the PowerPoint menu to begin the presentation development process. Then select the type of presentation you wish to create. Clicking on the "finish" button will take you to the "outline view" of your presentation format. Follow the prompts of the software to edit the outline, organizing your ideas by key words, phrases, or simple sentences into the format provided.

After completing the creation of your outline, the software offers opportunities for adding backgrounds, charts, graphs, or other artwork to your slides. Follow the prompts and graphics menus to enhance your basic outline.

Proofreading is critical before you are ready to save or print out your slides. Be sure all spelling, punctuation, and grammar are absolutely perfect, or your audience will undoubtedly spot the error. One small typographical error unchecked can severely reduce your credibility as a presenter.

Once you are satisfied with your presentation, print out your "slides" to create transparencies for use with an overhead projector. The software will also allow you to print your outline in the form of speaking notes, if desired. Ideally, a computer-enhanced presentation is made using an LCD projector that is attached to a lap top computer. This allows you to create animated slides. You can have "builds" in which one line is reveled at a time, and dissolves that fade out line when another comes up. It is also possible to scan photographs and artwork onto disks to incorporate. Using the LCD projector requires you to practice coordinating the changes in slides.

HOW TO PRESENT THE COMPUTER-ENHANCED SPEECH

Before you are ready to present the speech, be sure you have the necessary equipment needed, such as the overhead projector. Ideally, you should rehearse with this equipment in the room you will be using for the presentation if possible. Be sure to notice when to put each slide on the projector, when to change slides, and to check to focus for the audience's best viewing.

Delivery skills for this speech are no less important than for the other speeches discussed in this text. Volume, rate, and clarity are vitally important, as are gestures and posture. Rehearsal is a must until you are completely comfortable with the changing of the slides as well as the fluidity of your vocal delivery.

With adequate preparation, a computer-enhanced presentation can be quite impressive.

The following is a thumbnail layout of a PowerPoint presentation:

Title Slide

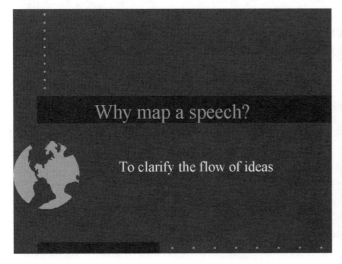

1

2

How to Begin

- Identify the main points you wish to make
- Create an outline of main ideas and sub-points

3

Making the Map

- How do ideas fit together?
  - Do ideas represent a time progression?
  - Do ideas build like a pyramid?
  - Are ideas like recipe ingredients?
  - Is there a problem and a solution, like in a mystery?

4

Making the Map, cont'd.

- Select a visual image that best fits your ideas
- Draw the image; label each part to that identify main ideas
- Do the ideas fit the image?
  - If no, rearrange the order; try another image
  - If yes, you correctly identified a relationship
  - Ideas should be easy for your audience to follow

5

Making the Most of Your Map

- Now you are ready to test your flow of ideas on a friend or classmate to check your success
- If the test audience agrees that your ideas are easy to follow, you may want to consider using your speech map as a visual aid, making your presentation even more audience-friendly

6

HOW CAN YOU EFFECTIVELY USE VISUAL AIDS?

1. Choose visuals that are clear and easy to see across a room.
2. Place them in view of all audience members.
3. Keep them out of sight until they are ready to be used. Place them out of sight after they are used.
4. Try using different media. Try, overhead transparencies, actual objects, videotapes, slides, or computer-generated graphics.
5. Practice with the visual aid so it can be used smoothly during the speech.
6. Face the audience and not the visual aid when presenting.

16

THE INTERVIEW

Time limits:

> 4-6 minutes for report of an interview.
>
> 1/2 -2 minutes for role-played telephone appointment.
>
> 5-10 minutes for a role-played interview.

Speaking notes: 25-50 words for interview report.

Sources of information: List the person interviewed.

Outline your speech: Prepare 75-100 word complete sentence outline.

Q

Question: Is loud and boisterous speech effective?

A

Answer: No. It may interfere with what you are saying.

Key Words:
Background data
Interview

Student Expectations: In completing this assignment each student will:
> ➤ *Prepare appropriate interview questions*
> ➤ *Conduct an interview to acquire information*
> ➤ *Understand the role of research in preparation of the interview*
> ➤ *Identify types of questions to ask employers when being interviewed for a job*
> ➤ *Understand the communication effects of interviewing by phone or in person*

PURPOSE OF THIS ASSIGNMENT

The **interview**, in some form or another, is an almost certain event in your life. Perhaps you have already interviewed for a job or are planning to do so. Unless you are that one person in a million, you will be interviewed (briefly or extensively) before you are employed. Whether or not you get the job, or any other favorable response, will depend on how you conduct yourself under interview circumstances. And if you are interviewing for other reasons, to gain information, for a report, to prepare a newscast, to prepare a legal brief for a case in court, or to sell an article, the maturity, skill, and judgment you exercise will bring success or failure. This experience will add to your chances

for success, help put money in your pocket, and give the confidence needed to do well.

EXPLANATION OF THE INTERVIEW

An interview is talking with another person or a group for a specific purpose. It is a series of questions and answers. Most are planned. Impromptu interviews, however, occur among business people and others often observed on the street, in a store, even in a home. Unplanned interviews possess characteristics of conversation while more formal interviews tend to proceed in a more structured manner. It is the latter we wish to discuss here since they impose restrictions on the parties involved such as making an appointment, having a limited time period for you to finish the interview, and having several separate meetings, which are scheduled before you complete your interview purpose.

One common element in an interview is talk; thus, if you can express yourself well things should go smoothly. If you cannot, you may have trouble. Another common element is your physical behavior, your appearance, your walk, your posture, subtle movements of your hands and feet, eye contact, and facial expressions. Everything you say and do tells something about you, and altogether it tells what you really are. It is your personality. Your thoughts and moods, attitudes and feelings, are all symbolized by your total behavior, and you can't hide them. You are kidding yourself if you think you have secretly mastered an art of deceit and won't be discovered. Business executives or sales personnel are quick to detect a phony.

Since the interview situation often places the parties involved close together, perhaps in a small office, the interview permits many personal judgments and subconscious reactions. In effect the interview places all participants in positions of judgment with everyone revealing themselves to other persons present. No one has yet invented a better way to formulate final evaluations of people whether it be a prospective employee or prospective boss.

Occasions for interviews occur in all kinds of employment, inquiries for information, sales situations, personnel work, special reports and surveys, and others.

Remember an interview may be conducted by a group such as when news reporters interview a governor or other official. In contrast to this, a school board may interview a prospective teacher, and the teacher may interview the board members. Or a single reporter might interview any executive or administrative group.

HOW TO CHOOSE AN INTERVIEW SITUATION

Select a topic that interests you and one you can complete. Avoid a person or group too distant to reach or who cannot grant the interview within a short time or at a time you can meet. Make your

choice and arrangements within twenty-four hours. Why so soon? You may learn that the person you want to interview is on vacation or ill; thus, you will be forced to contact someone else.

Since many of the people you might want to interview could have last-minute conflicts, schedule the interview several days ahead of your due date. Thus, if the person must cancel, you still have time to reschedule before the due date. For this assignment, think about a person who has a job you want to hold someday. Use the interview to learn about it. You can also interview someone who makes policies that affect you—school administrators, local and state officials. If you are interested in learning more about a historic or current events topic, interview an expert.

HOW TO PREPARE FOR AN INTERVIEW (THE INTERVIEWER)

1. Since you are the interviewer, make an appointment and if it is made in person be prepared to conduct it on the spot should the interviewee suggest you do so. If your appointment is by telephone, be pleasant and efficient by using a carefully prepared and rehearsed request constructed as follows: (a) make sure you are talking with the right person; (b) introduce yourself completely; (c) explain why you want the interview, also suggesting the amount of time needed, the date, hour, and place; and (d) leave your name, telephone number, and ask to be called should it be necessary for the interviewee to change the appointment. Sometimes a secretary will take your appointment.

2. Regardless of whether you are interviewing for a job or to acquire information for a report you should acquaint yourself with **background data** about your interviewee. Ask an assistant to send you information about the interviewee and the business.

Now comes the crux of your interview preparation. What is your purpose, and what do you want to know? You will determine the purpose first. Second, you will prepare a list of about ten lead questions and twenty specific inquiries that will bring out the information you want. Do not read your list of questions verbatim while interviewing. Memorize selected questions from it to be used as needed. You will refer to your list occasionally and originate other questions as the interview proceeds.

3. Dress neatly, carefully and appropriately. Avoid being conspicuous by your appearance. Casual school clothes are not suitable. Dress for an adult's approval who is used to seeing support staff and other employees attired for the business world. You can fail an interview before opening your mouth to speak if appearance suggests carelessness or disregard for the situation. A personnel worker who interviewed job applicants for a large mercantile business told the writers that some applicants appeared for interviews without regard to their appearance and seemingly with an attitude their appearance was a personal matter and none of the interviewer's business. They were not even considered and would have saved everyone's time by not applying.

4. Get the correct address and exact time for the interview. Be sure of this. Allow more time than needed to get there. You might have car trouble or traffic problems. If you are going to a location you haven't had to find before, do a test run before the interview date to make sure you can find it.

5. Study the background information and your list of questions. They should be partially memorized. Be sure you have your questions laid out with adequate space for writing responses to them or provide yourself with an additional notebook for recording the interviewer's answers. Also have a pencil or pen that works. Tape recording is a good idea, but be sure to ask permission to record when you make the appointment.

6. Think of your approaching interview as an enjoyable experience.

HOW TO CONDUCT AN INTERVIEW (TO ACQUIRE INFORMATION)

Arrive ten minutes early at the office of the interviewee. Inquire where to locate Mr./Ms._____, or tell the receptionist, if one is present, who you are and that you are there to meet your appointment. When informed that Mr./Ms._____is ready, go into the office, in-

troduce yourself if the receptionist fails to do this, shake hands (use a firm grip), politely wait to be seated when invited or seat yourself if your judgment tells you it is appropriate. The host may be busy at a desk and request you to wait a moment. You may stand or sit politely, or look over the office furnishings and arrangements casually, but don't fidget or pace nervously. You might glance over your list of questions to refresh your memory. When your host is ready you may sincerely comment on the office, the view, or something of general interest as an opening remark.

Start your interview by explaining why you are there. State your questions courteously, tactfully, and directly. Initial opening questions may concern (1) history of the business; (2) the nature of the business such as products sold or services performed; (3) number of employees, labor practices, qualifications of employees, vacations, employee benefits and; (4) advantages of this business. Do not press questions on any subject the interviewee obviously doesn't want to discuss. It's your obligation to direct the interview into the desired areas and bring the discussion back if it gets too far off the subject. Remember this is your interview. Bring the interview to a pleasant conclusion (perhaps by saying you have one more question), and do not overstay your time. Should the interviewee offer to show you the place of business, have a cup of coffee, or tour the grounds, accept graciously but

Interviews can open doors to jobs and can also be a way to gather information.

don't forget that time may be limited—don't overstay your invitation. Thank the interviewee when it seems appropriate and extend an invitation to visit your school.

While the interview is underway, take notes quickly and accurately. (Write clearly so you can read your notes later.) Listen attentively so you won't have to ask to have the information repeated, and should time run out request a later appointment to finish the interview. Be courteous at all times. Avoid random, nervous movements, any familiarities, excessive throat clearing, and mumbling. Don't fidget or do anything distracting while the interviewee is talking. Be attentive and provide nonverbal feedback. Thank the interviewee before leaving.

HOW TO INTERVIEW FOR A JOB

Let's suppose you must interview for a job. You will be the interviewee and an interviewer at the same time. Questions will be directed to you and you will ask questions about the work. Read again the preceding section on conducting an interview to refresh your thinking. Next, you should have a copy of your resumé which includes personal information, honors received, offices held, activities participated in, memberships, a record of your work experience, a list of at least three personal references with complete addresses and telephone numbers (a business person, teacher, or other influential person) and/or letters of recommendation. All of these may not be required but they should be available in neatly typed form and correct. Several extra copies of these records should be kept in your files. Before you are interviewed you may be required to fill out an application form, and, if so, fill it out completely answering every question fully. Be neat and accurate. Omit nothing, and don't assume that a stranger studying the form will be able to read your mind and fill in blank spaces. There are several good books available on resumé preparation. Check your school or public library.

When you go into the job interview conduct yourself as you would before any business or professional person. Greet the interviewer cordially, shake hands if appropriate, state your purpose, and ask generally what positions are available unless you are applying for a particular one. So you will know what is expected of you, ask about the qualifications, responsibilities, duties, and requirements of the offering. Most likely you will be asked questions about your experience, background, training and education. Answer these questions honestly and directly but don't belittle yourself. Suggest that the inter-

viewer might like to examine summaries of your personal history, training, experience and recommendations you have with you. Sit politely while the interviewer reads them. Besides the job you are applying for, they may be looking for someone to fill a special position that is not advertised. It's quite possible they would select you, especially if you conduct a superior interview showing alertness and intelligence. Or maybe they will try you out at something less important with the idea of moving you up if you are a superior worker. As the interview progresses you should be ready to talk and give answers or to wait with poise if anything unusual occurs. Sometimes interruptions are planned to test your reactions—the telephone rings, a secretary brings a message, an employee comes in. Or sometimes the interviewer asks a startling or unexpected question. Don't be surprised at anything—just respond intelligently and respectfully.

Before the interview ends, if you haven't been told, inquire about company policy concerning union membership, insurance, advancements, salary or wages, vacations, sick leave, and other important matters. If it appears appropriate you might ask to be shown around the buildings or grounds where you would work. In all instances when you inquire, avoid an attitude of distrust or suspicion—just be interested, courteous, alert.

Before the interview concludes, ask when you will be notified about the job. If you receive a vague or indefinite answer, ask if you may contact them or write them at a future date. It is only fair before you leave that you have their word you will be notified within a reasonable time.

When the interviewer indicates that the interview is ending, bring your remarks to a close, extend thanks again, and leave. Sometimes it may be necessary for you to close the interview—you can stay too long.

Here's a hint: If you don't fill out an application form, and you want the interviewer to remember you instead of one of a dozen other applicants, hand the interviewer a three-by-five card as the interview ends. On it, neatly typed, include your name, address, telephone number, education, work experience, and type of work you are interested in or qualified to do.

Assignment 1. (Appointment for job interview)
The instructor may develop the Interview Assignment as follows:

Two persons at a time sitting back-to-back eight to ten feet apart carry out an imagined telephone conversation. One is a business person, the other a student seeking an appointment for an interview. Other persons, appointed by the instructor, may occasionally answer the telephone instead of the business person. Don't overdo the role-playing—and keep it realistic. The instructor may send the student outside the classroom while the appointment situation is set up. The person seeking the appointment then enters the room, takes a seat, and proceeds to pantomime a phone call to the business person. Be sure to have a specific job description in mind when asking for the interview.

Note: If time permits, students should participate in Assignment 1 before doing Assignments 2 or 3.

Assignment 2. (The job interview)

Two persons role-play the job interview for five to ten minutes. The interviewee should enter the classroom door after the instructor has set up any special circumstances the interviewer will confront. The business person, a secretary, or someone else will admit the student who will take it from there. This should not be rehearsed by the participants since a real interview is not rehearsed; however, the participants should be well prepared to conduct their individual parts and try to make the entire experience true to life.

Assignment 3.

The appointment and interview aspects of this assignment should be role-played successfully before any student is permitted to actually complete the interview with a business person. Here's the assignment.

1. By telephone make an appointment with a business or professional person whom you do not know personally.

2. Complete an interview to learn about the business, its general operations, policies (labor, products, organization, etc), and future plans. Take notes. Prepare a five to six-minute oral report of the interview and what you learned for the class.

The instructor should keep a list of all business persons interviewed in order that future classes will not interview the same ones too often. A letter of appreciation from the interviewer and the instructor to the business person expressing gratitude for the cooperation is a good practice.

Assignment 4.

Students wanting work should conduct actual job interviews, then prepare five to six-minute oral reports of their experiences for the class.

CHAPTER 17

THE PANEL DISCUSSION

Participants: Three to six and a chairperson.

Time limits: 30 minutes for most classroom performances. Others vary according to the amount of time available.

Speaking notes: Participants usually find it necessary and convenient to have notes which provide data such as figures, facts, sources, etc., concerning the points of view and information they present. Sources of information: Three or more should be studied.

Outline of discussion: See "How To Prepare For a Panel Discussion" next page.

Question: Does a person who uses good grammar have much advantage?

Answer: Yes. People are judged partially by their grammar.

Key Words:
Cooperative effort
Panel discussion
Problem-solving

Student Expectations: In completing this assignment each student will:
➢ *Work as a group member to solve a problem*
➢ *Use the steps of a problem-solving process*
➢ *Understand the importance of open-mindedness in problem-solving*

PURPOSE OF THIS ASSIGNMENT

There is no better method for resolving the world's problems than by "talking them over." The panel discussion, when operating successfully, utilizes this method. It is democracy at work. Every citizen and, certainly, every student should have the experience of deliberately sitting down in the company of other persons to find the answers to problems of mutual concern. This assignment will give this vital experience; hence, you should study it carefully.

EXPLANATION OF A PANEL DISCUSSION

A **panel discussion** occurs when a group of persons sit down together to try to solve a problem or problems by pooling their knowledge and arriving at decisions satisfactory to the majority. If they reach these decisions, their purpose is fulfilled. This requires that the panelists enter the panel with

open minds and a willingness and desire to hear other viewpoints, opinions, and evidence. Thus, by gathering all possible information (facts) and by pooling it, the group can examine a problem bit by bit, point by point, and arrive at a logical solution. No one should consent to join a panel if they do so while harboring preconceived ideas, prejudices, and opinions, which they are unwilling to change in the light of evidence which they do not possess. An attitude of open-mindedness is the most valuable asset a panel speaker or anyone else can possess. This does not mean they are vacillating but rather that they will easily and gladly change their minds when confronted by information which perhaps they did not know was in existence.

A panel may vary greatly in the number of members; however, if there are too many participants, progress tends to be slow and laborious. It is, therefore, advisable to limit membership to a maximum of five or six persons besides the chair.

Occasions for a panel discussion are as numerous as the problems that face any group of people. Every club, every society or organization has recourse to the panel as a method of problem solving. Naturally, if an organization has a large membership, its problems will be submitted to committees which will in turn attack them through the discussion method, that is to say, the panel. Today radio and television often feature the panel as a public service. You should not be led to believe that every panel must have an audience or that certain TV programs dominated by sarcasm, acrimony, and quibbling represent true discussion. Such discussions are not in any sense of the word good panel discussions because they often lack the quality of open mindedness and a sincere desire to solve a problem.

HOW TO CHOOSE A PROBLEM FOR A PANEL DISUCSSION

If the problem is not assigned, the panel should meet under the leadership of the chair. At the meeting, various problems should be considered and a selection of a topic for discussion be made by majority vote. Think of school or community problems that affect you directly. The selection should be based on interest to the panelists and the availability of material for research and study. If the discussion will be conducted before listeners, then the audience should be considered when the choice is made. In either case the group should select a question they are capable of adequately discussing. Some sample discussion questions are as follows:

1. How may more people be encouraged to vote?
2. How may teacher's salaries be raised?
3. What should be done to improve high school and college curricula?
4. What should be done about cheating at school?
5. What should be the policy relative to paying athletes or granting them special privileges?
6. Should required courses in marriage be taught in high schools?
7. Should all physically and mentally capable students be required to attend school until eighteen years of age, or until graduated from high school?

HOW TO PREPARE FOR A PANEL DISCUSSION

Participants should give careful thought to the purpose of a panel discussion, which is problem-solving. They should prepare their material with this thought uppermost. Their attitude should be that of a farmer who sees a strange plant growing in a field. What should be done about it? Is it harmful? Is it valuable? Should it be dug out by the roots or cut off? Who can tell what kind of a plant it is? In other words, the student should not jump at conclusions immediately after selecting a problem, but, like the farmer, should find out everything possible about the question under discussion and then determine what opinions are most sound.

Let us assume for a moment that the problem has been selected and that the panelists are ready to begin searching for possible solutions. Here are the steps each participant should follow in arriving at possible answers:

The Problem: What should be done to decrease the number of divorces?

Procedure to follow in arriving at possible solutions: (Keep detailed notes on the following data.)

1. Find out all the effects of divorce, both good and bad. Ask your teacher and librarian to help you locate sources of information.

2. Find out what caused these good and bad effects.

3. Now that you know the results of divorces and what causes them, you should decide that anything you suggest as solutions to the problem must meet certain standards. For example,

   (a) Any solution must be fair to both the man and woman.
   (b) Any solution must be fair to the children of divorced parents.
   (c) Any solution must be legal and constitutional.

(d) Any solution must be acceptable to a person's religious beliefs.

4. State several tentative (possible) solutions to your problem of divorces. Be sure these answers meet the standards you set up. Under each suggested solution list both the advantages and disadvantages of it. Remember that you are not to be prejudiced for your solutions. You will soon say to the other panelists, "Here are my ideas with their good and bad points. This is what I believe on the basis of the information I could find. However, I'm willing to change my views if your information indicates I should."

5. Now select the one solution which you think is the best from all those you have constructed.

6. Suggest ways and means to put your best solution into action. For example, newspaper publicity, beginning with your school paper.

Note: Outline all of your points, one through six, using complete sentences. State all your sources of information, giving dates, authors, names of books or magazine, pages, volumes. Be sure to identify your authorities. Hand this outline to your instructor as evidence of preparation.

Now that you have gathered all of the information on your problem, outlined it, and learned its contents sufficiently well, you are ready to meet with other members of the panel to see what they have discovered. Each one of them has done the same thing you did in trying to find out what should be done to decrease the divorce rate. You will all get together and pool your knowledge. Obviously you will not all have the same information, because you did not all read the same magazines and books and talk to the same people. This means you will not agree with each other because your information is different. Your possible solutions will be different too. Nevertheless, you will pool your knowledge and after thoroughly talking it over and examining all the data carefully, you will decide on possible solutions that are agreed on by a majority of the panel. These solutions will represent the **cooperative effort** of all of you, rather than only one person.

HOW TO PRESENT A PANEL DISCUSSION

In presenting a panel you merely meet as a group and discuss the information and ideas each one has brought with them. To do this effectively, each participant should approach the panel with an open mind. You must have a desire to find the answers to the mutual problem of the members, not a desire to propound and seek adoption of your personal ideas and solutions. This attitude of open mindedness is probably the most important aspect of discussion.

Now let us assume that the members of the panel have assembled. The chair should have arrived first and previously placed the seats in a semi-circle so that each person can easily see everyone else during the discussion. The chair will sit near the middle of the group. If an audience attends to hear the panel, the chair should be sure the panelists are all seated in such a manner that they are visible to the listeners. The speakers, in turn, should be just as sure that their remarks are easily heard by everyone present, and they should direct their voices toward the audience as well as the panel.

Before the actual participation begins, each speaker should remember not to dominate the occasion, nor withdraw and say little or nothing. Each one should remember further that they will not become angry, impolite, sarcastic, or acrimonious. They will be very earnest and sincere, however, and even persistent if necessary.

The chair, in turn, will insist—gently, but firmly—on a policy of fairness. The chair will encourage the most timid to speak their minds and promote harmony and goodwill among the group. The chair permit some digression from the main question but direct the discussion in such a way that the main problem is explored. The chair will note the passing of time and make certain that the discussion progresses rapidly enough to be completed within the allotted time.

Now we are ready to begin discussion. The chair will make brief introductory remarks in which they will mention the occasion and reasons for discussing the topic at hand. The chair will introduce members of the panel (if there is an audience) and tell where each is from, their occupation, and anything else appropriate. If there is no audience, the chair should be certain that all members of the panel are acquainted with each other.

The procedure or the actual discussion should be entirely informal throughout. It should be a spontaneous give-and-take affair with free and easy questions, answers, and contributions from everyone without prompting from the chair. This does not mean the chair may not call on a member if they think that it is necessary to do so.

The points to discuss should develop in the following order through informal talk.

1. Define the terms. Be sure you all agree on what you are talking about.
2. Limit your subject if it is too broad. For example, perhaps you should talk about decreasing divorces in the United States only or in one state, one city, or among members of one religion. (Note: The statement of your question does not limit the discussion in this respect.)
3. Talk about the effects of the problem.
4. Discuss the causes of the identified effects.
5. Set up standards on which you will base any solutions to your problem.
6. Arrive at several tentative solutions or conclusions to your question. Be sure you discuss advantages and disadvantages of each one.
7. Select one tentative solution as the best one to put into action.
8. Decide on ways and means to go about putting your solution into action.
9. The chair should summarize briefly what the panel has accomplished.
10. If it is desirable, the chair will permit the audience (if there is one) to direct questions to the panel members. They will have to rule on questions that obviously have no bearing on the discussion or other questions that are out of order.
11. The chair will conclude the meeting with a brief summary at the end of the allotted or appropriate time.

Note: To follow through all of these steps will necessitate a constant alertness on the part of all panelists and the chair. Of course, if a number of meetings are scheduled, you may move gradually through the various stages of arriving at a solution. It is not wise, however, to prolong the sessions until the members become tired.

A good panel discussion starts with research and planning by the members.

LISTENING TO AND READING THE NEWS

NOTE: By regularly viewing television news, listening to radio news and reading newspapers and magazines, you will be introduced to a wide array of potential speech topics and will observe good writing and speaking practices.

1. Keep a place in a notebook to list ideas for potential speech topics you heard or read about in the news. Record the date you heard or read the news item. This will allow you to locate additional material in a variety of sources on similar dates.
2. Read a wide range of news magazines. Don't overlook specialized "news" publications such as sports magazines.
3. Go to the library and read a magazine you have never read before. If you live in a rural area or a small town, read a newspaper from a major city.
4. As you watch the news on television, observe the way the visuals complement the voiceover from the reporters. Think how you can use visuals to add life to your speech.
5. Listen to the news on the radio; a public radio broadcast is preferable. Listen to the way reporters use changes in inflection, volume, and tone to add life to the reports.
6. Read editorials and op-ed pieces (these are the articles appearing on the page opposite the editorial page). Analyze the way the writers build their arguments. Locate articles from two columnists or editorial writers on the same topic with different viewpoints. Analyze how they consider the other side in preparing their columns.

THE SYMPOSIUM

Participants: Three to four speakers and a chair.

Time limits for each speech: 5-6 minutes.

Speaking notes: None for the speakers. The chair may use notes in order to be sure that the order of speakers, topics for discussion, and other information do not become confused.

Sources of information: Three or more should be studied.

Outline of speech: None is required for instructor. Prepare your own to ensure proper organization.

Question: What should you do if you run out of breath?

Answer: Pause and take a breath. Slow down and breathe more deeply.

Key Words:
Proposition
Symposium

Student Expectations: In completing this assignment each student will:
  ➤ *Organize one speech topic among several speakers*
  ➤ *Participate in presenting a speech with several others*
  ➤ *Coordinate presenting a speech topic from several different points of view*
  ➤ *Coordinate answering audience-generated questions with several panel members*

PURPOSE OF THIS ASSIGNMENT

The **symposium**, one type of discussion, is being used more and more as a means of informing and enlightening the public. Many persons are unaware of the different types of discussions and the advantages or disadvantages inherent in each of them. Because it will be to your advantage to understand the workings and the technique of the symposium, it is offered here as a new speech experience for you.

EXPLANATION OF THE SYMPOSIUM

The symposium is a method of presenting representative aspects of a problem. Usually three or four speakers talk about one general question, with each speaker presenting views on a particular aspect. A chair acts as moderator and leader. They synchronize the different speeches so that unification of ideas rather than a series of unrelated lectures is present. Speakers are charged with the responsibility of fitting their remarks into the main question by making sure that they contribute to the **proposition** being explored.

The time allotted each speaker is the same, except that the length of the speeches may vary from a few minutes to fifteen or twenty each if time allows. Following the conclusion of the speeches, the participants may form a panel, after which the audience is invited to ask questions of the speakers. Either one of the latter procedures may be omitted—the panel or questioning by the audience. The whole program may continue as long as an hour and a half if time permits or more if the audience is quite active and the panelists capable.

The purpose of a symposium is to inform and stimulate the listeners. This purpose is accomplished by virtue of the fact that each speaker may support a given point of view. Occasions for the symposium may present themselves any time a group of persons meets. It may be the meeting of a club, a society, a religious, fraternal or business organization, an educational group, any civic gathering or other assemblage. Today radio and television utilize the symposium frequently on certain types of programs.

HOW TO CHOOSE A TOPIC

The members of the symposium should meet with the chair and then by general agreement decide on a proposition. They should choose one that is interesting to everyone, if possible. However, if all of the members of the group do not agree, the one most suitable to the majority should be the choice. It is not to be expected that you can choose a topic on which everyone is well informed. Be sure that your selection is one about which you can secure information by interviews and reading. Consider some of the following topics:

1. What should be done to conserve energy?
2. Should the United States have a program of compulsory national service?
3. What should be done about the nation's homeless?
4. Should scholarships be given to all high school graduates with outstanding records, regardless of financial need?
5. What should be done to decrease juvenile crime?

HOW TO PREPARE A SYMPOSIUM

First of all, it should be kept in mind that the individual speakers should prepare their speeches according to the suggestions laid down for any speech to inform or stimulate. All the steps of preparation should be included from audience analysis to rehearsal.

The mechanics of overall preparation may be as follows:

I. The members should meet with the chair.

A. The topic to be discussed should then be divided by mutual agreement among the speakers so that each one presents a different aspect of it. For ex-

ample, if the topic is "What should be done to improve the streets of our city?" The three speakers (if that is the number) could set up these questions:

(1) What should the city administration do to improve the streets?
(2) What should the citizens do to improve the streets?
(3) What should be done to improve the efficiency and use of present equipment?

II. Having agreed on the above divisions of the question, each speaker is next obligated to prepare the discussion making sure, of course, that they observe the time limits closely.

The chair should be well prepared on the entire subject, in order to direct discussion on it. A routine responsibility of the chair is to set up the order of speakers.

Having completed this, the chair must prepare brief introductory remarks. These remarks will include these facts: (1) a history and statement of the proposition; (2) reasons for its discussion; (3) relationship and importance of the topic to the audience; (4) definitions of terms of the proposition; (5) names, qualifications, topics, and order of the speakers; and (6) the manner in which the symposium will be conducted. The chair should be familiar with the point of view each speaker will take. The chair should also be aware of the necessity for a brief summary at the conclusion of the performance by the speakers and after the questions are asked by the audience.

Members of the media share ideas about the future of presidential debates in a symposium.

Let us assume now that everyone is ready for the symposium. A final check should provide answers to these questions: Does each speaker have sufficient authorities and accurate data to back up their information, ideas, and conclusions? Are these proofs in a form which they can use while they are being questioned by a member of the symposium or the audience? Does each member know how to answer questions from their own group or the audience, to meet objections, to restate arguments, to summarize their point of view? Will the speakers keep their head, their sense of humor, and remain polite when under fire? Does the chair know how to lead the symposium when they form a panel? Does the chair know how to lead the audience and direct questions to the speakers? Do they know what types of questions to permit as legitimate and which to rule out of order? If the answers to these questions are not known to the participants, they are obligated to discover them.

HOW TO PRESENT A SYMPOSIUM

Throughout the entire symposium, good speech practices should be followed. In addition to keeping these in mind, the procedure may be as follows:

1. The symposium members may be seated side-by-side with the chair at one end.
2. The chair will make introductory remarks, will introduce members of the symposium, and then will present the first speaker and the topic.
3. The first speaker will deliver a speech after which the chair will present the other speakers in a similar manner.
4. At the conclusion of the speeches the chair will briefly summarize the ideas of the speakers.
5. Following the chair's summary, the symposium will be continued according to one of the alternatives listed below:

(a) The speakers will form a panel for a limited time and discuss the ideas that were presented after which the chair will summarize briefly, then adjourn the meeting.

(b) The speakers will form a panel as indicated in (a) above, after which the audience will be permitted to question the speakers for a limited or unlimited time by directing questions through the chair. The chair will conclude the symposium with a brief summary followed by adjournment.

(c) Following the speeches and the chair's brief summary, the audience will be permitted to question the speakers (for a definite or indefinite time) by directing questions through the chair. At the conclusion of audience participation, the chair will summarize the matter of the individual speakers, and then adjourn the meeting. In this case there is no panel by the speakers.

CHAPTER 19

THE KEYNOTE ADDRESS

Time limit: 5 minutes.

Speaking notes: Write out a full manuscript with notes for emphasis and other delivery cues as suggested in this chapter.

Sources of information: Two or more. List them at the end of your written speech.

Outline of speech: Prepare a 75-100 word outline for instructor.

Question: How does a speaker decide on a topic for a keynote address?

Answer: The conference or organization's theme should guide topic selection.

Key Words:
Keynote
Manuscript

Student Expectations: In completing this assignment each student will:
- ➤ *Adapt a speech to a conference theme or a group's goals*
- ➤ *Practice generating enthusiasm and motivation*
- ➤ *Prepare a manuscript for delivery*
- ➤ *Understand distinctions between oral and written styles of communication*

PURPOSE OF THIS ASSIGNMENT

This assignment introduces you to an important type of speech that is given in a variety of business, professional, and political settings. The keynote address sets the stage for an entire conference or meeting. It provides a unifying theme and, often, a challenge to listeners. Most **keynote** addresses are carefully worded; thus, one of the important elements of this assignment is preparation of a full manuscript for the speech. Most of the speeches you have given thus far require an outline, and that is the preferred form of speech notes. However, when a speech must be carefully timed, and a message worded to fulfill many purposes, then a **manuscript** is desirable. The keynote address is a formal speech that is usually given to a large gathering. The speaker typically stands behind a lectern on a stage or platform and uses a microphone. Because of the setting and formality,

nonverbal delivery is affected. While you will not have a large audience for your speech, this speech should be given in an auditorium setting to provide the experience of being elevated and distant from the audience. Thus, this assignment fulfills several goals related to both content and delivery.

EXPLANATION OF KEYNOTE ADDRESS

The two short words that are joined together to name this type of speech tell you much about its purpose as well as what you are to accomplish with the assignment. Something that is "key" is important or fundamental. The word "note" has many meanings, but one is a call or a sound. A keynote address sounds or calls attention to something important. If you are a musician you know that the word "keynote" refers to the first tone of a scale that is harmonically fundamental to the scale.

A keynote address is usually the first address given at a conference, convention, or meeting. It is designed to identify the key issues that participants will address in all of their sessions and meetings. The address generates enthusiasm and motivation for the work the group must face. In some instances, especially at political conventions, it is intended to promote unity among subgroups of a party that supported different candidates. At a political convention the keynote reminds everyone that the primary elections are over, the winner has emerged, and it is now time for everyone to unify behind the party's nominee.

A good keynote address makes use of a conference theme or builds on the goals that the group's leaders have chosen for the meeting or for the length of their terms. The speaker should be aware of all of the events that take place during the conference because workshop titles or other activities might provide examples or starting points for developing challenges to the audience. The address also sets the tone for the meeting. If it is a meeting with an agenda that requires the group to solve a problem, then the speaker should challenge the audience to work together to meet that goal. If it is a conference that is intended to share information through workshops, then participants should be encouraged to take advantage of the learning opportunities. In other words, the speaker's goals are influenced by the meeting planners' and audiences' goals.

Keynote addresses can be persuasive or informative. Often they include humor to build good will with the audience. Keynotes are usually given by someone known to the audience either personally or by reputation as an expert on topics that audience members will address during their meetings. Occasionally keynotes are controversial; thus, a speaker should be aware that some members of the audience disagree. A good keynote, regardless of its persuasive or informative intent, prepares everyone in the audience for what is to come and motivates them to take full advantage of the speeches and workshops that follow.

HOW TO CHOOSE A TOPIC FOR A KEYNOTE ADDRESS
Most keynote speakers are assigned a topic that is either on a general theme such as computer literacy or multicultural education. In most instances, not only is a general theme identified for the speaker, but the conference theme is expected to be incorporated. An example of a conference theme is "Beyond the Three Rs: Computer Literacy in a Technological Age."

While a speaker is "assigned" a general theme or topic, the speaker must still narrow the focus of the address. The theme on computer literacy is broad. The speaker could approach it many ways. For instance, the speaker might develop the speech to call for a state-mandated computer literacy requirement for graduation from high school. Or the speaker might discuss novel ways that computer literacy is being incorporated throughout the K-12 curriculum. The composition of the audience, as with any other type of speech, should guide the speaker in the specific development of the topic.

Another source for a topic is the mission statement of the organization. If an elected official were asked to give a keynote address at the beginning of Boys' or Girls' State, then a logical place to focus the speech development would be on the mission or goals that the American Legion has for the activity.

For this assignment, class members should make a list of all of the organizations in your school. These can be local, state, or national organizations. Develop conference themes suitable for the missions of each organization. Select a theme for a hypothetical conference composed of students from schools throughout the city or state. Examples would be student government or Thespians.

HOW TO PREPARE A KEYNOTE ADDRESS
Decide the general purpose of your speech as either informative or persuasive or some combination of both. Review information in earlier chapters on both types of speech. Narrow your, topic and develop a specific purpose as you would with any other speech.

You will need to conduct research appropriate for the organization and for the theme. This will involve talking to the sponsor of the organization and members to learn more about the organization's history and mission. You will also need to do library or Internet research that is appropriate for your specific purpose.

Outline your speech. Then prepare a manuscript. When preparing a manuscript, it is best to talk through your speech as you would if you were giving it from an outline. Tape-record the speech. As you write your speech word-for-word, listen to the way you spoke it when giving it from an outline. Review the manuscript for sentences that ramble or ideas that are not clearly stated. Revise where needed.

As you prepare the manuscript make sure that you are using oral language. Oral style includes contractions, sentence fragments, or single-word sentences for emphasis. For example, "Well, don't," could be a complete thought in a speech if it follows a rhetorical question such as "Have you ever put off studying until the hour before an exam?" After a pause, the statement could be followed by a reminder of the problems that behavior could create for a student. Use words that sound natural to the ear. We tend to use smaller vocabularies when we speak than we do when we write. While you might want to use a thesaurus to write an essay, you want to use common language for a speech. Read the manuscript out loud to others. Ask them if it sounds natural. In other words, does it sound the way you talk, or does it sound as if you are reading? If it is the latter, go back to your outline and practice the speech again. As you rewrite, think about how you "said" the speech.

HOW TO PRESENT THE KEYNOTE ADDRESS
Because you will be giving the speech from a stage with the audience at a distance, it is important to maintain good eye contact. This means that you need to practice the speech several times to the point where it is almost memorized. It is important to remember that the audience doesn't have a manuscript to follow. If you say something differently from the way you wrote it, don't go back and repeat. It is likely that the way you said it was more natural than what you wrote. Prepare your manuscript using triple spacing and a font size of 18 or larger. You want to be able to read it easily

Prominent people, such as General Colin Powell, are popular keynote speakers.

and not lose your place. Be sure to number the pages since you will have multiple pages. Place the manuscript with the page you are reading from on the left and the remaining pages in a stack on the right. As you begin speaking from the page on the right, slide it to the left. Don't turn the pages over.

Since your nonverbals will be limited because you are changing pages every minute or so, you need to use vocal emphasis to get your point across. Because you will have two pages visible at all times, you can still use gestures, however, movement is limited unless you have large segments of the speech memorized and you have a portable microphone. If you have a stationary microphone, you must stay behind the speaker's stand. Speak at a natural rate and in a normal volume as the microphone will do the work of carrying your voice to all parts of the auditorium.

CONQUER THE ISMS THAT STAND IN OUR WAY
CRITICISM, SENSATIONALISM, AND PESSIMISM
by Haven E. Cockerham, Vice President of Human Resources, Detroit Edison
Excerpt from speech delivered to the Birmingham-Bloomfield Task Force on Race Relations and Ethnic Diversity, Birmingham, Michigan, October 31, 1997

Thank you, Ann, for that kind and generous introduction. Ann is a wonderful neighbor. And I'm sure you would agree that she is a valuable asset to the Birmingham-Bloomfield Task Force on Race Relations and Ethnic Diversity. Because this group represents such a wide and diverse range of organizations, I am honored that you chose me to give your keynote address. I hope I can provide some valuable insight to help better grasp the challenges that we face in this arena.

As residents of the city of Birmingham, my family and I have the highest regard for this group. Your commitment to build bridges and increase understanding have made the Birmingham-Bloomfield community a better place for all of us to live and work.

Through activities such as today's conference, you shine a spotlight on some incredibly sensitive issues that many people would simply rather not discuss—at least not in the open. Racism is too controversial... Sexism is too divisive. And you know what they say about politics and religion. Let's face it, it's a lot easier to just keep silent.

But like an old adage says: "Sometimes silence isn't golden—just yellow."

Regardless of race, ethnicity... or religion, as human beings we're all affected by the "isms" that permeate our society. Because the cautionary path of silence often leads nowhere, we must continue to place ourselves on the front line, and address today's important issues.

Earlier today, our panelists offered practical solutions to confront racism, sexism, classism and other divisive issues. But I'd like to discuss a few other "isms" that discourage us from taking active roles in the fight against prejudice and intolerance. These road blocks in the struggle for peace and unity are criticism, sensationalism and pessimism. We must conquer these "isms" that stand in our way.

The first "ism" is criticism. Companies, individuals and organizations that seek change should expect and prepare for criticism. As you know criticism is not always constructive or fair. Sometimes it's just plain hurtful whether it comes from your co-workers, from your neighbors, or from within your own household. Without a doubt, criticism is a heavy cross to bear.

For example, an Arab-American who tries to bridge political differences between Arab Christians and Arab Muslims in the Detroit area may hear criticism by members from both groups. But should he or she let criticism stop these efforts if they could improve the quality of life for nearly 275,000 Arab-Americans in Southeastern Michigan?

Maybe you are a member of the League of Women Voters and you speak out against disparities in the political opportunities offered to men and women. Do your efforts make you a "male basher?"

Or perhaps you are a member of the Anti-Defamation League, and you challenge individuals or organizations that make "anti-Semitic" remarks. Is it better to just keep silent and hope that prejudice will go away on its own?

I recall that a year or so ago some of the organizations here took part in the debate over SMART bus service linking Detroit and the suburbs. For example, you encouraged the city of West Bloomfield to rejoin the SMART regional bus system. The city was among 55 communities in metropolitan Detroit that opted out of the system in 1995.

We all know that the lack of public transportation can be an impediment for many low-income Detroiters to get jobs in the suburbs. Task force members readily tackled the racial ramifications of the debate. You educated the community about how regional bus transportation can build bridges and improve race relations between Detroit and the suburbs.

Residents approved the small property tax increase required for the city to rejoin the system. Many of you felt the sting of criticism from residents who opposed the city's support of the SMART bus system. But that didn't stop you. You stood by your convictions. By disregarding criticism, you opened the door to job opportunities for thousands of Detroiters, and helped bridge the racial gap between the city and suburbs. You should be proud of your courage and your achievements.

It may be easier to keep silent. But I cannot imagine what our world would be like if Dr. Martin Luther King Jr., Mahatma Gandhi, Susan B. Anthony or more recently Mother Teresa had been silenced by criticism, before they had a chance to make a difference.

Another "ism" that can silence our voices is sensationalism. Understandably, many of us are reluctant to take positions on high-profile issues. After all, being committed to change doesn't mean we want to see our faces on the six o'clock news. What would people think? Would we be subject to criticism?

Concerns about sensationalism are not unrealistic. Pick up the newspaper any day of the week, and you will read articles about racial quotas, religious wars, age discrimination lawsuits, sexual harassment charges and a host of other volatile issues that ignite our emotions.

Earlier this year, the media and opinion leaders debated the issue of having a federal government apology to African Americans for slavery. The debate triggered a wide range of discussion and sentiment. But most importantly, the publicity stimulated dialogue about race relations in this country. Hopefully some of that dialogue will help heal the wounds from one of the most shameful periods in our country's history.

You may have heard about lawsuits by current and former Detroit Edison employees, charging the company with race, and age discrimination.

In the early 1990s reorganizations to prepare DTE to compete triggered the lawsuits. The process was difficult and painful. We believe we were fair; but unfortunately many employees feel differently. Hopefully, we can resolve the lawsuits so we can focus our attention on the challenges and opportunities of competition in the electric utility industry.

Resolving internal issues under the watchful eye of the news media and the public can be a difficult task for any corporation or organization. But experience has taught me that you can turn sensationalism into a positive "ism"...

Sensationalism by its nature keeps diversity and related issues in our society on the front burner. If you let it, this "ism" can serve as a positive motivator for change. The best way to conquer the fear of sensationalism is to make it a learning experience—and move forward.

The third "ism" that distracts us from our goals is pessimism. It can gradually chip away at our spirits. Pessimism can extinguish the fire that heats our passion for the struggle against intolerance. We can grow tired and weary. Sometimes, regardless of how hard we try, the glass just looks half empty...

We are all discouraged from time to time...but we must continue to push forward, and rejuvenate our commitment to remove the barriers that keep us apart. It takes a tough mind and a strong spirit to conquer the stranglehold of pessimism.

I learned that lesson a long time ago. Growing up in the segregated south taught me about mental toughness and perseverance. When I was a high school student in 1963, I watched Dr. Martin Luther King Jr. deliver what may be the greatest speech of the 20th Century. Dr. King stood in front of more than 200,000 people gathered at the Lincoln Memorial, and captivated the nation as he presented his dream of racial equality.

But growing up in North Carolina, I had a difficult time visualizing Dr. King's dream. He saw hope, unity and understanding. I saw "Whites Only" and "Colored Only" signs in restaurants and at public facilities.

But as I grew physically, I also developed my mind, opened my heart and strengthened my spirit. Life's experiences have a way of building character. I began to understand Dr. King's dream and the requirements to transform dreams into reality.

Detroit Edison will join the nation next year in celebrating the 35th anniversary of the "I Have A Dream" speech. And I'm pleased to say that in 1997 my dreams—like Dr. King's—are not blocked by pessimism. Instead, I have embraced another "ism"—one that is more positive than the criticism, sensationalism and pessimism that can stand in our way and block our success. I am talking about constructive activism.

We must continue to embrace positive activism...

At Detroit Edison, we are doing our part by building a diverse and people-focused workforce for the future. A people-focused workforce attracts the quality of employees required for success in a competitive environment. We want all employees to feel they are treated fairly, and with respect.

At the same time we can better serve a diverse customer base. For example, more than a quarter of metropolitan Detroit's residents are non-White, including African American, Asian, Middle Eastern and other groups.

A diverse workforce also helps Detroit Edison build upon our long tradition of community involvement and leadership. Through positive activism, we can promote diversity awareness in our company and community. Here are a few examples.

Detroit Edison recently formed a Diversity Management Initiative to support an environment of trust among our highly qualified and diverse workforce.

Diversity training is a requirement of leadership training. The diversity training also is available companywide on a voluntary basis.

The closely-related Diversity Action Council is a "grass roots" outgrowth of the Diversity Management Initiative. The council consists of about a dozen employees representing all employee groups at DTE Energy: African American, Native American, Gays and Lesbians, physically challenged and others.

The council identifies and recommends solutions for company and industry diversity issues, such as increasing the use of minority-owned vendors. Norm Littles, our minority business administrator, creates successful alliances between major Detroit Edison suppliers, and minority- and women-owned businesses. He helps generate new opportunities and open new markets for minority suppliers. With Norm's help, last year Detroit Edison spent $53 million dollars with minority and women-owned vendors.

Earlier this year, we introduced an Ethnic Marketing group to better serve our Asian and Arab American customers. Southeastern Michigan is home to the largest Middle Eastern community in North America. . .

Our goal is to make Detroit Edison a model for a discrimination-free workplace just as the Birmingham-Bloomfield Task Force is a model for improving race relations and understanding diversity in the Detroit area.

I heard someone say: to avoid criticism, do nothing, say nothing, be nothing. I think that is too big a price to pay. I hope you will turn sensationalism and publicity into opportunities for growth and change. In summary, I urge you to engage your tough mind and spirit to conquer the negative "isms" of criticism, sensationalism and pessimism.

Together or separately, the negative "isms" of life will discourage and distract you from your mission. But if you are truly committed to the goals of this task force and I am confident that you are—you will not let them stop your positive activism.

Businesses, individuals and organizations like this one must continue to actively seek opportunities to dialogue about diversity in the workplace, with our families and friends, as well as in our schools, churches, temples and mosques.

Continue your work in the task force and the other organizations represented here today. You will inspire other communities in the Detroit area to carry the torch of racial healing and diversity awareness and acceptance.

I will close with a few words from Dr. King's speech. Because the words are as prolific and relevant in Birmingham, Michigan today, as they were in Washington, D.C. in 1963:

" I say to you today, my friends, that in spite of the difficulties and frustrations of the moment, I still have a dream. It is a dream deeply rooted in the American dream. I have a dream that one day this nation will rise up and live out the true meaning of its creed. We hold these truths to be self-evident: that all men (and women) are created equal."

Dr. King's words relay the most powerful "ism' of them all—and that is optimism. Thank you very much, and continue to fight for what you know is right.

UNIT IV

SPECIAL OCCASION SPEECHES

Speaking for a special occasion usually means that a particular context will frame the speaking experience. All of the speeches in this unit are examples of such contexts. Each comes with particular expectations from the audience that certain criteria will be met by the speech for each occasion.

After Dinner Speaking takes place, of course, in the context of a meal being served. People generally have lowered abilities to listen right after eating, so such speeches do not ideally include the dissemination of critically important information, nor the high-powered persuasion of policy-making efforts. More frequently, after dinner speeches are designed to entertain and celebrate the occasion for the dinner or special persons present. They can certainly impart information or persuade, but those are secondary purposes for this context in most cases. This chapter provides the student with the opportunity to design appropriate remarks for such an occasion, as well as to understand the complexities of planning such an event.

An occasion of more gravity would be the election of persons to hold responsible positions of leadership. The nomination and election of persons to those positions require remarks that inspire confidence from voters. In the chapter on *Nomination to Office and Acceptance Speeches,* students will have a chance both to nominate someone to an office with appropriate efforts to establish their credibility, and to accept a nomination or election with sincerity, assuring the voters they have made a good choice.

On many occasions there is need for a speaker to receive a formal introduction before they make their presentation. Formal introductions, though they are necessarily brief, have particular requirements of their own. The introducer's job is to set the tone for the speaker to be well-received by the audience, and to offer the evidence of the speaker's credentials in order to establish his or her authority to speak. *The Introduction Speech* prepares students for just such a task.

As we have said throughout the text, public speaking is about building and maintaining relationships between speakers and audiences. Nowhere is this more directly illustrated than in speeches of welcome and their responses. Formal greetings are often made in order to set a pleasant stage for the visits of special guests. The chapter on *Welcoming and Response Speeches* describes the important elements necessary to establish an atmosphere of hospitality and warmth between hosts and visitors.

Presenting and Accepting Gifts or Awards are usually occasions when people stop to recognize the outstanding achievements of someone who is a part of their community. Because it is important enough to take the time and resources to honor the person or persons, the speeches of presentation and acceptance must be carefully crafted to incorporate the elements that will make the audience feel they have accomplished their goal of proper recognition. This chapter helps the student understand what those necessary elements are and how to incorporate them into the speeches of the event.

Another occasion for recognizing the contributions of a particular person occurs when the person leaves the community after being an active participant in community life. In this context, the one who is leaving may need to offer a few remarks of appreciation for the time spent in the community. While the purposes of recognition may be similar, the emotions involved in this particular setting may be very different from other speeches of appreciation. *The Farewell Speech* introduces the student to the leave-taking context, and provides guidance for making appropriate remarks on that occasion.

Sooner or later we all experience the loss of someone important in our lives. When these occasions happen, people often gather to hear speeches in praise of that person's life and of their contributions to the community left behind. *The Eulogy* is a speech of praise given at funerals, retirements, and other settings recognizing similar significant events. This assignment offers the student an opportunity to study the elements of such a speech in order to be better prepared when such an occasion arises.

Two similar contexts offer the chance for persons to mark the present experience of a past event. *The Dedication Speech* is given when a particular place or object is set aside to commemorate an event of the past. *The Anniversary Speech* in given to mark the particular time or day of the event as one that continues to be honored in the memory of those present. These two chapters are designed to familiarize the student with important aspects of comments made in either setting.

The commencement ceremony is always a very full event with many important components. Despite the fact that many people hope the commencement speaker is brief, most would feel incomplete without the appropriate words presented in the ceremony on behalf of, and in honor of, the graduates. *The Commencement Speech* requires careful consideration of these diverse elements of this particular context. This chapter will help the student understand how a speech can best meet these competing needs on this special occasion.

An oral book review is a unique occasion for a speech because the topic is clearly determined by the text to be reviewed. Still, it is *not* appropriate on such occasions to, in effect, read the text or large portions of it to the audience. They have assembled to hear a concise, complete summary of the text, as well as the speaker's evaluation of the text. This chapter on *The Book Review* will help the student experience making such an evaluation and summary, and then presenting those results orally in an interesting way.

As you can tell, there are many special occasions for which spoken remarks are essential elements. This unit is designed to introduce the student to a wide variety of those occasions in order to provide experiences they may draw upon as they encounter these contexts throughout life.

CHAPTER 20

AFTER DINNER SPEAKING

Time limits: 3 minutes –This time limit is necessary in order that each person may be permitted to speak. Longer speeches may extend the time too much.

Speaking notes: 10-word maximum.

Hint: Although you are not required to prepare an outline or to read source materials, it will be wise to do both for your own benefit.

Question: What is the best type of speech for a beginner?

Answer: Generally an informative speech. Don't avoid other kinds, however.

Key Words:
After dinner speaking
Toastmaster

Student Expectations: In completing this assignment each student will:
  ➤ *Understand how an after dinner program is arranged and experience holding one*
  ➤ *Identify the duties of a toastmaster*
  ➤ *Determine an appropriate purpose for an after dinner speech*
  ➤ *Adapt a speech topic to a specific setting*

PURPOSE OF THIS ASSIGNMENT

One of the best ways to learn anything is actually to experience it. From the experience of preparing this speech assignment, you will gain first-hand knowledge of after dinner speaking. You will see how the program is arranged, how the order of serving is coordinated with the speeches, and how the toastmaster must carry on and keep events moving. You will acquire much other valuable information concerning after dinner speaking. You will learn it because you will help build the entire program and because you will be a speaker at the dinner.

This experience is proposed so that you may broaden your knowledge of the various types of after dinner speeches and their related activities.

EXPLANATION OF AFTER DINNER SPEAKING

After dinner speaking is giving a speech following a meal at which a group has gathered. The speech may have a serious purpose, or it may be designed to give entertainment and pleasure. The type of speech—informative, persuasive, entertainment, or a combination—which you present depends on the occasion, its objective, and the purpose for the dinner. After dinner speeches require that the speaker follow closely all the rules of good organization, particularly those for serious talks. An after dinner speech can be given formally while standing behind a podium, or it may be given while seated, if it is for a small group.

Occasions for the after dinner speech are many.

They may be business luncheons, club dinners, committee meetings, special breakfasts, promotional gatherings, campaign inaugurations, socials, celebrations, anniversaries, or any one of a dozen other occasions.

HOW TO CHOOSE A TOPIC FOR AFTER DINNER SPEAKING

Decide on the purpose of your speech. Be sure you can develop your topic to fulfill that purpose. Select something suitable and interesting to you, yet adapted to the occasion and audience. Adapt the theme, if there is one, for the occasion. As with any other speech, plan your topic well in advance.

SOME TOPIC POSSIBILITIES

Best Friends
Gendered Communication
A Success Story
Of All the Sad Words
Ten Years from Now
A Better World for All
Raising Parents

HOW TO PREPARE AN AFTER DINNER SPEECH

First of all, study this assignment carefully to learn fully the requirements of successful after dinner speaking. Follow previous information relative to speech organization, wording, and practice. Plan to use no notes. If you are a **toastmaster**, knowledge of and preparation for your task are the only assurances of a satisfactory performance.

The speaker's obligations: The preparation for this talk is no different from that of any other speech of the type you intend to present. Possibly your thoughts will be to entertain. If this is true, of course you will prepare a speech to entertain. Should you not be familiar with the requirements of this kind of speech, turn to Chapter 11. Follow this procedure for any type of speech you wish to deliver whether it be the speech to persuade, to inform, or to motivate.

Having ascertained your subject and the manner in which you will treat it, complete the preparation of your speech carefully. Before you consider yourself fully prepared, find out all you can about the program, when you will speak, who will pre-

cede you, and who will follow you. Then be sure that your speech is in line with the occasion.

It is not necessary and certainly not always advisable that a speaker plan to tell a joke on the toastmaster, regardless of what the toastmaster may do in the way of introduction. If the occasion calls for humor, a person should be ready to meet it. If it is doubtful what to do, play it safe. Good taste never offends. As far as risqué stories go, leave them at home. The world has a great storehouse of humor and stories for all who want them, and these are excellent for after dinner speeches.

To complete the preparation of your after dinner speech, practice it aloud several times before a mirror or tape record. It is a splendid idea to ask a friend or friends to hear you in rehearsal. Before you accept their advice or criticisms too literally, give some thought to their suggestions and the reliability of their advice.

The toastmaster's obligations are to see that everything is ready to go, to open the proceedings, to keep them going, and to close the meeting. Let us examine these duties separately.

First, to arrange everything, you should arrive at the meeting place early, at least by an hour. Then perform the following chores: (1) advise the servers in detail as to how the meal is to be served; (2) note the arrangement of the banquet room and suggest any changes desired; (3) inquire about a checkroom or other space for coats and make certain it is available and ready for use; (4) locate restrooms and be ready to direct persons to them; (5) shortly before dinner time, personally check place cards on the tables to be sure that the right number is available; (6) keep careful check on the guests as they arrive so that you will know when everyone is there; (7) indicate to the group when they are to go into the dining hall, that is, if they have been waiting in a lobby. If everyone has previously gathered in the dining room, be the first to seek your chair as a signal that the others should follow suit; (8) your general duty will be to see that guests are welcomed by yourself or another designated person, that they are introduced, their coats properly disposed of, and that they are entertained and put at ease; (9) during the banquet, constantly remain alert to see that all goes well, and (10) see that the committee pays for the banquet or makes definite arrangements to settle the account later. Also see that a tip is left for the servers. Of course, when there are several toastmasters, these duties may be divided among them. Everyone should know specifically what they are to do and should carry out each obligation conscientiously.

In regard to the actual work of introducing the speakers, considerable information must be gathered and set up several days early. This includes these necessary items: (1) the names of the speakers; (2) their topics; (3) data concerning speakers that will be suitable to use when introducing them; and (4) the order of the speakers. All this must be drawn together at a toastmasters' meeting and definitely agreed on by mutual consent. The act of introducing the speakers requires ingenuity and planning. A toastmaster should learn early, they are not to make speeches. This pleasure belongs to the after dinner speakers. The toastmaster merely presents each speaker by giving a short introduction. Thirty seconds usually suffices, sometimes less, but never more than a minute or two, at the maximum. At the banquet for this assignment the thirty-second limit should prevail. The introduction may be a clever statement or two about the speaker, their name, and topic. A fitting anecdote is in order if the occasion demands it. After the speaker concludes the speech, the toastmaster should get on with the show and not take time out to offer a response to some remark made by the speaker.

Throughout the evening's performances, the toastmasters should agree on matters such as when and whom to applaud and any other activities or procedures that should be initiated by the toastmasters.

HOW TO PRESENT AN AFTER DINNER SPEECH

Your presentation should reflect the type of speech you deliver. Generally speaking, a simple organization, graphic word pictures, sufficient humor, lively and animated delivery, and a forward motion of ideas characterize after dinner speeches.

Voice and bodily action should be in harmony with the speech occasion and environment. The chances are that you will not need to talk loudly to be heard, nor will you be permitted much bodily action because of room accommodations and arrangement. Care should be exercised when rising to speak, or your chair may scrape noisily on the floor making you appear awkward. To prevent this, see that your chair is far enough from the table that you may rise freely without moving the chair. When the chairperson, toastmaster, or president introduces you, rise and address the person according to the position they hold, such as, "Mr. Toastmaster," "Madam President," and the like.

If during the program some person appearing ahead of you unknowingly steals your speech, the best thing for you to do when you speak is to refer to their remarks in support of your statements. You can go ahead then with your own thoughts and elaborate on them as necessary and as was planned. "Ad lib" and improvise as the situation demands. Retain a sense of humor; use it if it is appropriate, and observe time limits. Remember that the program committee allotted only a certain amount of time to you.

GROUP PLANS TO BE MADE

To make this experience real, you should by all means hold this meeting at a local hotel, cafe, school cafeteria, or other place where the class can meet and eat without being crowded. The atmosphere should be absolutely real, no make-believe.

In order to prepare successfully for this dinner, the following arrangements should be completed by separate committees:

Committee No. 1:
The reservation and menu committee should set a date for the luncheon and reserve a suitable place to hold it. Committee members should check carefully the size of the room and whether or not there will be extra charge for the use of the room. Serving facilities should be ascertained and assurance should be received that the group will not be disturbed by customers, if they are in a public restaurant. It is to be noted also if there is lobby space in which to gather and check coats before going into the dining room. At least three different menus and their respective costs should be investigated

and submitted to the class. One menu should be adopted and a price limit established. Arrangements should be made for special dietaries needs, such as vegetarian meals. The time the meal will be served should be announced. It may be a noon or evening function, but preferably an evening one.

CNN's Bernard Shaw shares ideas in an informal after dinner presentation.

Committee No. 2:
The decorations committee decides what, if any, decorations are to be used. A fund must be established to cover any costs. Expenditure must be kept within the limits of this fund. The class may need to hold a fund raiser of approach the administration about possible funding support. If the later approach is used, invite the principal and spouse or guest to the dinner.

Committee No. 3:
The toastmaster's committee will consist of, approximately twenty-five percent of the class, who will act as toastmasters. They should be elected by secret ballot. Each class member will write on a piece of paper as many names as there are to be toastmasters. If five is the number of toastmasters, then the five persons whose names are written the greatest number of times will be declared elected. They in turn, will meet as a committee to decide the order in which they will preside and the order of those they will introduce. They will learn in advance the topic of each speaker, thus preventing overlapping talks. Each toastmaster should plan to introduce a series of speakers, after which they will present the next toastmaster who will continue in the same

manner. The first toastmaster will open the meeting and introduce guests. This may be done just before starting to eat, or it may be done at the first part of the program following the dinner. The last toastmaster, after introducing the speakers, should make appropriate closing remarks and adjourn the meeting. It is often embarrassing to everyone present if the last toastmaster does not make it absolutely clear that the banquet is concluded.

This use of several toastmasters may be somewhat unconventional but this arrangement gives more persons the experience as toastmaster. It adds variety to the program, provides opportunity for originality, and generally enhances the experience. It also suggests a basis for comparison of ideas as to what makes a good toastmaster.

Committee No. 4:
The fund raiser committee is responsible for finding someone to help with expenses and for collecting in advance the proper amount needed from each class member. They will divide and deliver this money to each committee chair whose group has incurred a debt which must be paid immediately following the dinner. Persons who have a plate reserved at the dinner but who do not come should expect to forfeit the price of the meal. Most hotels will charge for the places set.

SUMMARY
Needless to say, all of the above committees must coordinate their efforts and work as a unit. Each reports its activities so all may know what progress has been made. It is likely your instructor will act as coordinator. It will be wise to seek advice besides reading numerous references pertaining to banquet procedure.

The group may or may not wish to invite guests. It is highly desirable that parents, friends, teachers, or dates be invited. This makes the event a real banquet. While it is advisable to bring guests, those who do so should remember that they will be expected to pay for the guests' dinners.

Here are several points to investigate:
 1. How early should you arrive? (A minimum of five minutes early.)

2. What clothes should you wear? (Hint—better make this dinner informal.)

3. What is the proper etiquette? (Good manners and willingness to make conversation—do not "freeze up.")

4. When and whom should you applaud? (Follow the toastmaster's lead.)

5. What are the toastmaster's duties? (To set the pace for the entire banquet.)

6. When should the food be served? Between speeches? Just how? (Hint—better settle this point definitely and be sure your servers are correctly informed. It is desirable that speeches come after dessert.)

7. What should you do if you make a blunder? (Do nothing; go on.)

8. Supposing someone is late; what then? (Wait a few minutes then start the banquet.)

9. What if you should forget your speech? (Hint—do not ever memorize it. Have your main points in mind. Rehearse.)

10. How and when should you seat yourself? Where? (If there are no place cards, find your own seat.)

11. What should you do when the toastmaster dismisses the group? Linger? Just wait? (Go home, unless other arrangements have been made.)

WHAT IS MOST IMPORTANT
An After Dinner Speech by Tim Borchers

I was walking down the street one day when this weird looking bearded guy wearing a toga approached me, "You may be just the person I am looking for to carry out my quest." I walked faster, but he chased after me, "You are to tell the world of terrible destruction. The citizens of the world don't know how to think anymore." He looked real intense and kind of sad, so I let him continue. "The citizens believe everything told to them by bad people. There is only one way to save the world from impending doom. Someone must teach the world how to think again." I was wary. "Can I do that?" I asked. He replied, "You must at least try."

My buddy Plato once theorized people would blindly accept society's versions of importance, truth and reality without critically evaluating these ideas. Unfortunately, we do. Now we must begin to examine what we often take for granted. We must understand, first, how we allow capitalists to tell us what is important; second, how we permit society to tell us what is true; and finally, how we rely on the media to tell us what is happening in the world.

I was sitting in my civics class one day and, in between naps, I caught the teacher asking, "Anyone, anyone. Who can tell me the implications of the Supreme Court case *Mapp vs. Ohio.*" The guy sitting next to me, wearing a "Property of the Football Team" sweatshirt, raised his huge hand and said, "Uh...15 yards and a loss of down?" I thought, "football player, he's dumb." Then I thought for a minute. "In six years, he will have been drafted by the pros, making a million dollars a year. I'll be graduating from college, $50,000 in debt. I'm dumb!" Then I started to question our society—"Why do Madonna, Bill Cosby, Donald Trump, and Michael Jordan all make more money than our teachers?"

In the beginning of time, or when TV was invented, same difference, these other people became famous by appearing on the tube. As soon as they became famous, they started advertising products for capitalists. Advertising for capitalists made these people rich and consequently important. Let's face it, since teachers are never on TV or in the movies, they don't get corporate endorsements, and voila! aren't important. Could you imagine? "Hi! I'm Tim Borchers, former student, now I'm a teacher. When it comes to shoes, I wear Nike Wing Tips. When it comes to education, Just Do It!"

By now you're asking, "I can't play football, or basketball and I'm not a money-grubbing unethical capitalist swine. So how do I know what's important?" First, we need to write our Representatives and Senators. Tell them to support legislation abolishing capitalism! I don't suppose that will work, so let's make it simple: think! Don't accept the societal hierarchy created by capitalists. Stand up and say, "Teachers are more important than football players." Establish for yourself what is important.

Knowing what's important is not enough, we must also see how society is full of them. . .it. . . stereotypes—society's statements of truth. I asked Plato when stereotypes started. He said he didn't' know. So I turned to Dr. Seuss. He said, "Once there were two kinds of people in the world. The star bellied sneetches had bellies with stars. The plain-bellied sneetches had none upon thars. When the star-bellied sneetches went out to play ball, could a plain belly get in the game? Not at all!" We haven't advanced very far from the days of the sneetches. Television and movies perpetuate stereotypes until we don't know what's true.

Fortunately, there is a solution. Critically evaluate what society says. That's right, we have to think. Don't start stereotypes, don't repeat stereotypes. And if you hear someone repeating a stereotype, tell them to knock it off. Tell them to solve the greenhouse effect, make world peace, or go read a book.

You're asking, "What's the final thing we do without thinking?" It is this: we accept the media's perspective of what's happening in the world. Trying to figure out what was happening in the world, I bought a recent news magazine. I was flabbergasted: on the cover, Seinfeld!! No presidnet, no congressional sleaze stories, not even a measly story on world trade. The news magazine was an anomaly, I thought, so I bought a another one, long known for its in-depth reporting. Again, Seinfeld.

Doris Graber, in her book *Mass Media and American Politics*, argues that the press indicates how much importance we should attach to public issues. This is called the media's Agenda-Setting function. So if all we hear is Seinfeld, we think it's important. If all we see is the presidency, we think it's important, and if all we see is news about free trade, we think it's important.

You won't know what's going on in the world by reading news magazines, so you must determine what's important based on what you think and not the amount of press an issue gets. A social studies instructor of mine once said, "Develop your perception of reality based on information-gathering from a cross-section of media." Sorry, spending five minutes a day reading *USA Today* won't work.

We've reached a point where we don't know what's important, "true" or "really" happening in the world. Rather depressing, but here's some advice: Don't let the Donald Trumps of the world think for you. Cognate, muse, ponder, meditate, create, don't watch so much TV, read a book, don't eat sweets, wear your seatbelt. And above all, remember the ideals that make our country great—knowledge, discipline, and individuality.

CONCLUSION

The conclusion is an extremely important part of a speech. It is important to leave the audience with a strong, straightforward impression.

1. Summaries are the most common type of conclusion. If using a summary conclusion, be brief and recap only the main points.
2. Attention-getting materials or anecdotes also make effective conclusions.
3. Review the introduction and see if there is a way to tie the conclusion to it. For instance, if you quote a famous person in the introduction, refer back to the quotation to summarize or quote a similar thought from the same or a different person.
4. Always keep in mind the purpose of the speech and develop an appropriate conclusion. If the purpose is to persuade, an appeal at the end may be effective. If the purpose is to entertain, an amusing story may be the most effective. An appropriate quotation can also be a good way to end a speech.

CHAPTER 21

NOMINATION TO OFFICE AND ACCEPTANCE SPEECHES

Time limits: 2-3 minutes. Keep your speech within the allotted time.

Speaking notes: Do not use them.

Source of information: To nominate someone else, simply be accurate in your statements regarding the qualifications of the one you are nominating. To accept a nomination, you are the only source needed.

Outline your speech: Prepare a 50-100 word complete sentence outline.

Question: If your remarks draw applause, what should you do?

Answer: Be very happy, wait until it subsides, then go on.

Key Words:
Confidence
Nominating speech
Acceptance speech

Student Expectations: In completing this assignment each student will:
- ➤ *Determine an appropriate candidate for a particular office*
- ➤ *Generate arguments that will establish confidence in the candidate*
- ➤ *Organize and present the speech in a clear, concise and confident manner*
- ➤ *Identify the necessary elements for a speech of acceptance*

PURPOSE OF THIS ASSIGNMENT

How many times have you heard the remark, "I wish I had nominated Mary for president last night; I almost did. She'd be better than Bill." But the sad fact remains that Mary, well qualified and capable, was not nominated. Why? Probably because the person who wanted to nominate her lacked the knowledge of what to say in order to nominate her effectively. This experience should show you what to do and how to present both an effective nominating speech and an acceptance speech, should the occasions ever arise for them.

EXPLANATION OF THE NOMINATING AND ACCEPTANCE SPEECHES

A **nominating speech** is one in which a speaker places the name of another person before an as-

sembly as a candidate for office. The speech is usually not long, most often lasting only a few minutes. In presenting the candidate to the audience, the speaker tells why the candidate is especially fitted for the office in question. Before a nomination can be made, the chairperson of the assembly must announce that nominations are in order, and the nominator must be formally recognized to speak.

A speech in which you accept a nomination for an office is one in which you publicly recognize your own nomination or election to the office. Your purpose is to establish **confidence** in you in the minds of the audience. An occasion of this sort is potentially important; anything you say may be used for or against you. If you are surprised by the nomination, it is wise not to say anything about your unpreparedness for you could easily say the wrong thing.

HOW TO CHOOSE A CANDIDATE FOR A NOMINATING SPEECH

First, you must have confidence in the ability of the person whom you nominate. Second, be sure that the person is acceptable as a candidate. Choose someone reasonably well known with a good record. For this assignment, think about organizations to which you belong and nominate an officer. Another possible choice is to nominate a person for a political office. You can research campaign literature to help you.

HOW TO CHOOSE A SUBJECT FOR AN ACCEPTANCE SPEECH

Base your decision on your own interest in the office and in the suitability of your goals to those of the audience and organization. Think about the clubs and organizations to which you and your classmates belong. If you hold an office or have held one, recreate that situation.

HOW TO PREPARE THE NOMINATING AND ACCEPTANCE SPEECHES

In the nominating speech, all of the elements of the speech should point in one direction: Elect this candidate! Careful organization should be worked out. Name the office, and set forth its specific requirements and needs. Then show that your candidate has exceptional fitness to satisfy all needs and demands of the office. Be specific. Mention training, experience, abilities of leadership, outstanding traits of character. Clinch your point by summarizing and stating that the person is undoubtedly best suited for the office.

In the **acceptance speech**, be sure to adhere to all the rules for preparing and constructing a speech. Since the purpose of this speech is to establish yourself as a leader, speak in well-chosen words of appreciation for the honor conferred on you by the nomination or election. Do not talk about yourself; rather, speak of the organization and its

importance. Commend its history, its achievements, and its principles. Explain how these have made it grow and will continue to operate in the future. You may refer to the names of great people of past fame in the organization and promise to uphold their ideals. Finally, pledge your loyalty and support to the organization. State frankly that you accept the nomination or office with a complete realization of its responsibilities and that you intend to carry them out. It would be appropriate to make a concluding remark repeating your appreciation for the honor. Caution: *In no way* should you let the audience down by causing them to feel they have made a mistake.

Rehearse your speech aloud until you have the sequence of ideas well in mind. Give particular attention to the introduction and conclusion.

HOW TO PRESENT NOMINATING AND ACCEPTANCE SPEECHES

You must have confidence in yourself. Your attitude should be one of dignity, friendliness, sincerity, and enthusiasm. Attention should be paid to your dress so that it is appropriate to the occasion, the audience, and yourself.

The words of your speech must be vivid, descriptive, and meaningful. Talk loudly enough to be heard by all; speak clearly and distinctly, neither too fast nor too slowly. There must be a fluency and readiness of speech that fairly shout to the audience that you know what you are talking about.

Your emphasis, spontaneity, and sincerity must be manifested by your entire body. This will be shown by what you do, the way you look, and how you sound. You should avoid giving the appearance of being overly confident, overbearing, or conceited. Have a lively, energetic, unhesitant manner, as well as a pleasant, confident voice and a sincere desire to communicate. Then you will make a good speech.

NOMINATING SPEECH
by John R. Knorr

In the past years, the Medical Practice Board of Missouri has made many innovative moves, a few of which have been nationwide firsts. These moves have often been spearheaded by a single person. Tonight I am proud to put before the Board such a person for nomination to be chairperson of the Allied Health Advisory Committee, Nell Healy, R.N. Ms. Healy through her work as Head of Nursing at Washington University Hospital has seen the health care field from many sides. She not only has the foresight that being a chair demands, but also the experience to convert the future into the present. Ms. Healy was at the head of the lobby for the Nurse Training Act that was adopted by the Missouri Legislature last month.

Ms. Healy has shown the Board that there is more to the health care field than patient care in understaffed hospitals. There are dedicated people today who would go into the nursing field if only given the chance. This is because the most vital programs of Nursing Education can't presently give them that chance.

As chairman of the Allied Health Advisory Committee, Ms. Healy will be an advisor to the Missouri Legislature on health care matters. She will be at the head of a branch of the Medical Practice Board that everyone will be proud to represent.

Ms. Healy has shown through her expressed views that the patient and the patient's health are our highest priorities. This post needs a chair with this outlook. For these reasons I am proud to put before the Board Ms. Nell Healy for nomination to be chairperson of the Allied Health Advisory Committee.

ACCEPTING A NOMINATION
by Tom J. Mayer

Mr. President, officers, and fellow members of F.F.A., all of you are dedicated to a purpose which can be realized: The purpose of strengthening the agricultural backbone of our country and restoring the farm family to its rightful position. We have seen our parents and grandparents toil long hours to nurture life in once fallow tracts of land. The recognition they deserve still lies fallow, but the Future Farmers of America are seeing more than the vision of our parents— we are seeking the culmination of world events that must place the fruits of our labor in utmost demand.

The heritage of the farmer in this country is rich. Cities, towns, even countries have been fed, and they receive the fruit of our greatest office, that of provider. Each one of us stands in the gap as provider for the world. Let us stand boldly in recognition of the office handed us by our parents, and make them as proud to be called our parents as we are to be called their children.

The nomination to the office of national president of Future Farmers of America is a special privilege, and one I accept with much pride and appreciation. The challenge demanded by this position is great, not only because of the decisions concerning future operations, but because of the standards realized by all of you. I accept this nomination with confidence in the foundation of our heritage and the progressive attitude of our membership.

ACCEPTING AN OFFICE
by Mary-Alice Shaw

President Ugaki, members of the Board, and delegates: Three years ago I was attracted to the Intermountain Hospice Support Group for personal reasons. I admired the unique combination of compassion and professionalism evident within the organization, and I appreciated the fact that your support existed for those of us left to deal with terminal illness at some level in our lives.

As I look around at those of you here today, I see the past three years reflected back at me. I see the tears shared, the small joys experienced, and the patience and understanding given so readily and so often. I see a concept which has grown and flourished and gained validity and worldwide recognition.

I have endeavored to contribute as much of my abilities and talents and time as I could toward our common goals, and I have been proud to be a part of the whole. The challenges have been difficult, the failures few but palpable and the satisfactions many, but the people involved have impressed me the most.

I've come to respect each of you with whom I've worked for your cooperative spirit and extensive knowledge and extreme caring. Your willingness to teach me what you could was gratifying. Your criticisms were valid and offered in a constructive manner. You supported my ideas and projects, and you gave me that important pat on the back for encouragement when most needed. This has all provided me with one of the most positive work environments imaginable, and I thank you for that.

Just when I thought I had the best of situations, you topped it by asking me to accept the position of Regional Coordinator. I'm pleased and humbled by the realization that you know I can do this most important job for you and do it well.

We have difficult decisions ahead of us. There are many questions on controversial subjects to be answered. There are sensitive ethical and moral realities to be faced. I appreciate your confidence in my ability to make those decisions wisely.

I willingly accept that challenge. I am excited by the responsibilities which await us, and I know that together we can accomplish so much in the field of terminal care giving. I am honored to be able to represent you as your Regional Coordinator. Thank you.

CHAPTER 22

THE INTRODUCTION SPEECH

Time limits: 1-2 minutes.

Speaking notes: Key ideas, dates, events, or quotations only.

Sources of information: They may be fictitious or real.

Outline your speech: Prepare a 50-100 word complete sentence outline.

Question: When I pick a topic, do I have to know everything about it?

Answer: No. You should research it thoroughly so you may speak with authority and possess a basis for your views.

Key Word:
Salutation

Student Expectations: In completing this assignment each student will:

➤ *Understand how to set the tone of a speaking event for another speaker*
➤ *Be able to establish the credibility of another speaker with the audience*
➤ *Identify the variety of information that may be required in an introduction of another speaker and where to locate that information*

PURPOSE OF THIS ASSIGNMENT

Many untrained speakers are asked to give introduction speeches. Some of the introductions are well done. Far too many are haphazard and embarrassing, because the person making the introduction is untrained. This brings criticism upon the person who must present a speaker, and it also weakens programs that feature lecturers. Of all the types of speeches you may make in the future, it is probable that one of them will be the introduction of a featured speaker. This assignment will provide an introduction speech experience.

EXPLANATION OF THE INTRODUCTION SPEECH

An introduction speech is one in which a chairperson or other person introduces a speaker to an audience. The purpose is to bring an audience and speaker together in the proper spirit. Several of the requirements are: the speech should be short; it should make the audience and speaker feel comfortably acquainted; it should interest the audience in the speaker and the subject; it should put the speaker at ease, announce the subject, and give the speaker's name.

The introducer should avoid attempts at being humorous. Never embarrass the speaker either by heaping too much praise upon them or by belittling them. The person introducing a speaker should not call attention to self nor say or do anything to detract from what the speaker plans to say. The person who once said, "Get up, speak up, shut up," probably was thinking of the individual who makes introduction speeches; and the introducer can hardly go wrong if they follow this advice.

Occasions for the introduction speech arise every time a speaker is introduced. They probably number in the millions annually.

HOW TO CHOOSE A SUBJECT FOR AN INTRODUCTION SPEECH

You will have to decide for yourself as to the type of imaginary audience and occasion you will use. You will also find it necessary to arrive at some decision concerning the specific person you plan to introduce. Be sure that your speaker is a suitable one for the occasion. Some possible situations include introducing (1) a college president to a high school audience; (2) the mayor to a public gathering; (3) a war hero to a school assembly; (4) a Hollywood celebrity to your school; or (5) a sports star to an athletic banquet.

HOW TO PREPARE AN INTRODUCTION SPEECH

In preparing this speech you may draw your information from four sources: the speaker, the subject, the audience, or the occasion. Not all of these may be necessary in every speech; however, they are all often suitable if not required sources. You will not need much material, but that which you have must be accurate and pertinent. Know how to pronounce the speaker's name correctly. Discover any background the speaker has that should be known by the audience. This may concern education, special training, travel experience, special honors, membership in organizations, important positions held, books written, or any other notable achievements. Of course, for a famous and well-known person, little need be said, possibly nothing. An example of the latter is the introduction often heard: "Ladies and Gentlemen, the President." However, almost all speakers require more to be said than the Presidents of the United States, governors, and other high state officials. You should know the title of the speaker's subject. As with the name, you must have it right. But you should say nothing about the speech that will tend to "steal the thunder" of the remarks. You should inquire thoroughly into the personnel of your audience so that you may adjust your remarks to them. The occasion of the address should be well-known to you. From the four sources just mentioned and a fifth, yourself, you will construct your introduction speech. Short though this speech is, what you say must really "count." Thus, you must organize and arrange it carefully, selecting those bits of information that are most important.

Before you set your ideas, you should confer with the person you are going to introduce, and in conference, arrive at a definite understanding regarding what you plan to say in your introduction speech. After this point is decided, then rehearse aloud until you are confident that you are thoroughly prepared.

HOW TO PRESENT AN INTRODUCTION SPEECH

When the moment arrives for you to introduce the speaker of the evening, rise calmly, take your place on the platform, pause until the assembly grows quiet, and then deliberately address the audience in your normal voice, yet speak loudly enough for all to hear. Avoid straining or using greater force than is needed. You may say, "Ladies and Gentlemen," or use some other **salutation** or form of introduction appropriate to the audience and the occasion. Your body language and gestures will be limited. There will likely be no necessity for using either more than moderately. Your voice should be well modulated, the words spoken clearly, and your pronunciation correct—especially that of the speaker's name.

A speech of introduction should be brief and highlight the speaker's major accomplishments.

Keep in mind your part of the occasion. People did not come to hear you or see you. You are only a convenient but necessary cog in the events surrounding the speaker. Your poise and confidence and appropriate but brief remarks are all that are expected or wanted from you. You may greet the audience and mention the occasion, extend greetings, and note the fact that there is an exceptionally good audience (if there is). If there is a poor audience, do not remark about it and do not make any apologies.

At the moment you present the speaker, announce the name and subject somewhat as follows: "I am happy to present Dr. A, who will address you (or speak to you) on_____(mention the subject)." Then turn to the speaker with the words, "Dr. A." You may bow slightly or nod and take your chair when the speaker rises and approaches the front of the platform.

If you are chairperson of the assembly, it will be appropriate for you to express publicly the appreciation of the audience to the speaker at the conclusion of the address.

A SPEECH OF INTRODUCTION
by Brent Peterson

Principal Norton, coaches and lettermen of Valley High School. Meeting this evening as a group of athletes we all recall during many basketball games a most unforgettable shot, the "dunk." It is a privilege to have with us such a man who thrilled many spectators. A little six-foot guard through hard work perfected his shot—the free throw—and became known as "Dunker" to match his own name, Bob Dunkin.

Bob, a three-year basketball letterman at Northside High in Kennington, attended banquets similar to this one. Upon receiving the free throw trophy after making seventy-six percent of his free throws, at the banquet his junior year Bob announced, "Next year I'll shoot ninety percent." The following year persistent Bob made ninety-two percent of his free throws due to his consistent practice during the summer. Coach Dunkin conducts summer basketball camps to develop the abilities of young ball players because he is interested in them.

A competitive college athlete said, "You must always give one hundred percent effort; if you don't, someone, somewhere will, and he will beat you." "Dunker" Dunkin made that statement and has always gone the extra mile in all his life's endeavors and has rarely been beaten. At State U, "Dunker" was all-conference twice, led the conference in free-throw shooting and his team to a berth in the NCAA tournament.

Bob Dunkin's life is the story of persistence, hard work, and success. It has been said, "No chance, no destiny, no fate can circumvent or hinder or control the firm resolve of a determined soul." Athletes, I want you to meet and hear this determined man who will speak to you concerning the value of reaching your own potential. Coach Dunkin.

WELCOMING AND RESPONSE SPEECHES

Time limits: 1-3 minutes.

Speaking notes: None, or key ideas only.

Sources of information: None required. If used, they may be real or fictitious.

Outline your speech: Prepare a 50-100 word complete sentence outline.

Question: How does one overcome talking too fast?

Answer: Give individual words and phrases greater emphasis. Utilize more pauses. Articulate words distinctly. Make a conscious effort to speak slower.

Key Words:
Felicitations
Genuineness
Tribute

Student Expectations: In completing this assignment each student will:
> ➤ *Learn how to promote friendship through a public speech*
> ➤ *Understand the importance of a response to a welcome*
> ➤ *Identify common interests and values of hosts and guests*

PURPOSE OF THIS ASSIGNMENT

The speeches of welcome and response are of sufficient importance that you should know how they are organized and what they should do. They occupy a high place in speech making, because on their effectiveness hinges much of the public relations among groups that convene daily throughout the country. You may be asked to give or respond to a speech of welcome at any time in your community, and you should be familiar with how to do so in order to be ready to promote goodwill when the opportunity arises.

EXPLANATION OF WELCOMING AND RESPONSE SPEECHES

A speech of welcome is one made publicly to a single individual or to a group of individuals with the purpose of extending greetings and promoting friendship. The person or persons being welcomed should be made to feel that they are sincerely wanted and that the hosts are delighted to have them. Warm hospitality should be expressed with such **genuineness** that the listener enjoys a spirit of gladness as a result of being the guest of a gracious host. The speech is characterized by brevity, sincerity, geniality, and simplicity.

A speech in response to a welcome is simply to reply to the **felicitations** expressed by a host. Its purpose is to cement goodwill and friendship, and express these mutual feelings that exist between the groups. It is short, courteous, and friendly. Often the response is impromptu in nature and as such places a burden of doing fast thinking and uttering logical thoughts on the person who presents it. It also demands sincerity and respectfulness from the speaker. Practice in speech fundamentals will serve you well on such occasions as these.

HOW TO CHOOSE TOPICS FOR WELCOMING OR RESPONSE SPEECHES

Select an occasion that interests you. Decide what organization you will represent and what position you will hold in that group. Select one you know something about or one about which you can easily secure information. Recall situations in which you have heard a speech of welcome and response, or select one of the following:

1. A native son or daughter returns home to visit.
2. A newly elected school superintendent arrives in your community.
3. A banquet is held for new teachers.
4. The governor visits on state business.
5. New officers join the student council.
6. A sister city from another country sends a delegation to visit.
7. An organization holds a big convention in your city.

A good welcoming speech makes guests feel important and prepares them for events to follow.

HOW TO PREPARE WELCOMING AND RESPONSE SPEECHES

First, keep clearly in mind the purpose of the occasion and the talk. If you are welcoming others, your purpose is to make guests glad to be there; if you are responding to the welcome, your purpose is to express your appreciation of hospitality extended.

To welcome others, mention the organization you represent, its character, the work it is doing, and points of interest about it. Pay **tribute** to your guests for their work, and tell of advantages they will gain by visiting you. Note who the guests are, where they are from, and whom they represent. Comment briefly on common interests your organization holds with them. Express anticipation of pleasant associations and mutual benefits. Invite your guests to feel at home and to participate fully in your community.

To respond to a welcoming, you will generally strive to make the welcoming overshadow your own personality. Address the hosts and those associated with them; acknowledge the greeting of welcome and the hospitality of the organization; express sincere thanks for their courtesies. Extend greetings from your organization and show how the occasion is mutually advantageous. Predict future pleasant associations with the host organization. Mention that you have been made to feel most welcome and at home. Thank your hosts again for their hospitality, extend best wishes, then be seated.

Keep in mind that not all of the items listed here are needed in every speech of welcome or response. The particular situation will dictate your choices.

HOW TO PRESENT WELCOMING AND RESPONSE SPEECHES

Let the occasion govern your presentation here as well. If it is formal, act and speak appropriately. If it is informal, adjust yourself and your remarks appropriately. In either case, be genuine. Feel what you say. Your attitude and demeanor must be a combination of appreciation and friendliness. Portray the same gentility you would to receive people into your home or to be received in someone else's home.

Speak loudly enough to be heard. Use your normal voice as much as possible. Speak clearly. Pronounce all names distinctly and correctly. Smile pleasantly as is fitting. Maintain your poise by observing an alert posture. Your spoken language should be simple, vivid, appropriate, and devoid of any slang or redundancy. Be brief but complete.

Here are a few additional suggestions: (1) have a few serious thoughts in your speech even though gaiety fills the air. Do not resort to telling nothing more than a series of anecdotes; (2) Do not apologize—accept your responsibility and meet it as a mature person by having something worthwhile to say.

WELCOME TO WESTERN AMERICA HIGH
A Welcoming Speech by Setits Raclile

Principal Rogers and delegates to the Seventh Regional Government Conference. It is my pleasure as senior class president to welcome you to our school where we hope you will learn a lot of new information and have a good time doing it. This is the first time you have honored Western America High School by selecting us as your host, and I'm glad to tell you we are both proud and happy to have you here today.

Our achievements and our problems are no doubt similar to yours, and they make us either joyous or perplexed, depending on whether we are doing something notable or having trouble. I do believe however, every achievement by schools represented here today should be shared so we may all benefit from each other's successes. And I believe just as strongly we should discuss those problems we all face every year. By doing this we can learn from each other how to improve our individual governments and thus improve our schools in this region.

I told you Western America High is pleased to have you as our guests and to show you we really mean it, our school governing council has arranged free bus tours over Exhibition Scenic Drive during our afternoon recess. Just climb on a bus in the parking lot, and you'll get the ride of your life with more hairpin curves and thrilling views than you ever dreamed of. Then tonight at 8 o'clock in this building, there will be a delegates' free dance with an outstanding band, which our students will attend to help make your evening more enjoyable.

Once again I want to tell you how glad we are that you are here. We will do our best to help you have a successful conference and a pleasant visit, thus we will all profit greatly from this wonderful experience. When you leave tomorrow we want you to take our friendship and best wishes with you, but until then have a good time and thank you for joining us.

RESPONSE TO A SPEECH OF WELCOME
by Yenan Noscaasi

Fellow delegates and Principal Rogers. I want to thank Mr. Raclile for his most friendly remarks and tell him we do feel the sincere welcome he speaks of. Already there seems to be present among us a spirit of cooperation and strong desire to exchange information helpful to every school represented at this conference. I truly believe that if each of us can gain only one new idea from our various group meetings and the guest speakers we will all return home with the satisfaction of having attained something worthwhile.

We all trust that our presence here will in a sense express the esteem we hold for Western America High School. It's a privilege to come here to share our experiences and thoughts with Western's students and delegates in their outstanding facilities. We can all see how much preparation they have made for us and also see they are doing everything possible to make this conference a success.

As representative-at-large from all schools present, I want to thank Western America High for arranging our housing and meals; also for the bus tour coming up this afternoon and the big dance tonight. I'm sure everyone will enjoy these events. By having a good time together and exchanging ideas we will have a conference second to none. So to our hosts I want to say on behalf of all of us "thanks for everything."

TOPIC IDEAS

1. Make a list of everything you know more about than other people might. Perhaps you have a hobby or have lived in several different cities. If so, prepare a speech about your hobby or about the special features of a city where you once lived.
2. Interview your parents, grandparents, or an elderly neighbor. Ask about interesting fads or historical events that they remember. Use these ideas as a basis for research.
3. What do you want to learn more about? Use a speech as a way to learn it.
4. What do you have strong feelings about? What has someone said lately that you disagreed with? Write a speech and support your viewpoint.
5. What is something that your classmates need to know about: finding a summer job? job opportunities for those not going to college? how to resolve differences without physical violence; how to better understand individuals with different racial, religious, or ethnic backgrounds? Use ideas such as these for informative speeches.

CHAPTER 24

PRESENTING AND ACCEPTING GIFTS OR AWARDS

Time limits: 1-3 minutes.

Speaking notes: key words for presenting; none for accepting.

Sources of information: None required. They may be real or fictitious.

Outline your speech: Prepare a 50 - 75 word complete sentence outline.

Question: Should pitch vary much during a speech?

Answer: Yes. It will add variety to keep your listeners' interest.

Key Words:
Acceptance speech
Homage
Presentation speech

Student Expectations: In completing this assignment each student will:
➤ *Identify the appropriate elements in a speech to present or accept an award*
➤ *Understand the role of modesty and gratitude in accepting an award or gift*
➤ *Recognize several different types of occasions for acceptance or presentation speeches*

PURPOSE OF THIS ASSIGNMENT

The ritual of publicly presenting and receiving gifts and awards has been conducted for centuries. Every time the occasion occurs, someone must make the presentation speech. Just as often, the recipient is expected to say a few words of acceptance.

It is not easy to make a public presentation or acceptance graciously, to handle the situation with ease, and to utter thoughts that symbolize the spirit of the event. Yet, at any time, you may find yourself in either of these positions. Frequently, recipients are not told in advance that they will be honored; hence, they can be embarrassed if they do not know how to accept with simple sin-

cerity. This assignment is designed to help you know what to do on either occasion.

EXPLANATION OF THE PRESENTATION SPEECH

A **presentation speech** is one made in conjunction with the presentation of an award or gift. It is short, sincere, and commendatory of the recipient. It requires tact and good taste because an audience will always encompass divided attitudes toward the recipient. Others, no doubt, are just as worthy of the gift or award. Intense rivalry may have been present in seeking the award. Feelings and emotions may have been running high. To understand the tenor of the audience, to avoid embarrassing the winner, and to use a language appreciated by all or even a majority requires a simple, yet artistic quality of speech.

Occasions for this type of speech vary. One of these is when a prize is won in a contest. The presentation may be formal; the winner may or may not be known in advance. Emphasis will be placed on the interest in the award, the careful consideration of the judges, and the delicate position of all involved.

Another occasion is when an award or gift is given to an organization such as a school, church, society, or group. It is likely to be formal, though there will be no surprise. Emphasis here will be on the symbolism or utility of the gift.

A third occasion commemorates a recognition of service. The element of surprise may or may not be present, but emotions are likely to run high. The speech should not make it difficult for the recipient, but sufficient tribute should be paid to the one who is being honored. Shortly after times of national crisis or emergency is a frequent occasion for such presentations.

A fourth kind of presentation also revolves around recognition of service, but the occasion is more light-hearted. Surprise is often present. There is no rivalry, but rather good fellowship and possibly a little sadness. Examples of this kind include retirements or members moving from a community. Emphasis is placed on the happy side of fellowship. Some regret for the departure is expressed, but hope for the future is given a prominent place.

EXPLANATION OF THE ACCEPTANCE SPEECH

A speech made by the recipient of a gift or award is a sincere expression of appreciation of the honor accorded. It should establish the person as a friendly, modest, worthwhile individual to whom the people may rightfully pay tribute. Its purpose should be to impress the donors with the worthiness of the receiver and to make them happy in their choice. There can be no artificial or hollow remarks.

It should be noted that in some instances no speech is necessary. The only essential propriety required is a pleasant "thank you," accompanied by an appreciative smile. To do more than this when it is not appropriate to do so is awkward. The recipient must decide on each occasion whether or not a speech is wanted or needed.

Occasions for **acceptance speeches** arise, potentially, every time an award or gift is presented. Possibilities for presentations and their accompanying speeches are unlimited.

HOW TO CHOOSE A TOPIC FOR PRESENTING AND ACCEPTING GIFTS OR AWARDS

You have undoubtedly been present for an award presentation and acceptance or have observed one on television. You may wish to select an occasion with which you are familiar. If no experiences immediately come to mind, consider one of the following possibilities: Presenting or receiving

1. A scholarship
2. A cash prize for winning a sales contest
3. A prize for writing poetry
4. A donation of funds for a new park
5. A medal for outstanding community service
6. An environmental award for a school or group
7. A championship award to a team
8. An Eagle Scout award

HOW TO PREPARE A PRESENTATION SPEECH

Make certain you are fully aware of the occasion and any particular requirements governing it or the presentation. Keep in mind that it is an honor to present the award or gift, and not an occasion to speak on your pet subject. Remember that you are speaking on behalf of all those who have sponsored the award or gift. It is your responsibility to say the things they would want to have said on their behalf. By all means observe proper speech construction.

In preparing the talk, keep several things in mind. First, do not overpraise the individual, but pay deserving tribute with wise restraint. Second, pay appropriate **homage** to the audience, referring to the occasion that brought everyone together, a brief history of the event, and the purpose and symbolic value of the award or gift being presented. Third, do not over-emphasize the gift itself or its value. Instead, stress the work or merit which it represents. Finally, recount the recipient's personal worth and tell how this worth was recognized or discovered. If you personally know the honoree, mention the fact that you are intimately aware of the person's service or merit.

Awards should be presented with sincerity.

Prepare your ideas by rehearsing aloud until you have them thoroughly in mind. Do not memorize your speech (which would hinder your fluency in delivery), but be sure to know what you are going to say.

HOW TO PREPARE AN ACCEPTANCE SPEECH

This speech will necessarily be impromptu on some occasions; hence little preparation can be made other than formulating a basic pattern of ideas about which you will speak. If you are warned or informed early that you will receive a gift or award, then, of course, you should certainly prepare a speech. In this case, all principles of good speech construction should be followed.

In either case, there are several important points to be noted. First, utilize simple language. Second, begin by expressing a true sense of gratitude for the gift or award. If you are truly surprised, you may say so; however, the surprise must be genuine. Next, modestly disclaim total credit for the award. Give credit to those who assisted you in any way, for without them you would not have achieved your success. No one is completely isolated. Praise their cooperation and support. Do not apologize for winning or disclaim your worthiness as this would be insulting to your audience and, in particular, those who selected you for the tribute. Accept the award or gift modestly and graciously.

The nature of the gift or award will determine what you say next. You may express appreciation for its beauty or significance, but do not overpraise or overvalue the gift itself. Do not express disappointment in any manner.

Conclude your remarks by speaking of your plans for the future, especially as they may relate to the gift or award or the work associated with it. As a final word you may repeat your thanks for the recognition.

HOW TO PRESENT THE SPEECH

Your attitude and manner must convey the sincerity of the occasion. There must be no ostentation, flamboyancy, or show in your speech or actions. Dress appropriately in respect of the occasion. The presenter should call the recipient to the platform. The recipient moves forward politely and alertly, neither hurrying nor loitering.

Be sure you stand so that the audience can see and hear you. Do not obscure the gift; let the audience see it. Be sure to speak loudly enough to be heard by all, especially if you are turned partially away from them to present or receive the award. Observe all the elements of acceptable stage presence. If the recipient is to return to the audience after the presentation, and the gift is small, carry it in your hand; do not stuff it into a pocket.

SPEECH PRESENTING A GIFT OR AWARD
by Valerie Ritter

Fellow Parents and Athletes: This awards banquet has been an annual event for several years. Some of you here tonight will look forward to many more banquets such as this, while others will reminisce of the banquets past. These are special nights for athletes and parents, for it is because of you that these banquets are held. As President of the Scholarship Selection Committee, it is with great pleasure that I am able to present this award.

This evening there is a student present who has earned recognition by means of his outstanding performance as an athlete. This recognition presented by the University is an annual event arranged to provide financial assistance for students with athletic ability.

The recipient is a transfer student from the College of DuPage located in Glen Ellen, Illinois. He has been active as an athlete throughout his school years. Tonight I wish to present Mr. Rich Kielczewski with a scholarship recognizing his ability in the game of tennis.

Rich is honest and hard working and is dedicated to the sport of tennis. He always seems to put forth more effort than is originally necessary. He is also a qualified and very competent tennis instructor.

Rich has entered many amateur tournaments. Among those in which he has captured the crown are the Chicago District Tournament and six consecutive conference titles. He has also received recognition of the people of Illinois by being ranked sixteenth in the state.

I have known Rich for a long time and have many times witnessed his stunning ability to overcome his opponent. I personally know of no other person more deserving of this tennis scholarship. In view of these outstanding qualities and accomplishments, I am very pleased to present Rich Kielczewski with this scholarship on behalf of Northwest Missouri State University.

SPEECH ACCEPTING A GIFT OR AWARD
by Sherri Dunker

Three years ago if anyone had told me I would someday join a sorority, I would have laughed in her face—there was just no way I was going to become a part of those, quote "cliquey snobs." But to this day I bless the friend who persuaded me to find out what sororities were really about. They weren't snobs at all but beautiful people with the same fears, frustrations, and hopes many women have.

Now I am very proud to say that I too am a sorority woman, and with honor I accept this "Most Spirited Kappa Delta Award." This sorority has taught me more than any text or instructor, and it's given me my "people" degree in college.

Kappa Delta has shown me the importance of budgeting time wisely, accepting and utilizing criticism, respecting and listening to others' ideas, social etiquette, and especially leadership experience. Incalculable are KD's gifts, but I'll never forget the most precious of all—my vast circle of sisters who genuinely care. You accepted me for what I am and have helped me build my self-confidence. Thanks for standing by me through my moments of despair and making college life a pleasant life.

I truly believe in you, Kappa Delta, and all for which you stand—the most "honorable, beautiful and highest!" (Open Motto of Kappa Delta) I shall treasure this award and when I glance upon it long after I have graduated, I shall remember all the glorious memories and sisters of Kappa Delta. Thank you.

SPEECH ACCEPTING A GIFT OR AWARD
by Ed Ashcraft

(The recipient was completely surprised to receive this award.)

Thank you Dr. Ellis, thank you Ladies and Gentlemen. I really don't know what to say, I am at a complete loss for words.

My principal called me this evening on the phone and told me he would be at the school board meeting this evening, to give the board some input on our needs in the Science Department. He asked if I could be there in case he needed some off-hand information about our department. Of course, I said I would be happy to attend, since we had discussed these needs many times.

As you have heard, Mr. Soderquist gave us quite an in-depth list of our needs, plus some methods for improving our department. When he finished his presentation, I assumed he managed to get through it without my help. But I felt good about being there, just in case I was needed.

But I certainly did not expect this. The Golden Apple Award for the most outstanding teacher? Me?

I've held so many differing types of jobs in my life, but I knew the first day I walked into a classroom that this would be where I would spend the rest of my life. I look forward to Monday morning, getting back to my kids. To receive such a prestigious award for something I enjoy doing so much, well. As my students would say, "This is too much, man!"

I certainly want to thank my principal for recommending me for this award. Also, all of my fellow teachers, who voted for me. I can't thank the school board enough for this great honor.

I will keep my Golden Apple on my desk. Each morning I will take a minute to remind myself of the great trust that's been placed in me. I will do the best that I can to honor that trust. Thank you again.

CHAPTER 25

THE FAREWELL SPEECH

Time limits: 4-5 minutes.

Speaking notes: Do not use any for this speech.

Sources of information: None required. They may be real or fictitious.

Outline your speech: Prepare a 75-100 word complete sentence outline.

Question: How fast should you talk when giving a speech?

Answer: The rate varies with the ability to talk distinctly – 125 to 150 words per minute is about average; however, these figures vary considerably.

Key Words:
Farewell speech
Mood
Redundancy

Student Expectations: In completing this chapter each student will:
> *Identify the necessary elements of a speech of leave-taking*
> *Analyze various emotions present in a farewell situation and determine how to adapt a speech to them appropriately*
> *Organize and present a speech of leave-taking*

PURPOSE OF THIS ASSIGNMENT

Many times a person is the guest of honor at a farewell party. The guest of honor is invariably asked to say a few words as a last expression before leaving. Too often, what is said may be only a mumbling of incoherent remarks, because the guest has never had a previous experience of this kind and does not know what is appropriate at such a time. This speech assignment will give you an experience that will point the way when you are called upon to make a farewell speech.

EXPLANATION OF THE FAREWELL SPEECH

A **farewell speech** is one in which a person publicly says goodbye to a group of acquaintances. It should express the speaker's appreciation for what acquaintances have helped them accomplish and for the happiness they have brought them. It may be given at a formal or informal gathering, a luncheon or a dinner. Frequently, on this occasion, the guest of honor will receive a gift from the group. A common informal party occurs when "the boss," a superior, or some other leader calls an informal meeting following the day's work, at which time the person who is leaving will receive commendation, favorable testimonials, and possibly a gift. They, too, will be expected to "say something." The formal occasion is, of course, much more elaborate and is surrounded by formalities from start to finish.

Occasions for the farewell speech are of one general kind—leave taking. Situations may vary greatly; however, a few of the usual ones are retirement after years of service in a certain employment, taking a new job, promotion to a different type of work that demands a change in location, concluding service in an organization, leaving school, or moving to another community for any reason whatsoever. The occasion, whatever its nature, should not be treated with too much sadness. It should be approached with true sincerity and honesty. Feelings of deep emotion may be present, and they should be expressed in a manner in keeping with the occasion and all persons present.

HOW TO CHOOSE A TOPIC FOR A FAREWELL SPEECH

Think about the situations outlined in the previous section. Do any of these appeal to you? Have you ever moved from one community or school to another? Was there something you wanted to say to someone you were leaving behind? Select a situation that is realistic for you as a result of your experiences or observations. If you are having difficulty formulating your own topic, consider the following:

1. Going home from a foreign country.
2. Moving to a new location—any reason.
3. Going back home after completing a year's job.
4. Leaving for South America to study rain forests.
5. Going to New York to become an actor.
6. Leaving for college on an athletic scholarship.

HOW TO PREPARE A FAREWELL SPEECH

Remember that this is a special occasion and that old friends are honoring you. Remember, too, that there may be an atmosphere of considerable sentiment and emotion, or there may be one merely of friendly gaiety. This means you must carefully analyze your audience, their probable **mood,** and the general atmosphere. If you are likely to be presented a gift, plan your remarks so that you may accept it graciously. Sincerity must dominate your utterances whatever they may be.

Farewell speeches usually follow a well-defined pattern with appropriate variations which the speaker deems necessary. It is advisable to begin your talk by referring to the past, the time when you first arrived and why you came to the community. A bit of humor or some interesting anecdotes may be in good taste. The way you were made welcome or to feel at home might be an excellent recollection. Continue your thoughts by pointing out how your ideals and those of the audience, though not completely attained, inspired you to do what you did, and that work remains still to be done.

Express appreciation for their support of your efforts which made your achievements possible. Commend the harmony and the cooperation that prevailed. Tell them that you will always remember your associations with this group as one of the outstanding events in your life. Speak next of your future work briefly but sincerely. Explain why you are leaving, and what compelled you to go into a new field or location. Show that your work just completed will act as a background and inspiration to that which lies ahead. Continue by encouraging those who remain, predict greater achievements for them, praise your successor if you know who he is, and conclude with a genuine expression of your appreciation for them and a continued interest in their future. Remember, if you received a gift, to give a final word of thanks for it.

In your speech omit any and all references or illusions to unpleasantries or friction that may have existed. Do not make the occasion bitter or sad. Be happy and leave others with the same feeling. Smile. Make sure that a good impression will follow you.

HOW TO PRESENT A FAREWELL SPEECH

In this speech fit your manner to the mood of the occasion and audience. Do not go overboard in solemnity, emotion, or gaiety. Be appropriate. Use a friendly and sincere approach throughout. Adjust your introductory remarks to the prevailing mood; then move into your speech. Speak loudly enough to be heard by all. Use bodily action suitable to the audience, the occasion, the speech, the environment, and yourself.

Be sure that your language is appropriate to the five requirements just given. Avoid ponderous phrases, over-emotionalized words and tones, **redundancy**, and flowery or florid attempts at oratory. Let everything you do and say, coupled with a good appearance and alert posture, be the evidence that you are genuinely and sincerely mindful of their appreciation of you at your departure.

FAREWELL SPEECH
by Reed Adams

Fellow faculty members, students, parents, and guests. I am greatly honored by your presence tonight. I have always had a rule to live by when leaving a place to move on in the world, that is to just leave and try to forget the people left behind as soon as possible. However, that will not be possible for me to do with you.

For the last eight years you have shared in my joys and my sorrows. We have shared in change but have learned that change just for change does not work. You people as the community have brought my family and myself from vagabonds of the educational system to actual professionals in that field. I am certain it is your ideals and your school that have made this change in me. Without this change I would not have the opportunity that has now availed itself to me.

I remember my first day at this school just like it was yesterday. I had such high hopes of how I was going to change the whole education system, but my first day at school changed that. The students entered the room and took their seats, but it seemed my techniques of teaching would not work. It seemed that the harder I tried the more the students seemed to resent me and what I was trying to teach them. Then one of the students came up to me at the end of the day and said that he really would have enjoyed my class if he had not had so much on his mind.

I asked him if it was something I could help him with and he said he wished that I could, but I was a little bit too old to be on the football team. I had been so wrapped up in changing the system that I had forgotten to listen and learn what was happening in the school. The biggest game of the season was the first one with us playing Western High. The whole student body was more interested in that than what I was trying to teach, so that's how we got our ten minute rap sessions at the first of every class.

We have had good times, bad times, broken hearts, and romance, but the most important thing we have learned is that we are people and we all make mistakes. That is why we accept other people and their mistakes, as well as our imperfect selves. I am indebted to you all for the wonderful example you have set for me and my family in this area.

Next fall you will continue in your education. Some of you to become doctors and lawyers and others to find jobs out of high school, but whatever you do, I hope you will remember, as I will, the wonderful experiences and academic achievements as well as the sports of Highland High School.

The new house we have purchased in Mississippi has a large mantel in the center of the room and this plaque you have given me tonight will go there beautifully. We had been wondering what we where going to put there. Thank you very much and may whatever you believe in bless and keep you happy.

CHAPTER 26

THE EULOGY

Time limits: 5-6 minutes.

Speaking notes: 10-word maximum.

Sources of information: Two are required, preferably three. For each source give the specific magazine, book, or Internet site it was taken from title of the article, author's full name, date of publication, and the chapter or pages telling where the material was found. If a source is a person, identify the source completely by title, position, occupation, etc. List these on the outline form. For Internet sites include the address (URL).

Outline your speech: Prepare a 75-150 word complete sentence outline.

Question: What is a pleasant voice — high, low, medium?

Answer: A well-controlled voice of any pitch which is not extremely high or low may be "pleasant." It is not so much the pitch as how it is used.

Key Words:
Character studies
Commemoration
Eulogy

Student Expectations: In completing this chapter each student will:
➤ *Select appropriate information to include in the speech*
➤ *Understand the importance and role of sincerity in a speech of praise*
➤ *Organize and present a speech of praise of another person*

PURPOSE OF THIS ASSIGNMENT

The speech is assigned so that you may learn by doing and become familiar with the speech of eulogy. Frequently a person is called upon to eulogize or praise someone. There are several ways to do this. Of course, the type of eulogy you may be asked to present will depend on different aspects of the speech situation. But whatever that requirement may be, you will be better prepared to do a creditable job if you have had previous experience. This assignment will provide that experience.

EXPLANATION OF THE EULOGY

The **eulogy** is a speech of praise that is delivered in honor or **commemoration** of someone living or dead. Sometimes eulogies are presented for

animals, particularly dogs, horses, and others. A more fanciful and imaginative eulogy would be one to inanimate objects, such as the sea or the mountains. Some eulogies are written to trees and flowers, but these, too, are abstract and fanciful in nature.

The purpose of a eulogy is to praise and evaluate favorably the subject being eulogized; it commends and lifts up the finer qualities and characteristics of the subject eulogized. It stresses the personality of the person (or thing) that it concerns; it tells of their greatness and achievements, their benefits to society, and their influence upon people. It is not merely a simple biographical sketch of someone. To illustrate the point, imagine a eulogy of a great oak, in which the speaker tells the date on which the acorn sprouted, and a later date when the tiny plant emerged from the soil. Next the number in inches it grew each year thereafter, are given, and finally the number of leaves it developed in forty years. Compare this with the eulogy of a person, and you can see why a biographical sketch is not a eulogy. Actually, it sounds like a scientific report on a person (or tree).

Occasions for eulogies are many. For persons who are living, the speech may be given on a birthday, at a dinner in honor of an individual, at the dedication of a project someone has created and/or donated. Eulogies often appear at the formal announcement of a political candidate or at an inauguration. For persons who are dead, not considering funeral tributes, eulogies are offered on birthday anniversaries or in connection with notable events or achievements in individuals' lives. Sometimes eulogies in the form of **character studies** are presented as evidences of good living. They become lessons of life.

HOW TO SELECT A PERSON TO EULOGIZE
First, it is essential that you eulogize someone whom you greatly admire and who, in your opinion, is living or has lived a commendable life. This is necessary, for your eulogy to be completely sincere. Second, select someone about whom you can secure adequate information. Finally, think twice before deciding to eulogize a tree, the sea, the mountains, or an animal, as these are probably more difficult to eulogize than a person. It is wiser to select a person as a subject to eulogize.

SOME TOPIC POSSIBILITIES
A Well-Known Person in Your Community
A Past President
A Leader for Minority or Women's Rights
A Grandparent or Other Relative
A Classmate
A Religious Leader
A Teacher

HOW TO PREPARE A EULOGY
The purpose of a eulogy is a set objective, a tribute—regardless of the time, place, or occasion. Since eulogies are intended to stimulate an audience fa-vorably toward the subject and to inspire them to nobler heights by virtue of the examples set by the person being praised, the speaker is not required to determine a purpose in preparing a eulogy.

Having selected the person to be eulogized, you should decide upon the method which you will use in developing the eulogy. Your method and whether or not the individual is living will determine the material that is necessary. Let us examine several different methods of constructing a eulogy.

First, you may follow a chronological order, that is, you will take up events in the order of their development. This will permit a study of their growth and orderly evolution of character in the subject. As you touch upon these broad and influential events in the subject's life, you will point to them as evidences of (1) what the person has accomplished, (2) what they stood for, (3) the nature of their influence upon society, and (4) their probable place in history or in the memories of friends and family. In building your speech chronologically do not end by composing a simple biographical sketch. If you do, you will have an informative speech but not a eulogy. It is not enough to list the significant happenings in a person's life chronologically and consider that you have built a eulogy. You must state how they reacted to the events in their life and what happened as a result of them.

For example, if you were eulogizing Franklin D. Roosevelt (chronologically), you would recount, as one event, how he was stricken with infantile paralysis when a grown man, but you would not merely make a statement regarding the tragedy that befell him and then pass on. Rather, you would show how his illness became a challenge to him, how he resolved to live a great life despite a pair of useless legs, and how he did overcome his handicap. You would show that, as a result of his illness, he became more resolute, more determined, more kindly. Other incidents should be given similar treatment.

A second method of developing a eulogy might well be labeled the period method. It is the one which covers the growth of an individual by treating different periods in his or her life. It is very broad and makes no attempt to enumerate the many life events with their attached significance. Instead of this, using Franklin D. Roosevelt again as an example, you could speak of him as he grew through: (1) boyhood, (2) college life, (3) early political life, (4) late political life.

In following this method you would attempt to bring out the same basic points mentioned above—namely, (1) what they accomplished, (2) what they stood for, (3) their influence upon society, (4) their likely place in history. Although this treatment is broad, it is quite effective.

It should be emphasized at this point that, regardless of which method you use, there are certain necessary points to be observed. A discussion of these follows. First, omit the unimportant events, the small things, and the insignificant details. Second, in developing your speech, point out the struggles which they met in order to achieve their aims. Avoid overemphasis and exaggeration when you are doing this. Third, show the development of ideas and ideals. Fourth, describe relations and services to others and indicate their significance.

It is not necessary to cover up for an individual but rather to admit the human element in the person. In doing this, mentioning the human element is enough. It need not be dwelt on nor apologized for. It can be shown that despite weaknesses or shortcomings a person was great. It can be shown that a person lived above these frailties of human nature. But whatever the qualities of your subject, be honest in your treatment. It is only fair to assume that the good outweighed the bad by far, or you would not have elected to eulogize them.

In giving a eulogy at a funeral or memorial service, it is often appropriate to recognize family and friends and offer words of comfort. This is best accomplished by letting them know how the person touched many lives and will live on through the influence he or she had on others.

In constructing your speech, be sure you pay careful attention to your introduction and conclusion. Aside from these, do not neglect the logical organization and arrangement of the remainder of your talk. Actually, a eulogy is a difficult speech to prepare. However, if you go about it knowing what

you wish to put into it, you should have no particular trouble. When you have the eulogizing speech ready for rehearsal, it will be advisable to practice it aloud until you have thoroughly mastered the sequence of ideas. Do not memorize the speech word for word.

Materials for eulogies may be found in Who's Who, histories, biographies, autobiographies, encyclopedias, newspapers, magazines, and similar sources. Consult your librarian for assistance.

HOW TO PRESENT A EULOGY

Your overall attitude must be one of undoubted sincerity. Be a true believer in the person about whom you speak. Aside from your attitude, you will, of course, observe all the requirements of good speech. There should be no showiness or gaudiness in your presentation that will call attention to you instead of your ideas about the subject of your speech.

You will need to be fully aware of the occasion and atmosphere into which you will step when you deliver the eulogy. It is your responsibility to know what will be required of you in the way of carrying out rituals or ceremonies if they are a part of the program. Since you will be in the limelight, you

Family or friends are often called upon to speak at funerals or memorial services.

should fit easily into the situation without awkwardness. Naturally you must adjust your bodily actions and gestures to your environment—and your audience. Your voice should reach the ears of all present.

If you are sincere, well prepared, and mean what you say, the eulogy you present should be inspirational to all who hear it.

TRIBUTE TO THURGOOD MARSHALL
A Eulogy by Senator Carol Moseley-Braun
Delivered to the United States Senate, Wahington, D.C., on January 26, 1993.

Mr. President, Thurgood Marshall died last Sunday of heart failure. I still have great difficulty believing it. I know he born over 84 years ago, and I know that he himself said he was "old and falling apart," but it is nonetheless hard to conceive that a heart as mighty and as courageous as his is no longer beating.

Thurgood Marshall epitomized the best in America; he was, in fact, what this country is all about. That may seem to be an odd thing to say about him. After all, he himself was very aware of the fact that the United States did not, and in too many instances still does not, live up entirely to its founding principles. He knew that the phrases of the Declaration of Independence, "that all men are created equal" and are endowed "with certain inalienable rights," including those to "life, liberty and the pursuit of happiness...," were not, all too much of the time, the principles that govern everyday life in America.

Thurgood Marshall was born in Baltimore in 1908. He lived and felt the humiliation of racism, of not being able even to use the bathroom in downtown Baltimore simply because of the color of his skin.

But Thurgood Marshall was not defeated by racism. He knew that racial inequality was incompatible with American ideals, and he made it his life's unending fight to see that this country's ideals became true for all of its citizens.

And what a fight it has been. It took Thurgood Marshall from Baltimore's segregated public schools to Lincoln University, where he graduated with honors, to Howard University Law School, to the NAACP, to the circuit bench, to the U.S. Solicitor General's office, to become the first African-American member of the U.S. Supreme Court.

That quick biography does not begin to measure the battles Thurgood Marshall fought and won, and the strength, conviction and power he put into that fight.

Thomas Jefferson said that "A little rebellion, now and then, is a good thing, and as necessary in the political world as storms in the physical." Thurgood Marshall took Jefferson at his word, and played a key role in creating a rebellion in American, a rebellion not of violence, but of law. What Marshall did was to use the U.S. legal system to bludgeon and destroy state-supported segregation.

What Marshall did was to use the courts and the law to force the United States to apply the promises made every American in our Declaration of Independence and our Bill of Rights to

African-Americans who had little or no protection under the law up until the Marshall legal rebellion. What Marshall did was to make the 13th, 14th, and 15th amendments to our Constitution the law of the land in reality, instead of just an empty promise.

The history of the civil rights movement in this country is, in no small part, the history of Marshall's battles before the Supreme Court. As lead counsel of the National Association for the Advancement of Colored People, Marshall appeared before the Supreme Court 32 times, and won 29 times. His legal skills, grounded in sound preparation and sensitivity to the evidence helped him win such landmark decisions as *Smith vs. Allwright*, *Shelley vs. Kramer*, *Sweatt vs. Painter*, and the biggest case of them all, *Brown vs. Board of Education*.

I am somewhat reluctant to dwell on Thurgood Marshall's many successes, because I know he would not like that. He would not like it because he knew only too well that there are many more battles that must be fought and won if America's founding principles and American reality are to become one and the same for every American of every color. In his dissent in the Bakke case, Marshall said:

"The position of the Negro today in America is the tragic but inevitable consequence of centuries of unequal treatment. Measured by any benchmark of comfort or achievement, meaningful equality remains a distant dream for the Negro."

However, the fact that the battle is not yet won does not lessen Marshall's many accomplishments. He was a man who worked and fought to make a difference, he was a man who did make a difference.

He certainly made a difference in my life, opening doors of opportunity measured only by merit. He helped ensure that I was able to attend public schools and the University of Chicago Law School, and not schools for blacks only. His work helped make my election to the U.S. Senate possible. He opened closed doors and created new opportunities for me and for many, many others. His life was the most convincing evidence that a change is possible.

I want to close, Mr. President, by quoting Thurgood Marshall one more time. In the Bakke case, he said:

"In the light of the sorry history of discrimination and its devastating impact on the lives of Negroes, bringing the Negro into the mainstream of American life should be a state interest of the highest order."

I share his view. Elimination of racism is not just an interest of African-Americans, but of all Americans. Only then will we be able to tap the full potential of our people. Only then will we live the greatness of the American promise.

I hope we will all remember Thurgood Marshall by continuing his lifetime to struggle. I hope we will all remember Marshall by dedicating ourselves to the principles and goals he dedicated himself to: making American opportunity available to every American. And as we work toward those goals, I hope we can all live our lives as completely as he did, enjoy ourselves as much as he did, and poke as much fun at ourselves as Thurgood Marshall did all of his life.

I will miss Thurgood Marshall. America will miss Thurgood Marshall. I am proud to have the opportunity, in some small way, to continue his work, and to try to build on his legacy.

CHAPTER 27

THE DEDICATION SPEECH

Time limits: 3-4 minutes.

Speaking notes: This is a short speech—you do not need any.

Sources of information: Two are required, preferably three. For each source give the specific magazine, book, or Internet site it was taken from, title of the article, author's full name, date of publication, and the chapter or pages telling where the material was found. If a source is a person, identify the source completely by title, position, occupation, etc. List these on the outline form. For Internet sites give the address (URL).

Outline your speech: Prepare a 75-150 word complete sentence outline.

Question: What is fluency?

Answer: It is the readiness and ease with which words are spoken.

Key Words:
Commemorative
Dedication speech

Student Expectations: In completing this chapter each student will:
> *Identify the required elements of a dedication speech*
> *Identify ideals to be celebrated*
> *Present a speech with dignity appropriate to the occasion*

PURPOSE OF THIS ASSIGNMENT

You may not give a speech at dedication ceremonies for a long time, then again the occasion for a speech of this kind may arise sooner than you had thought possible. But regardless of when you are called on for this type of speech, one thing is sure, and that is that you must know its requirements. The dedication speech occurs on an occasion and in an atmosphere that requires very strict observance of certain aspects of speechmaking. This speech assignment is designed to give an experience like the "real thing," so that you give a credible performance when the opportunity presents itself.

EXPLANATION OF THE DEDICATION SPEECH

The **dedication speech** is one presented on **commemorative** occasions. It is generally brief and carries a serious tone. It employs excellent language, demands careful construction, fine wording, and polished delivery. Its purpose should be to commemorate, to honor an occasion, and to praise the spirit of endeavor and progress that the dedication symbolizes. The speech should thrill the audience with pride regarding their community, ideals, and progress. Occasions for the dedication speech usually involve a group enterprise. Common among these are occasions such as: erecting monuments, completing buildings, stadiums, and baseball parks, or laying cornerstones and opening institutions. Similar events considered as marks of progress are also occasions for dedication speeches. Lincoln's Gettysburg Address is one of the finest dedication speeches ever made.

Ribbon cutting ceremonies are a common occasion for a dedication speech.

HOW TO CHOOSE A TOPIC FOR A DEDICATION SPEECH

This will involve a bit of imagination on your part; however, choose an occasion that you wish were actually true, really being enacted. For instance, think about someone you consider to be a hero or heroine and dedicate a statue to that person. Would you like to have a new community center in your neighborhood where you could play games with your friends? Then, create a ceremony to break ground, lay a cornerstone, or dedicate a completed building. If you are having trouble developing a topic, consult your teacher for additional suggestions.

HOW TO PREPARE A DEDICATION SPEECH

First, know your purpose. It must dominate this speech the same as the purpose dominates every speech. This means that you are to compliment the ideals and achievements which the dedicated structure symbolizes, thus setting it apart for a certain purpose.

These are the points to cover in the speech. Give a brief history of events leading up to the present time. Mention the sacrifice, the work, the ideals, and the service that lie behind the project. Next, explain the future use or work, the influence or significance that will be associated with the structure being dedicated. Place the emphasis upon what the object dedicated stands for (ideals, progress, loyalty) rather than upon the object itself.

The above thoughts will constitute your material. Now, organize your speech carefully. Pay particular attention to the introduction, the conclusion—yes, everything in your speech. It must have order. To accomplish the organization of the speech you will first outline it. Wording it follows. Do this meticulously. Be understandable and simple in language. The speech is serious, not frivolous. Leave your humor at home.

You are now ready to practice. Do this orally. Rehearse aloud until you have definitely fixed the order of the speech in your mind. Avoid complete word-for-word memorization. You may memorize certain words and phrases, but you should not memorize the entire speech. When you have mastered an effective presentation, you will be ready to speak. Remember to include appropriate bodily action, gestures, and voice in your practice.

HOW TO PRESENT A DEDICATION SPEECH

The attitude of the speaker should be one of appropriate dignity. Emotion and sentiment should be properly blended to fit the noble sentiments that will be present. The adequacy and poise of the speaker would be obvious from appearance, bearing, and self-confidence.

Body language must be keyed to the tone of the speech. The environment surrounding the speaker may permit much action or limit it severely. If a public address system is used, the speaker cannot move from the microphone. The speaker can and should utilize gestures.

Whether speaking with the aid of a microphone or not, the voice should be full and resonant and easily heard. If the crowd is large, a slower speaking rate should be used. Articulation must be carefully attended, yet not so much so that it becomes ponderous and labored. Voice and action must be in tune, neither one overbalancing the other. The speaker must be animated, alive to the purpose, desirous of communicating, and capable of presenting a polished speech.

Four score and seven years ago our fathers brought forth upon this continent a new nation, conceived in liberty, and dedicated to the proposition that all men are created equal.

Now we are engaged in a great civil war, testing whether that nation so conceived, and so dedicated, can long endure. We are met on a great battlefield of that war. We have come to dedicate a portion of that field as a final resting-place for those who here gave their lives that that nation might live. It is altogether fitting and proper that we should do this.

But in a larger sense, we cannot dedicate—we cannot consecrate—we cannot hallow this ground. The brave men, living and dead, who struggled here, have consecrated it far above our poor power to add or detract. The world will little note, nor long remember, what we say here, but it can never forget what they did here. It is for us, the living, rather, to be dedicated here to the unfinished work which they who fought here have thus far so nobly advanced. It is rather for us to be here dedicated to the great task remaining before us—that from these honored dead we take increased devotion to that cause for which they gave the last full measure of devotion—that we here highly resolve that these dead shall not have died in vain—that this nation, under God, shall have a new birth of freedom and that government of the people, by the people, and for the people, shall not perish from the earth.

CHAPTER 28

THE ANNIVERSARY SPEECH

Time limits: 5-6 minutes.

Speaking notes: It is advisable to use none. Try it.

Sources of information: Two are required, preferably three. For each source give the specific magazine, book, or Internet site it was taken from, title of the article, author's full name, date of publication, and the chapter or pages telling where the material was found. If a source is a person, identify the source completely by title, position, occupation, etc. List these on the outline form. For Internet sites give the address (URL).

Outline your speech: Prepare a 75-100 word complete sentence outline.

Question: How do you speak fluently?

Answer: Fluency varies greatly. Whatever your fluency is you will be wise to accept it. Thorough preparation, much oral rehearsal, and experience will help.

 **Key Word:**
Anniversary speech

Student Expectations: In completing this assignment each student will:
➤ *Identify the necessary elements of an anniversary commemoration*
➤ *Create and present a speech that celebrates an historical event*

PURPOSE OF THIS ASSIGNMENT

The experience of presenting an anniversary speech now will prove helpful to you at some later time when you meet the real situation requiring knowledge of its structure and presentation. A speaker is often disturbed, nervous, and ill at ease when speaking on an occasion not previously experienced. Feelings of uncertainty probably spring from lack of familiarity with the environment. In your case, having known what it is to give an anniversary talk at least once, you should find future performances considerably easier and perhaps enjoyable.

EXPLANATION OF THE ANNIVERSARY SPEECH

The **anniversary speech** is one presented in commemoration of an event, a person, or occasion of the past. Its purpose is to recall and remember the past so that we may more adequately serve the present and courageously prepare for the future. It will weigh the past, observe the blessings of the present, and look to the future optimistically. Elements of loyalty and patriotism usually are contained in the remarks.

This talk is similar to the dedication speech. The speaker should be a good person, both in character and ability. The person should be fully acquainted with the history, the present status of the anniversary, and future plans as they pertain to it. You might think of the anniversary as a birthday celebration and incorporate all the ideals and ideas associated with such a day.

Occasions for anniversary speeches arise whenever the passing of time is marked by a pause in which people lay aside their work long enough to note what has been accomplished. The remembrance of Independence Day, Presidents' Day, Armistice, Thanksgiving, Martin Luther King's birthday, Labor Day, birthday of a national, state or local figure, are all examples of such occasions. Observance of the progress during a certain number of years of a business firm, a school, a church, a city,

Holidays such as Independence Day include many anniversary speeches commemorating historic events.

state or nation, or any organization, may form the basis of an anniversary speech. During recent years, state centennials marked by regional and state fairs have proved themselves worthwhile as anniversaries. Every day is the birthday of somebody or something; hence every day is a potential anniversary, whether it is observed or not.

HOW TO CHOOSE A TOPIC FOR AN ANNIVERSARY SPEECH

If you have a particular loyalty or devotion, it would be advisable to construct your speech around it at an imaginary or real anniversary. National holidays are natural events for anniversary speeches. They recognize historical events or individuals. Use this assignment as a way to learn something about the history of your school or community. For other suggestions, consult your teacher. Be sure you are interested in the topic you select for your speech.

HOW TO PREPARE AN ANNIVERSARY SPEECH

Remember that your purpose is to commemorate. Keep this purpose in mind constantly. Your thoughts must be constructed to achieve this end. Second, the organization of your speech is important. Here you must observe all the characteristics of adequate speech composition. You should include the following points: tell why you are especially interested in this anniversary; show historically that the people and their ideals are responsible for the organization's celebration; and trace the development of these ideals.

Anecdotes, stories, incidents, and humor are appropriate and impressive if properly used. The past should vividly live again for your audience. Turn next to the present; compare it with the past. Avoid references to or implications of partisan or class views. Speak broadly for all the people by utilizing a spirit of friendliness and goodwill. Bend your energies toward unity and interest for the common good. Speak next of the future. By virtue of a splendid past and a significant present, the future holds promises of greater things to be. Speak confidently on this thesis. Indicate that the cooperation of all persons directed toward a determined effort for a greater service to all human beings is the goal all are seeking. Show the relationship of this anniversary to the welfare of the state and nation.

After having constructed the speech, be sure to rehearse it aloud until you have fixed the order of points in your mind. Do not memorize it. Practice body language and gestures while rehearsing, but be sure to avoid mechanical movements.

HOW TO PRESENT AN ANNIVERSARY SPEECH

Speak sincerely. If you cannot and do not mean what you say, you should not speak. Your body language and your voice, should evoke sincerity. Maintain good eye contact with your audience. You should be easily heard by all and be completely in their view. Your dress should be appropriate to the occasion. Observe time limits.

50ᵀᴴ ANNIVERSARY OF THE UNITED NATIONS
By Boutros-Boutros Ghali, Secretary General of the United Nations
Delivered to the General Assembly, United Nations Headquarters, New York, New York, October 22, 1995

I welcome the heads of the States and Governments of the world. Welcome to your home—the home of the world's peoples. Welcome to the forum of the United Nations—the forum of peace, understanding and development. Welcome to you all, and heartfelt greetings to the world's leaders.

We meet to commemorate 50 United Nations years. How can we shape the next 50 years to serve people's needs?

The world of the twenty-first century will confront two great opposing forces—globalization and fragmentation. A new dialectic has already begun.

Globalization will generate an array of problems. Financial flows of vast magnitude sweep across the world. Alarming environmental events will expose the planet to permanent damage. Transnational criminal activity will grow. The global communications revolution will generate pressures which our institutions were not designed to address.

Fragmentation also will characterize the future. The remote, and impersonal forces of globalization will cause people to seek refuge in smaller groups. Fragmentation can breed fanaticism, isolationism, separatism, and the proliferation of civil war.

The United Nations can help deal with the dialectic of globalization and fragmentation and help solve the problems it will create.

This is because the United Nations was designed to be both the world Organization and the Organization of its Member States and their peoples designed, therefore to respond both to global concerns and to the needs of member states and their peoples. As if in training for precisely this moment the United Nations in 50 years has gained enormous experience in dealing with both globalization and fragmentation.

In response to globalization, the United Nations defined human rights for the global community. It fostered the progress of international law. It transformed the law of the sea. Through a continuum of global conferences it is promoting international consensus on new global issues of disarmament, environment, population, social development, migration, and the advancement of women.

In response to fragmentation, the United Nations has been called to respond to civil wars: Katanga, Cambodia, El Salvador, Angola, and Mozambique. To prevent fragmentation, the United National is promoting democratization—both within and among States.

Within States, issues of identity and ethnic separatism will be decided by the ballot box and the parliament, not by the gun and ethnic cleansing. Among States, democratization will promote a climate of peace, helping to prevent the outbreak of conflict.

But the United Nations cannot play this role if the present trend continues. The United Nations is trapped by a second dialectic. The problems, of globalization and fragmentation have caused vast responsibilities to be given to the United Nations. But the United Nations has not been given the resources required to accomplish the tasks imposed.

The financial crisis is a symptom of a deeper problem: Member States simply do not regard the United Nations as a priority. This is sad news to report to the commemorative session.

I appeal to you to give the United Nations a firm financial base. If steps towards this cannot be set in motion by the end of this year, I urge you to give serious consideration to calling a special session of the General Assembly to deal with the financial crisis of the organization.

This commemorative session is a time for you, the leaders of the Member States, to consider what it is you want from the United Nations. I respectfully ask you to do this. Thank you.

HOW CAN AN INTRODUCTION GET THE ATTENTION OF THE AUDIENCE?

1. Use a quotation. Sometimes a familiar quotation or a quotation from a familiar person can help the audience get involved with your presentation.
2. Use an important fact or statistic. Find a striking fact or statistic that will immediately catch the interest of the audience so they will say, "I didn't know that."
3. Tell a story or a joke. This will sometimes help break the ice and grab the attention of the audience.
4. Use an action. Actually do something that will attract the attention of the audience.
5. Ask a question. This will often get the audience to think about your topic and draw them in so they want to hear more.
6. Combine any of the methods. Use an action and a story, or ask a question and present a fact. Try your own combinations.

CHAPTER
29

THE COMMENCEMENT SPEECH

Time limits: 5-7 minutes.

Speaking notes: 10-word maximum.

Sources of information: Two are required, preferably three. For each source give the specific magazine, book, or Internet site it was taken from, title of the article, author's full name, date of publication, and the chapter or pages telling where the material was found. If a source is a person, identify the source completely by title, position, occupation, etc. List these on the outline form. For Internet sites give the address (URL).

Outline your speech: Prepare a 75-100 word complete sentence outline.

Question: How important is the speech introduction?

Answer: Very important! It is the audience's first impression of you as a speaker.

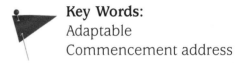

Key Words:
Adaptable
Commencement address

Student Expectations: In completing this assignment each student will:
➤ *Determine the objectives of a commencement address*
➤ *Create and deliver a commencement speech*

PURPOSE OF THIS ASSIGNMENT

How many times have you been to a graduation of a friend or relative only to hope that the speeches are short so you can get on with the ceremony? Unfortunately, this is the way many people feel about the speeches presented at graduation ceremonies. The speaker is not really the highlight of the ceremony. But the commencement speech need not be boring for the audience. A well executed **commencement address** will cause the audience to reflect on the past and inspire them to action in the future. This speech has its own unique difficulties. The speaker must be able to adapt to a dual audience of parents and relatives along with the students. The ability to adapt to both audiences and present an interesting, stimulating speech is the focus of this assignment.

EXPLANATION OF THE COMMENCEMENT SPEECH

Occasions for commencement speeches are not as numerous as are those for other types of speeches. Commencement ceremonies usually limit their speakers to a special guest, the senior class president, the valedictorian or salutatorian. But they are nonetheless a very important part of the whole ceremony. There are several objectives for the commencement speech. The speech should congratulate the students and family members on their accomplishments which led to graduation. The importance here is to not neglect parents and relatives in the audience who had a part in the student's education. It is important to emphasize both groups' accomplishments. A similar objective is to pay tribute to the teachers and administrators who helped the students through the education system. Another objective is to reflect on past memories and traditions.

This part of the speech is one most appreciated by the students in the audience. Stories about the things that have happened over the years and special memories are reflected by the speaker. The caution here is not to present stories that are too "inside" for the rest of the audience to understand. The speech should have a serious overtone, but humorous anecdotes and stories can help liven up the presentation. A third objective is to issue a challenge to the graduates for the future. The speaker must inspire the audience to do great things as they embark on a new chapter in their lives.

SUGGESTED TOPICS FOR A COMMENCEMENT SPEECH

The occasion of a commencement speech generally dictates the topics that are included in the presentation. Therefore, the speaker needs to find appropriate examples and inspiring stories to include in the speech. A future challenge should also be one of the topics that the speaker should cover.

HOW TO CHOOSE A TOPIC FOR YOUR COMMENCEMENT SPEECH

One of the most important things to remember about choosing a topic is that it needs to be **adaptable** to the variety of audience members. The speaker will be dealing with the students who are eager to graduate, along with the different generations of parents, grandparents, and friends. Many of these people have attended these types of ceremonies before and have certain expectations of commencement speeches. The student speakers should remember that "inside" stories of past experiences may not be of interest, or make much sense, to anyone other than their classmates.

HOW TO PREPARE YOUR COMMENCEMENT SPEECH

As with any speech presentation, careful attention should be paid to organization and supporting material. The speaker should prepare examples and stories which support the themes of the presentation. The examples should be vivid, interesting and make the principles of the speech come alive. Quotations from philosophers or other respected

individuals may be utilized. Use of contrast may be helpful as the speaker issues challenges for the students' new endeavors. Commencement is a beginning along with an ending and may be contrasted with other beginnings. The speech must leave the audience with a sense of accomplishment and an eagerness to move into the future. Therefore, organization of the presentation must build to these points.

Student speakers should pay tribute to family, teachers, and administrators who helped them succeed.

A guest speaker should attempt to impart some personal wisdom, which comes with age, to the audience. The audience is being prepared for something the speaker will have already been through, and for the problems that will be faced by the students. The speaker becomes the expert, leading the younger generation into their new world. A senior class president, valedictorian or salutatorian becomes the representative of the student body at the commencement ceremony. Their presentations should reflect the themes that are important to their classmates. They should bring back memories of happy times, sad times and important times in their lives. The examples and stories need to relate well to both the students in the audience and the parents and relatives who are in attendance.

HOW TO PRESENT THE COMMENCEMENT SPEECH

Since the commencement speaker is not the real highlight of the ceremony, the speaker needs to grab and hold onto the attention of the audience. The speaker must be dynamic and enthusiastic. But at the same time the speaker must be sincere and earnest.

Many times the student speaker must deal with the emotions that are present during this time. Practice is essential. Practice in front of people should be a requirement. The parts of the speech that need to be inspiring should be delivered in that enthusiastic, dynamic tone. Other parts of the speech which call for earnest reflection, and sincere gratitude also need to be delivered in the appropriate tone. The speech should also be long enough to get the message across but not too long so that the audience feels trapped or begins to feel bored. The speaker must remember that there are other parts to the ceremony. A long commencement speech is generally not well received by the audience.

All other presentational skills for speaking to large audiences should be observed. Speakers may wish to review the chapter dealing with speaking from a microphone prior to presenting this speech. Also prior to presenting, a review of the chapters which cover speeches to persuade and convince might be helpful.

CHOICES AND CHANGE: YOUR SUCCESS AS A FAMILY
A Commencement Speech by Barbara Bush, Former First Lady of the United States
Delivered at Severance Green, Wellesley College, Wellesley, MA, June 1, 1990.

Thank you President Keohane, Mrs. Gorbachev, trustees, faculty, parents, Julie Porer, Christine Bicknell and the Class of 1990. I am thrilled to be with you today, and very excited, as I know you must all be, that Mrs. Gorbachev could join us.

More than ten years ago when I was invited here to talk about our experiences in the People's Republic of China, I was struck by both the natural beauty of your campus and the spirit of this place.

Wellesley, you see, is not just a place, but an idea, an experiment in excellence in which diversity is not just tolerated, but is embraced.

The essence of this spirit was captured in a moving speech about tolerance given last year by the student body president of one of your sister colleges. She related the story by Robert Fulghum about a young pastor who, finding himself in charge of some very energetic children, hit upon a game called "Giants, Wizards and Dwarfs." "You have to decide now," the pastor instructed the children, "Which are you. . . a giant, a wizard or a dwarf?" At that, a small girl tugging on his pants leg, asked, "But where do the mermaids stand?"

The pastor told her there are *no* mermaids. "Oh yes there are," she said. "I am a mermaid."

This little girl knew what she was and she was not about to give up on either her identity *or* the game. She intended to take her place wherever mermaids fit into the scheme of things. Where *do* the mermaids stand... all those who are different, those who do not fit the boxes and the pigeonholes? "Answer that question," wrote Fulghum, "And you can build a school, a nation, or a whole world on it."

As that very wise young woman said,..."Diversity, like anything worth having requires *effort*." Effort to learn about and respect difference, to be compassionate with one another, and to cherish our own identity, and to accept unconditionally the same in all others.

You should all be very proud that this is the Wellesley spirit. Now I know your first choice for today was Alice Walker, known for the *The Color Purple*. Instead you got me—known for the color of my hair! Of course, Alice Walker's book has a special color, and for four years the class of '90 has worn the color purple. Today you meet on Severance Green to say goodbye to all that, to begin a new and very personal journey, a search for your own true colors.

In the world that awaits you beyond the shores of Lake Waban, no one can say what your true colors will be. But this I know: You have a first class education from a first class school. And so you need not, probably cannot, live a "paint-by-numbers" life. Decisions are not irrevocable. Choices do come back. As you set off from Wellesley, I hope that many of you will consider making three very special choices.

The first is to believe in something larger than yourself, to get involved in some of the big ideas of your time. I chose literacy because I honestly believe that if more people could read, write and comprehend, we would be that much closer to solving so many of the problems plaguing our society.

Early on I made another choice which I hope you will make as well. Whether you are talking about education, career or service, you are talking about life, and life must have joy. It's supposed to be fun!

One of the reasons I made the most important decision of my life, to marry George Bush, is because he made me laugh. It's true, sometimes we've laughed through our tears, but that shared laughter has been one of our strongest bonds. Find the joy in life, because as Ferris Bueller said on his day off:

"Life moves pretty fast. Ya don't stop and look around once in a while, ya gonna miss it!"

The third choice that must not be missed is to cherish your human connections: your relationships with friends and family. For several years, you've had impressed upon you the importance to your career of dedication and hard work. This is true, but as important as your obligations as a doctor, lawyer or business leader will be, you are a human being first and those human connections, with spouses, with children, with friends, are the most important investments you will ever make.

At the end of your life, you will never regret not having passed one more test, not winning one more verdict or not closing one more deal. You will regret time not spent with a husband, a friend, a child or a parent.

We are in a transitional period right now, fascinating and exhilarating times, learning to adjust to the changes and the choices we, men and women, are facing. I remember what a friend said, on hearing her husband lament to his buddies that he had to baby-sit. Quickly setting him straight, my friend told her husband that when it's your own kids, it's not called babysitting!

Maybe we should adjust faster, maybe slower. But whatever the era, whatever the times, one thing will never change: fathers and mothers, if you have children, they must come first. Your success as a family, our success as a society, depends not on what happens at the White House, but on what happens inside your house.

For over 50 years, it was said that the winner of Wellesley's annual hoop race would be the first to get married. Now they say the winner will be the first to become a C.E.O. Both of these stereotypes show too little tolerance for those who want to know where the mermaids stand. So I offer you today a new legend: the winner of the hoop race will be the first to realize her dream, not society's dream, her own personal dream. And who knows: Somewhere out in this audience may even be someone who will one day follow in my footsteps, and preside over the White House as the president's spouse. I wish him well!

The controversy ends here. But our conversation is only beginning. And a worthwhile conversation it is. So as you leave Wellesley today, take with you deep thanks for the courtesy and honor you have shared with Mrs. Gorbachev and me. Thank you. God bless you. And may your future be worthy of your dreams.

Reprinted with permission from *Vital Speeches of the Day,* July 1, 1990, p. 549

CHAPTER
30
THE BOOK REVIEW

Time limits: 10-15 minutes.

Speaking notes: 50-word limit.

Outline your speech: Prepare a 75-100 word complete sentence outline.

Question: How do you enunciate correctly?

Answer: Sound the letters t, d, p, b, k, g, ch, s, sh, distinctly, especially those in the middle and at the end of words. Stress syllables properly.

Key Words:
Oral book review
Purpose

Student Expectations: In completing this assignment each student will:
➤ *Analyze and evaluate a text*
➤ *Understand methods of preparing a review*
➤ *Present the review from minimum speaking notes*

PURPOSE OF THIS ASSIGNMENT

There are two reasons for this book review assignment. The first reason is that you should have the experience of preparing and presenting a book review so you will know first hand how it is done when called on to do it in an English class. While you are doing this, you will gain much valuable information and enjoyment from the book you are reviewing. The second reason is that as a class project you will, add much to the knowledge of all of the members of the class. Because each member will review a separate book, many different authors' ideas will be presented. This in turn will provide a general fund of information that would otherwise be unattainable.

EXPLANATION OF THE BOOK REVIEW

An **oral book review** is an orderly talk about a book and its author. This requires that you provide pertinent information about the author as well as what was written. Generally speaking, you should include an evaluation of the work relative to composition and ideas. The ends of your talk will be to inform, to stimulate, to entertain, and, possibly, to convince. The book reviewer is expected to know the material well, to be informed regarding the methods of giving a review, and to be able to present the information in an organized and interesting manner. These requirements demand an unusually thorough preparation.

Occasions for the book review can occur almost anywhere. They arise in scholastic, civic, religious, and other organizations. In practically any kind of club or society, school or church, a book review often forms the basis of a program.

SUGGESTED TYPES OF BOOKS FOR A REVIEW

For this particular experience it is suggested that each student select a different book. It is easier if it is fiction as contrasted to non-fiction or a textbook. You may want to use a book you are reading for another class or a book you have recently read. You probably won't have time to read a new novel before you speak. Whatever the book, it should be approved by the instructor before you start to prepare your speech.

Books to serve as the subject for a book review are abundant. Select a book of interest to you and your audience.

HOW TO CHOOSE A BOOK FOR REVIEW

First of all, follow your instructor's assignment. If you are asked to review a specific type of book, such as science fiction, go to the library and select such a book. If your instructor leaves the assignment open ended, select a book that you enjoyed reading—one you couldn't put down. If you have

time to read a book before the assignment is due, check *The New York Times* review of books and the list of best sellers. Finally, go to a bookstore or library and peruse the latest titles.

HOW TO PREPARE A BOOK REVIEW

Every speech must have a **purpose**. The book review is no exception; for this reason, you should determine your purpose whether it is to inform, to entertain, to convince, to stimulate. Now you ask, "What should go into a book review and how should you go about organizing your material?" Succinctly, your procedure may follow this order if you consider it suitable. Tell about the author—age, family background, education, when the person first published, anecdotes about the author, quotations about the author, home town, prizes won for writing, or why this book was written.

Now, about the book. Why did you choose it? When was it written? Under what circumstances? Why was it written? Is it biographical, historical, fiction, what? What do the reviewers say about it? (Ask your librarian to show you lists of book reviews such as those in *The New York Times, Christian Century, Saturday Review of Literature, New Republic, The Nation,* and others.) What is your opinion? Formulate your own. Do not plagiarize someone else's evaluation of the book. Give examples and comments in answering the following questions: Are the plot and organization well constructed? Is the writer's style interesting? How are situations and characters portrayed? Do the characters seem real and alive? Does the story move forward to a climax? Is the information interesting and useful? Do you recommend the book? Why?

One of the best ways to master the above information is to read the entire book or sections that you are preparing to review several times. First, read it through for enjoyment. The second and third times read for information you plan to use in your review. As for getting your material in mind, use your own method. It is advisable that you should make a careful and detailed outline, after which you rehearse aloud until your sequence of thoughts has been firmly fixed in mind. If you use quotations, limit them to one hundred and fifty words each.

HOW TO PRESENT A BOOK REVIEW

First of all, have the review "in your head." Do not stand before your audience with the book in your hands so that you can use it as a crutch while you give your review by following previously marked pages, or occupy time by reading. This is not reviewing. Use the book only for your quotations. If you use notes, limit yourself to three words or fewer for each minute you speak.

Utilize all of the aspects of good speech—friendliness, animation, vigor, communicative attitude, bodily action and gestures that are appropriate, a voice that is easily heard and well modulated, correct pronunciation, clear articulation, vivid and descriptive language, a neat appearance, poise and confidence. Utilize these and you cannot fail.

SPECIAL HINTS

1. Be sure you have an excellent introduction and conclusion.
2. Be sure your speech is logically organized all the way.
3. Do not fail to evaluate the book.

UNIT V

CONTEST SPEAKING

Contest speaking, if entered from an educational perspective, can help a student sharpen particular communication skills relatively quickly. In this unit we present chapters on some of the most common speaking contest events. If regional events are not available in your area, you might consider setting up a small contest within your class or school.

Oral Interpretation is an event that teaches the student how to understand the emotions and deeper meanings implanted in a text, and to express those meanings to others in a reading of the text. This chapter offers suggestions for selecting and preparing an appropriate example for the student.

Extemporaneous Speaking gives the student an opportunity to develop the ability to analyze current events and develop a presentation of that analysis in a relatively brief amount of time. This event offers more preparation time than impromptu speaking, but still requires the student to learn to think and organize ideas quickly — an invaluable tool for all of life's experiences.

For students who wish to learn how to conduct fair and orderly business meetings, many speaking tournaments offer an event called *Parliamentary Law* or *Student Congress*. These events require a good grasp of parliamentary procedures and offer the student a chance to apply that knowledge in the context of a lively debate on a topic of particular interest to many. This chapter explains the events in detail so that students may begin their participation in such events.

Finally, many opportunities in life invite us to formally *Debate* particular topics in decision-making bodies to which we belong. The contest version of formal debate is particularly ordered to present two strong sides of any issue, providing each side the chance to directly address the position of the other. This chapter explains that ordering and teaches the student how to prepare to participate in this event.

Competition has a way of "getting the adrenaline going" so that the communication skills involved are seen through a fresh perspective. In so doing, it provides the student with a new way to rehearse and develop important skills that will benefit the competent communicator for years to come.

CHAPTER
31

ORAL INTERPRETATION

Time limits: 4-5 minutes.

Sources for reading aloud: Consult school librarian or your instructor.

Question: How can one project to be heard better?

Answer: Use your diaphragm the way singers do rather than strain your vocal cords. Consult your vocal music teacher for diaphragm breathing techniques.

Key Words:
Oral interpretation
Pantomiming
Paraphrasing
Variety

Student Expectations: In completing this assignment each student will:
➢ *Research an author's background*
➢ *Discover the meaning and feelings intended by the author of a selected text*
➢ *Understand the process of formal oral interpretation presentation*
➢ *Rehearse and present an oral interpretation to an audience*

PURPOSE OF THIS ASSIGNMENT

Many persons find themselves in a quandary when confronted with a situation that demands oral reading. Too often they seemingly have no idea about the way oral reading should be done. As a result, excellent literary productions go unread or are so poorly read that much of their beauty and thought are lost. No one expects you to master the field of oral interpretation after concluding one appearance before your classmates, but certainly you should have a much clearer understanding of what is involved in reading aloud. This reading experience will help you improve your oral read-

ing from the standpoint of personal enjoyment and ability to read for others.

EXPLANATION OF ORAL INTERPRETATION

Oral interpretation, as we use the term here, is reading aloud from the printed page with the purpose of interpreting what is read so that its meaning is conveyed to those who are listening and watching. The purpose may be to inform, to entertain, to arouse, to convince, or to get action. Successful oral reading demands that the speaker must know the material well enough that they can interpret fully and accurately the ideas, meanings, and beauties placed in the composition by the author. To do this capably, a burden of careful, almost meticulous preparation is placed on the reader.

Much attention must be given to understanding what the author is saying; the reader assumes the responsibility of discovering and interpreting the author's meaning through voice and actions.

Occasions for oral reading are practically limitless. Any gathering at which it is appropriate to read aloud is suitable. School, church, and civic gatherings are common scenes of oral reading. Clubs, societies, private groups, private parties, and even commercial organizations, such as the radio, utilize oral reading largely for entertainment. We are not considering the hundreds of newscasts and other types of radio and television programs which are read daily in the category of oral reading. One of the most common scenes is in a household with small children.

HOW TO CHOOSE A SELECTION FOR ORAL INTERPRETATION

Choosing a selection is not easy; it is hard work. First of all, be sure to make your choice of a selection for reading early enough that you will have adequate time to prepare it. Your selection should be made on several important bases. Among these are the following: The selection should be suitable to you as its reader. In other words, choose something that you are capable of preparing and later interpreting. For this particular reading experience, it will probably be advisable that you do an interpretation that does not require characterization of several individuals. Of course, if you have had sufficient experience so that you are qualified to portray different characters and make the necessary transitions involved in more difficult interpretations, then go ahead with such a choice of subject. Give close attention to your prospective audience and the occasion. Your choice of a selection must be applicable to both. This means that you need to analyze both your audience and the occasion carefully; otherwise you may read something entirely inappropriate. You must ascertain the kind of environment in which you will be required to read. The size of the building, the seating arrangement in relation to you, the reader, outside noises, building distractions, and other fac-

tors will definitely influence your selection. If you observe closely all these bases of choosing a topic, you have a good chance of presenting a credible oral reading.

Sources of material are available in your school library. Check for poetry, prose readings, and interpretations. Your instructor and the librarian will gladly help you.

HOW TO PREPARE AN ORAL INTERPRETATION

Some important steps in preparation are these: Know the meaning of every word, as well as the use of all punctuation. The author wrote a certain way for a reason. Learn all you can about the author so that you may understand why certain words, punctuations, and phrases were used. Try to understand the philosophy and point of view. Acquire a knowledge of the circumstances surrounding the writing of your particular selection. Do the same for the setting of the article so that you may enjoy its perspective more adequately. Try hard to capture its mood.

Adequate preparation may necessitate your **paraphrasing** and **pantomiming** the selection to better understand its meaning. This will assist in obtaining a more complete comprehension of what the authors meant and what they might have done had they read their own poetry or prose.

Practice reading aloud until you have the entire selection well enough in mind that you can give most of your attention (eighty to ninety percent) to your audience by maintaining eye contact. This will necessitate a form of memorization that will permit you to use the printed copy as a guide only. Mark your manuscript with suggestions for changes in volume or pace. Use either words or a system of underlining to remind you that you need to slow down or read more rapidly. Highlighting pens can also be used to indicate vocal changes.

HOW TO PRESENT AN ORAL INTERPRETATION

Do not forget that the audience is watching you at all times. This includes before and after you read. All this time, they are observing you and forming opinions. Thus it is imperative that you constantly maintain an alert, poised, and friendly appearance. When you rise to read, your confidence and poise should be evident. Do not hurry to your position, but rather take your place easily and politely without hesitation. Pause a few seconds to glance over your audience before beginning to read. Avoid being stiff and cold and unfriendly. Begin your presentation by telling why you made your particular selection; tell something about the author so that the listeners may better understand

Oral Interpretation can bring a poem or short story to life mainly through verbal and nonverbal techniques.

the writer; provide information concerning the setting of the prose or poetry; and include anything else that will contribute to appreciation and enjoyment of your reading.

Your body should be appropriate to your selection both in posture and action. Any activity and gesture that will add to the interpretation of your reading should be included. Whatever will assist in imparting the mood, emotion, and meaning should be a part of your interpretation. Be careful

that you do not make the reading an impersonation.

Naturally, your voice must tell and imply much. Its **variety** as to pause, rate, pitch, melody, and intensity should be in keeping with what you are interpreting. All of these qualities should have been determined during the periods of rehearsal. If you can feel the emotions and meanings, so much the better.

Your book, or your reading material, should be held in such a way that it does not hide your face nor block the flow of your voice. Your head should not move up and down, as you glance from book to audience. One hand placed palm down inside the book will permit you to mark your place with a forefinger. The other hand held conveniently under the book palm up will act as a support. You need not hold your book in exactly one position, especially while you are looking at your audience. The point to remember is to raise your book in preference to dropping your head in order to read. The audience wants to see your face to catch emotions and meanings portrayed by its changing expressions. For ease in handling your material, type or photocopy the section of the book you are reading and place it in a folder. Use a music stand to hold your manuscript.

If you are reading several selections, treat each one separately. Allow sufficient time between numbers that the audience may applaud and relax slightly and otherwise express enjoyment of what you have done. When concluding a reading, pause a second or two before politely returning to your chair. Avoid quickly closing your book and leaving the stage when you are three words from the end of the last line.

By keeping in mind your audience, the occasion, your material and its meanings, the environment in which you are reading, and your place in the entire picture, you can do an excellent interpretation.

Using a Video To Improve Your Speech Performance

1. Set up the camera so that your entire body is in the picture. This allows you to observe your posture, stance, and movement.
2. Have some close-ups of the upper body and face to allow you to observe your gestures and facial expressions.
3. Tape the entire speech. Replay and watch it using a speech evaluation form. Review the strengths and weaknesses of your verbal delivery only.
4. Play the tape again without the audio and evaluate your nonverbal communication.
5. Practice the speech again without taping it. Work on the areas you noted as needing improvement.
6. Tape the speech again. Be sure to keep the first practice session on the tape. Watch the first practice and the second in sequence. Did you make improvements as desired? If not, work more without the tape.
7. Tape a final practice when you feel you have the speech ready for presentation. View it concentrating on what improvements you made.

CHAPTER 32

EXTEMPORANEOUS SPEAKING

Time limits: 6-7 minutes.

Speaking notes: Key words only.

Sources of information: Two are required, preferably three. For each source state the specific magazine, book, or Internet site it was taken from, title of the article, author's full name, and date of publication, if available. If a source is a person, identify the source as completely as possible, including full name, title or position, occupation, and date of interview.

Question: Should a person try to speak like someone he or she admires?

Answer: No. Develop your own effective speaker style and personality.

Key Words:
Extemporaneous speaking
Organizational method
Preparation time

Student Expectations: In completing this assignment each student will:
➤ *Understand the procedures of tournament extemporaneous speaking*
➤ *Critically analyze a current event or issue*
➤ *Determine an opinion on a current event or issue*
➤ *Organize speech materials in a limited amount of time*

PURPOSE OF THIS ASSIGNMENT

Many forensics tournaments include an event in **Extemporaneous Speaking.** The skills created and developed by participating in this event include the ability to organize your thoughts relatively quickly, to critically analyze current events, to formulate your opinions and ideas about national and international issues, and to express these opinions concisely and effectively to others.

EXPLANATION OF EXTEMPORANEOUS SPEAKING

In this event you may be given the option to choose either national or international issues. Interna-

tional issues would include topics dealing with other countries, or with U.S. foreign relations.

You may draw up to three topics, then select one of those on which to prepare your speech. Typically, you will have thirty minutes for your preparation. During the **preparation time**, you are allowed to consult source materials such as newspapers and magazines, or notes you may have made in advance from broadcast sources. You are not allowed to consult another person, however.

At the end of the designated preparation time, you are expected to present your speech to a judge and, possibly, an audience. The judges know you have had a limited amount of time to prepare. Still, a smooth delivery of well organized ideas and a clear, concise thesis statement will be expected.

SUGGESTED TOPICS FOR EXTEMPORANEOUS SPEAKING

Write one suggestion on a piece of paper for each of the following general categories: national issues, economic issues, international issues. They should be suitable to those who will be asked to use them as speech topics. Your instructor will ask you to supply a topic from time to time as needed during the class. Examples of suitable topics for extemporaneous speaking are (1) Will the recent crime bill passed by Congress reduce violent crimes by juveniles? (2) Is the U.S. economy stable, or ready for a major "course correction"? (3) How should the U.S. respond to the human rights abuses committed by China? (4) Are college costs excessive? (5) Should children under the age of 18 who commit murder be tried as adults?

HOW TO CHOOSE A TOPIC FOR EXTEMPORANEOUS SPEAKING

There is one general rule to follow in selecting a topic, if you have a choice. The rule is this: Choose the topic on which you are best prepared to speak. Consider your audience and the occasion as well when you are making a choice of topic.

HOW TO PREPARE FOR AN EXTEMPORANEOUS SPEECH

Like impromptu speaking, naturally you cannot use standard speech preparation practices for an unknown topic. However, unlike impromptu speaking, extemporaneous speaking does allow you a small amount of preparation time before you speak. Therefore, several suggestions are in order to help you make the most of that time.

First and foremost, to be a competent extemporaneous speaker you must keep up regularly with current events. A minimum effort in this regard is to attend to at least one radio or TV newscast per day, or read through a daily newspaper. More than one source per day will add to your ability to see the same issues from differing points of view.

Second, review the material in Chapter 12 on *How To Prepare for an Impromptu Speech*, as many of the same organizational principles apply to extemporaneous speaking as well.

Third, have someone help you rehearse by suggesting a topic in one of the three areas named above, and timing your preparations. Part of developing these speaking skills to their maximum effectiveness is simply a matter of practicing the process over and over again. The more opportunity you have to rehearse, the stronger your skills will become.

Contest extemp speakers usually speak without notes.

HOW TO PRESENT AN EXTEMPORANEOUS SPEECH

As in impromptu speaking, your attitude toward your audience and your subject has a tremendous impact on your effectiveness at extemporaneous speaking. Maintaining poise is important. (You may wish to review the suggestions for this in the *How To Present an Impromptu Speech* section of Chapter 12.)

Once your topic is selected, review your knowledge of that particular issue, making notes about the key ideas you recall. If you have brought clippings of current news publications with you that are filed by topic, you may use those to review and cite as sources in your speech. Take a moment now to think clearly about what position you want to take on the topic. Write out a very clear thesis statement that tells the audience both what you think is important about the topic, and how you are going to show that in your talk.

Next, decide what **organizational method** will both fit your topic and make it easiest for the audience to follow what you are saying. Do not feel you must always have three main points. Some topics require only two, and to try to fit them into three can cause you to misuse your speaking time unnecessarily. Organize your key ideas on the issue, checking to be sure they make sense (logically fit together) in that particular method.

Finally, you will need a few minutes of your preparation time to plan an attention-getting introduction and a solid conclusion. Do not neglect this part of your preparation as it will be the parts of your speech that your audience will likely notice the most! Search through your information on the issue to find a startling statistic or poignant story that could really capture your listeners' imaginations. Use such an example to begin your speech, followed by your thesis statement and a preview of your main ideas. Your conclusion should restate your thesis, summarize your main points, and if possible, refer back to that opening attention-getter.

When you are ready to speak, begin by making eye contact with the judge(s) and several members of the audience, if present. Begin your introduction with confidence, being careful not to speak too fast. Use gestures when appropriate, but avoid movements that only serve to communicate nervousness. You may wish to cross the room as you progress to a new main point. However, do not make these moves if they do not feel natural to you. "Staged" speaking movements are always obvious and serve to reduce your credibility rather than enhance your message.

Extemporaneous speaking can be a very valuable skill to have in the job market today. Keeping up with current events helps demonstrate that you are aware of a world larger than yourself which can be very attractive to colleges and employers you wish to impress. With sincere effort, you can master these skills in a relatively short time, reaping the benefits for years to come.

PARLIAMENTARY PROCEDURE AND STUDENT CONGRESS

Time limits of speakers: Unless otherwise stated in the organization's constitution, five minutes is generally recognized as the maximum amount of time any person may occupy the floor to speak upon a proposal in one speech.

Student motions: Each student will be required to place at least three motions before the assembly and seek their adoption. Motions which are adopted should be reported to the instructor.

Question: How will knowing parliamentary procedure help my communication skills?

Answer: Impromptu speaking, organization, and critical thinking skills are all developed through parliamentary debate.

Key Words:
Amendments
Incidental motions
Motion
Order of business
Parliamentary procedure
Precedence of motions

Student Expectations: In completing this assignment each student will:
➤ *Be able to identify and explain basic rules of parliamentary procedure*
➤ *Identify the basic duties of parliamentary officers and participants*
➤ *Understand the parliamentary process of conducting business*
➤ *Compose and deliver a formal motion and arguments in its support*

PURPOSE OF THIS ASSIGNMENT

A great many persons attempt to lead an assembly in which group discussion is paramount, or they endeavor to participate in a group discussion when they are totally uninformed regarding orderly and proper parliamentary procedure. The results of haphazard procedure are notorious. Ill-will, ruffled feelings, rife confusion, impeded progress, and circuitous thinking are but a few of the byproducts of such incidents.

By mastering the rules of **parliamentary procedure**, you will be enabled to take your place in any gathering whether you chair or participate. Furthermore, you will be qualified to assist in carrying on all matters of business pertaining to the group's needs.

These experiences are offered in order that you may learn thorough usage of parliamentary rules, the proper procedure for conducting or participating in a deliberative assembly.

EXPLANATION OF PARLIAMENTARY PROCEDURE

Parliamentary procedure is a recognized procedure for conducting the business of a group of persons. Its purpose is to expedite the transaction of business in an orderly manner by observing definite rules. These rules may and do vary according to the constitutions and by-laws adopted by a group. In the many state legislatures and the national Congress, parliamentary procedures are basically the same, but differ in numerous interpretations. The rules of each assembly determine the procedures which prevail for that assembly. There is no one set of rules which applies to all assemblies, despite the fact they may all adopt the same text on parliamentary procedure. The rules followed by a group are their own rules, adopted by themselves, interpreted and enforced by themselves. Kansas and Indiana legislatures might adopt *Roberts Rules of Order* as their rule book for conducting business, yet in actual practice differ widely. In fact, the House and Senate in the same state legislature normally operate under different regulations. This is true of the two houses in the national Congress. One of the obvious divergences here is the Unlimited Debate Ruling in the Senate (this is the reason for the Senate filibusters) and the Limited Debate allowed in the House. There are other dissimilarities which need not be dis-

project, a corporation office, or any one of ten thousand other places, the opportunity for practicing parliamentary procedure arises. The formality which governs the extent of the use of parliamentary procedure is dependent upon the group and their knowledge of its rules. Generally, the larger organized groups are more formal and observe their regulations more closely than do small informal gatherings.

HOW TO USE THE CHART OF PRECEDENCE OF MOTIONS AND THEIR RULES

The best, if not the only, way to prepare for participation in parliamentary law is to be familiar with the precedence of motions and their applications. This can be done with a reasonable amount of study through the use of any standard parliamentary law book. Without this knowledge, you

Mock legislatures are modeled after state and federal legislative bodies.

cussed here. The fundamental point is that assemblies do operate under definite laws and regulations. Occasions for using parliamentary law arise any time a group meets to transact business. Whether the occasion is a meeting in a church, a school building, a community center, a housing

will flounder in any assembly and slow down the entire proceedings. You will find the fundamentals discussed in the following paragraphs; however, it is necessary that you study a parliamentary text in considerable detail if you wish to master many of the technicalities.

CHART OF PRECEDENCE OF MOTIONS AND THEIR RULES

Key to Abbreviations:
No-S – No second required
Und. – Undebatable
Int. – May interrupt a speaker
2/3 – Requires a 2/3 vote for adoption
Lim. – Limited debate
1/3 S - 1/3 second required

PRIVILEGED MOTIONS

1. To fix the time to which to adjourn......................................Lim.
2. To adjourn (unqualified)..Und.
3. To take a recess..Lim.
4. To rise to a question of privilege.......................Int., Und., No-S.
5. To call for orders of the day..............................Int., Und., No-S.

SUBSIDIARY MOTIONS

6. To lay on the table...Und.
7. To move the previous question (this stops debate)......................Und., 2/3
8. To limit or extend the limits of debate........................Lim., 2/3
9. To postpone definitely..Lim.
10. To refer to committee..Lim.
11. To amend..1/3 S
12. To postpone indefinitely...Lim.
13. A Main Motion –
    a. "To reconsider" is a specific main motion..............................Lim.

INCIDENTAL MOTIONS
(These Have No Precedence Of Order)

To suspend the rules..Und., 2/3
To withdraw a motion..No-S., Und.
To object to a consideration........................Int., No-S., Und., 2/3
To rise to a point of order.............................Int., No-S., Und.
To rise to a point of information (parliamentary inquiry).....Int., No-S., Und.
To appeal from the decision of the chair........................Int., Lim.
To call for a division of the house........................Int., No-S., Und.
To call for a division of a question.................................Und.

Here are fundamentals you should know:

Precedence of motions—This term means that motions are debated in a certain order. To ascertain the meaning of this, study the chart entitled *Chart of Precedence of Motions and Their Rules*. You will notice that number 13 is a main motion. An example of a main motion would be a motion "That the Parliamentary Law Club have a party." This main motion is what the assembly must discuss. It is the *only* main motion that can be under discussion. It must be *disposed* of before any other main motion can legally be entertained by the assembly. If the group, after discussion, votes to have a party, the main motion is disposed of. If it votes not to have a party, the motion is disposed of. But supposing the Club does not want to adopt the motion as it stands. This raises another question.

Amendments—You see, as the motion stands, it simply states that the "Parliamentary Law Club have a party." It does not say *when*. It is obvious that a change will have to be made. Now look at number 11 on the *Chart of Precedence of Motions*. It is "To amend." It is in a position *above* the main motion of the chart. Hence, someone moves "to amend the main motion by adding the words 'Saturday night, June 16.'" This is in order. It is discussed and voted on. If it carries, the group has decided to add the words "Saturday Night, June 16" to the motion. If it fails, the main motion stands as it was originally made and is open to discussion or ready to be voted on. Assuming for a moment that the amendment carried, the business before the house becomes that of disposing of the *main motion as amended*. It is debated and voted on.

If an assembly wished to, it may amend an amendment in the same manner it amends the main motion. It then discusses and votes on the amendment to the amendment. If this does not carry, the amendment remains untouched. If it does carry, the amendment *as amended* is next discussed and voted on. If it, in turn, does not carry, then the main motion remains unchanged and the amendment plus the amendment to it is lost. If it does carry, the main motion as amended is debated and voted on. It is illegal to change an amendment beyond adding one amendment to it.

Other motions—Supposing the group decided to amend the main motion by adding the words "Saturday night, June 16," but still is not ready to decide definitely about having a party. You will note that number 10, the motion directly above number 11, is "to refer to a committee." When a motion is referred to a committee, all amendments automatically go with it. The motion "to refer" will be debated and voted on. If it carries, the main motion is *disposed of* and the house is ready for another main motion. If the motion "to refer to a committee" fails, then the main motion remains before the house as though the motion "to refer to a committee" had never been offered.

Now look at your *Chart of Precedence of Motions* again. You will note many more motions are listed above number 10. The higher you move up this list, the smaller the number of the motion is, but the more important it becomes, until you arrive at the very top of the list, at number 1. This is the most powerful motion of all. The motion on the chart may be placed before the assembly any time during debate on a main motion, provided you always put a motion on the floor that has *precedence*. In other words, John moves a main motion; Susan immediately moved number 9, to postpone the main motion definitely; Adam moves number 6, to lay the main motion on the table; Mary follows by moving number 3, to take a recess. This is all in order. However, when Adam moved number 6, Mary could not move number 8, since Adam's motion, number 6, had precedence.

Actually, the precedence of motions in its simplest form means that a person may place any of the motions on the floor at any time they are in order if it follows the rule of precedence. You have to understand that the numbers appearing before each motion are not put there to count them. Those numbers tell you exactly what motion has precedence over other motions. The most important motion, as far as having power over other motions is concerned, is number 1, to fix the time to which to adjourn. The second most important motion in order of precedence is number 2, to adjourn – unqualified; next is number 3; then number 4; and so on, clear down to number 13, the main motion itself.

Now let us look at the *Chart of Precedence of Motions* once more. You see the thirteen motions divided into three specific groups; namely, *Privileged Motions* from number 1 through number 5, *Subsidiary Motions* from number 6 through number 12, and last you see *Main Motion*, number 13, which can be a motion about anything from abolishing taxes to having a party. Here is the point you should get from studying these thirteen motions. After you have a main motion on the floor, there are seven actions you can take on it. These are the motions numbered 6, 7, 8, 9, 10, 11, 12. They are called subsidiary because they pertain to things you can do to a main motion. At a glance you can see that an assembly can do anything from postponing a motion indefinitely to laying it on the table and taking it off again. These motions do not conflict with the ruling that you can have only one main motion before the house at a time. They are not main motions. They are the ways you change (amend) or dispose of a motion (postpone indefinitely, refer to a committee, lay on the table...). Of course, you can dispose of a motion by adopting or rejecting it. It is obvious that once you have a main motion before the assembly, you have to do something with it, and rules concerning precedence of motions tell you how to do it.

If you will now examine the privileged motions, 1 to 5, inclusive, you will see that they do not do anything to a main motion. They are the actions a group can take while it is disposing of a main motion. For example, if the club were discussing a main motion to have a party, someone could move number 3, to take a recess. If the group wanted to take a recess, they would vote to do so and then recess for five minutes, or whatever time the motion to recess called for. When the recess was over, they would convene again and resume discussing the main motion where they left off when they voted to recess.

The section entitled **Incidental Motion**s is largely self-explanatory. You will note that it concerns those things a person would normally do during debate on a motion. For example, if the assembly were debating the motion "to have a party," you might want to find out whether it was in order to offer an amendment to the main motion at that time, because you were not quite sure of the status of such a move. In this case you would "rise to a point of information," sometimes called "point of parliamentary inquiry." If you observed an infraction of the rules which the chair overlooked, you would immediately "rise to a point of order." You will notice that most incidental motions require "no second" and also permits you to interrupt a speaker. This is true because certain matters must be clarified while debate is in progress. Otherwise too many corrections would have to be made after a motion was adopted or defeated.

IMPORTANT INFORMATION YOU SHOULD KNOW

1. *The chairperson's duties:* To call the meeting to order, to conduct the business of the assembly, to enforce rules, to appoint committees and their chairpersons, to appoint a secretary for each meeting if one is not elected. The chairperson refrains from discussing any motion before the house.

2. *The secretary's duties:* To keep an accurate record of all business transacted by the house. This includes all motions, whether carried or defeated, who seconded the motions and the votes upon them. Also a record of all committees appointed and any other actions of the assembly.

3. *If the chairperson wants to speak on a proposal:* He or she appoints a member to substitute, then assumes the position of a participant in the assembly. The chairperson must gain recognition from the newly appointed chairperson, make remarks on an equal basis with other members of the group, and then resume the chair at any time desired.

4. *To gain recognition from the chairperson:* Rise and address the chairperson by saying "Mr./Madam Chair," depending on the sex of the chairperson. The chair will then address you by name, or may nod to you, point towards you, or give some other sign of recognition. You are not allowed to speak until you get the chair's permission to do so, in other words, recognition.

5. *How to place a motion on the floor:* Gain recognition from the chair; then state your motion by saying, "I move that _____."

6. *How to dispose of a motion:* Either adopt or reject it or apply subsidiary motions to it.

7. *How to second a motion:* Simply call out the word "second." You need not rise or have recognition from the chairperson.

8. *How to change (amend) a motion:* Gain recognition: then say, "I move to amend the motion (or amendment) by adding the words_____" or "by striking out the words _____" or "by striking out the words _____ and inserting the words _____."

9. *How to stop rambling or extended debate:* Move the previous question, number 7, on all motions before the house. This will include the main motion and any subsidiary motions.

10. *How to ask for information:* Rise without gaining recognition, interrupt a speaker if necessary, and say, "Mr./Madam Chair, point of information" or "I rise to a point of parliamentary inquiry." When the chair says, "State your point," you will ask your question.

11. *How to ask a member of the assembly a question:* Gain recognition; then say, "Will the speaker yield to a question?" The chair then asks the person if he or she will yield. If the member says "yes," you may ask one question. If not, you cannot ask your question.

12. *How to exercise personal privilege:* Rise without recognition, interrupt a speaker if necessary, and say, "Mr./Madam Chair, personal privilege!" The chair will say, "State your privilege." You may then ask to have a window closed because a draft is blowing on you, or you may ask whatever happens to be your privilege.

13. *How to call for "division of the house:"* Without rising to gain recognition, simply call out, "Division of the house." This means that you want the voting on a measure to be taken by a show of hands or by asking members to stand to indicate their vote. "Division of the house" is called for when a voice vote has been taken which was so close it was hard to determine what the vote actually was.

14. *What does "question" mean when called out?* This means the person who calls out "question" is ready to vote. It is not compulsory that the chair put the motion to a vote. However, this is generally done if enough persons call out "question." This has nothing to do with the motion for the previous question.

15. *How do you reverse a ruling made by the chair?* Just as soon as the chair makes the ruling, the person who disagrees with it calls out without recognition, "Mr./Madam Chair, I appeal from the decision of the chair." A second is necessary to make the appeal valid. If it is forthcoming the chair asks the person who made the appeal to state the reasons for doing it. This done, discussion follows after which the chair asks for a vote from the assembly by saying, "All those in favor of sustaining the chair raise their hands," then after counting the votes says, "those opposed the same sign." The vote is announced by saying, "The chair is sustained by a vote of seven to three" or "The chair stands corrected by a vote of six to four."

16. *How is a meeting adjourned?* Adjournment may be made by the chair who declares the meeting adjourned, or it may be made after the motion to adjourn is placed on the floor, voted on, and carried.

17. *How do you know what order of business to follow?* The assembly agrees upon an order of business. It is the chair's duty to see that it is followed unless rules are suspended by the group, which will permit a change temporarily.

18. *How do you suspend the rules?* A motion is put before the house "that the rules be suspended to consider" certain urgent business. If the motion carries by a two-thirds vote, the rules are suspended.

19. *How do you vote on a motion?* The chair asks for a vote. It may be by voice ("yes" and "no"), roll call, show of hands, by standing, or by ballot.

20. *How does a person object to the consideration of a motion?* Rise without recognition, interrupt a speaker if necessary, and say, "Mr./Madam Chair, I

object to the consideration of the motion (or question)." No second is required. The chair immediately asks the assembly to vote "yes" or "no" as to whether they want to consider the question. If two-thirds vote against consideration of the question, it cannot be considered. The objection must be made immediately after the motion to which the member objects is placed before the assembly.

21. *How do you conduct nominations for office?* The chair opens the floor to nominations for a certain office. A member rises and says, "Mr./Madam Chair, I nominate _____." The secretary records nominations. After a reasonable time, the chair rules that all nominations are closed, or someone moves that all nominations to be closed. This is a main motion. It is seconded, debated, and voted on. If it carries, nominations are closed. If not, they remain open. The chair may rule a quick "motion to close nominations" out of order if it is obviously an attempt to railroad a certain party into office before other nominations can be made.

22. *How does a chair receive a motion and put it before the assembly?* If it requires a second the chair waits a short time to hear the second. If it does not come, the motion is ruled dead for want of a second. If a second is made, the motion is repeated as follows: "It has been moved and seconded that the Parliamentary Law Club have a party Friday night. Is there any discussion?" This officially places the motion in the hands of the assembly.

HOW TO CONDUCT A PARLIAMENTARY SESSION
Your instructor will advise you in this matter. However, every class member should take a turn acting as chair at one time and secretary another. It is advisable that the chair be appointed by the instructor until the class learns how to nominate and elect a chair. The following steps may then be carried out:

1. The chair should appoint a committee to draw up a proposed constitution and by-laws. (The committee may be elected if the group wishes to do it this way.) If time is limited, the instructor may dispense with drawing up a constitution and by-laws.

2. An **order of business** should be set up. Normally, it will be something similar to the following:

   A. Call the meeting to order.
   B. Read the minutes from the preceding meeting. Make any necessary changes, then adopt them.
   C. Ask for old business. This may be unfinished business.
   D. Ask for committee reports.
   E. Ask for new business.
   F. Adjourn.

3. In carrying out practice parliamentary sessions, it is necessary that motions be placed before the assembly. Each student is required to put at least three main motions on the floor and seek their adoption. Examples of motions would be:

   (a) A motion to petition teachers that all written examinations be limited to one hour.

   (b) A motion that tardy students should pay a twenty-five cent fine for each time tardy, the money to be contributed to a school social building fund.

Your instructor will give you a form on which to write your motion.

A STUDENT CONGRESS
A student congress may be composed of a house and senate with different speech classes acting in each capacity or one group may form a unicameral legislature. In either instance the group's purpose is to formulate bills, discuss them, and adopt or reject them by vote. To accomplish these activities the group must know parliamentary procedure and conduct its business in an orderly manner. This involves (1) determining the scope of legislation to come before the assembly, (2) organizing the legislature by electing officers, forming committees, and assigning seats, (3) holding committee meetings to consider and/or draft bills, and (4) debating and disposing of bills brought before the assembly.

THE FIRST MEETING OF THE GENERAL ASSEMBLY

At the first meeting of the general assembly a temporary chair and a temporary secretary are appointed or elected. Both will take office immediately. The instructor will act as parliamentarian unless one is elected or appointed. The temporary chair will then open the meeting to nominations for a permanent chair (speaker of the house or president of the senate) who will take office as soon as elected. The chair will call for nominations for a permanent secretary who will be elected and take office at once. As next business the presiding officer will appoint standing committees and a chair for each. The assembly may then discuss matters relative to its general objectives and procedures. Adjournment of the first meeting follows.

COMMITTEE MEETINGS

Committee meetings are next in order and, though informal, parliamentary procedure is advisable with an elected or appointed secretary to keep minutes for the group. A committee may originate its own bills and consider bills submitted by members of the assembly which the speaker of the house or president of the senate has referred to them. It will report bills out or "kill them" in committee, according to votes taken after discussion in the committee.

SAMPLE RESOLUTIONS AND BILLS

Keep resolutions and bills short, under 175 words. A resolution is a recommendation of action and does not carry the weight of law as it has no enforcement and penalty clause. A resolution must have a title, and a body. A preamble is optional. The body is composed of sections and each line is numbered.

A RESOLUTION LIMITING STUDENT DRIVERS AT CENTRAL HIGH SCHOOL

1 WHEREAS, Space is limited around Central
2 High School, and
3 WHEREAS, Parking on the street is limited to
4 one hour, and
5 WHEREAS, Student enrollment is increasing
6 each year, and
7 WHEREAS, Many students are within walking
8 distance of Central High School, therefore,

9 BE IT RESOLVED BY CENTRAL HIGH SCHOOL
10 SPEECH CLASS THAT:

11 SECTION I. The governing officials of Central
12 High School should prohibit
13 all students living within one mile of this school
14 from operating a vehicle to
15 and from school as a means of transportation.

This resolution introduced by

_____

A BILL PROVIDING FOR LIMITING STUDENT DRIVERS AT CENTRAL HIGH SCHOOL

1 BE IT ENACTED BY THE CENTRAL HIGH
2 SCHOOL SPEECH CLASS, THAT:

3 Section I. All students living within one mile of
4 the school shall not operate a
5 vehicle to and from school as a means of trans
6 portation.
7 Section II. Any exceptions to Section I must be
8 approved by the school board
9 upon petition.
10 Section III. The policy will take effect at the
11 beginning of the next school year
12 after passage.
13 Section IV. Any student in violation of the policy
14 will serve a three-day in-school
15 suspension.

This bill introduced by

_____

THE GENERAL ASSEMBLY IN DELIBERATION

Some student congresses follow the procedures and rules of their state legislatures. Others follow established rules of parliamentary procedure by designating a certain text as their guide. In either case, an agreed upon procedure must be used. To have a successful general assembly, members should know parliamentary procedure and how to use it. Especially important to know are precedence of motions, how to apply the privileged and subsidiary motions. Incidental motions, which have no order of precedence, are of vital importance in the general conduct of the assembly's deliberations and should be thoroughly familiar to all participants.

Under a bicameral student congress the requirement is that each bill must pass the house in which it originates. It is then filed with the secretary of the other house after which the presiding officer of the house refers it to the proper committee. If reported out of this committee and passed by the second house it may be considered as "passed" unless there is a governor who must act on it before it can be considered as "passed." When a governor is used, a lieutenant governor is ordinarily elected and serves as presiding officer in the senate. It thus becomes doubly important that all plans be laid before a student assembly convenes for the first time in order to know what officials to elect, what their duties are, what committees to set up, and what all procedures will be relative to activities of the congress.

A SUGGESTED ORDER OF BUSINESS
The following order of business meets most student congress needs:

1. The meeting is called to order.

2. Minutes of the last meeting are read and adopted as read or corrected.

3. The presiding officer announces the order in which committees will report and the group decides on (a) time limits for individual speakers and (b) the total time allowable on each bill.

4. The spokesperson for the first committee reads the bill, moves its adoption, gives a copy to the secretary. Another members seconds. If the bill belongs to an individual, he or she presents it in a similar manner when granted permission by the chairperson. A friend seconds. Whoever presents a bill then speaks for it. The bill is debated and disposed of according to the rules of the assembly.

5. Each succeeding committee reports and the process of discussing and disposing of each bill is continued until all bills have been acted upon.

6. The secretary announces the bills that were passed and those that were defeated.

7. The assembly conducts any business that is appropriate.

8. Adjournment is in order.

DEBATE

Time limits: 1st **Affirmative** Constructive– 8 minutes

cross-x of 1st Affirmative by Negative– 3 minutes

1st Negative Constructive– 8 minutes

cross-x of 1st Negative by Affirmative– 3 minutes

2nd Affirmative Constructive– 8 minutes

cross-x of 2nd Affirmative by Negative– 3 minutes

2nd Negative Constructive– 8 minutes

cross-x of 2nd Negative by Affirmative– 3 minutes

1st Negative Rebuttal– 4 minutes

1st Affirmative Rebuttal– 4 minutes

2nd Negative Rebuttal– 4 minutes

2nd Affirmative Rebuttal– 4 minutes

These time limits are standard for competitive debate. They may be shortened proportionately for class debates.

Speaking notes: Use notes sparingly, but efficiently. They are necessary in good debating.

Sources of information: You will need many. In your debate you will be required to state your sources of information to prove the validity of your statements.

Outline of speech: Prepare a 75-150 word complete sentence outline to be handed to your instructor before the debate starts.

Number of speakers on a team: Two speakers on a team is the conventional number.

Q

Question: Should a person slap or pound a speaker's stand?

A

Answer: Generally no, unless it is done lightly.

Key Words:
Affirmative
Constructive speeches
Cross-examine
Debate
Disadvantages
Harm
Inherency
Negative
Plan
Rebuttals
Resolution
Stock issues

Student Expectations: In completing this assignment each student will:
  ➤ *Express ideas and defend them under direct challenge*
  ➤ *Understand how to support arguments with evidence*
  ➤ *Understand how formal debates are organized and conducted*
  ➤ *Prepare and deliver a case on one side of a proposition*
  ➤ *Analyze and cross-examine an opponent's case*

PURPOSE OF THIS ASSIGNMENT

This assignment is proposed because many persons want the experience of debating. It is proposed also because debating can be done in speech classes without the long periods of training undergone by competitive debaters. This does not mean that long periods of practice are not desirable. They are. Such training produces truly superior speakers. But debating can be done effectively and with good results in speech classes. It provides excellent experience in communicating, since it pits two or more speakers with opposing ideas against each other. It tests your ability to express these ideas and to defend them under direct challenge. This teaches tact, resourcefulness, ability to think on one's feet, and it teaches that ideas must be backed by evidence, not by mere conjecture and opinion. Experience of this kind is beneficial and should be a part of every speech student's life.

EXPLANATION OF A DEBATE

A **debate** is a speaking situation in which two opposing ideas are presented and argued. The ideas represent solutions to a problem. The proponents of each solution attempt to convince the audience that their idea should be adopted in preference to all others. Actually, a debate, in the sense used here,

Debate is an excellent way to develop critical thinking skills.

consists of two opposing speeches to convince. A debate team may be composed of one or two persons depending on the debate format. Two-person teams are the most common for topics that deal with a policy change and this exercise is structured for that type of format.

Debates are divided into **constructive speeches** and **rebuttals.** Constructive speeches introduce the arguments and position of each speaker while the rebuttals review and extend the constructive issues. Refer to the time limits on the previous page for the order of speeches. It is at once apparent that the affirmative team leads off and closes the debate. While this may seem like an unbeatable advantage, both teams have the same amount of time allotted to them, and the second negative constructive followed by the first negative rebuttal is a powerful advantage for the negative.

After each of the constructive speeches a member of the opposite team will be given 3 minutes to **cross-examine** or question the speaker. Each team member will take turns asking questions. One negative team member will cross-examine the first affirmative speaker, and the other negative team member will cross-examine the second affirmative after the constructive speech. The same is true when the affirmative cross-examines the negative. The purpose of cross-examination is to gain additional information from the speaker or to clarify what the speaker said. Cross-examination is not a time to argue; it is a time for questions to be asked and answered.

Occasions for debates occur in practically all academic classes, although regularly organized debate groups and speech classes enjoy them most frequently. Inter-school debates among high schools are nationwide, as are intercollege contests. Debates provide excellent program material in schools, over TV, radio, before civic organizations, churches, business groups, or clubs. Any group of persons willing to listen to a sound discussion of opposing ideas always welcomes good debate. For sheer enjoyment with, perhaps, some thought thrown in, humorous debates are a fine type of entertainment. Even though they are light in treatment of subject matter and their purpose is to entertain, they require the same skillful preparation that the regular debate does.

TOPICS FOR DEBATE

Topics for debates are worded in a statement of resolve that asks for a change to be made in the way we currently do something. The affirmative team supports the topic. The negative team defends the present way of doing things. The topic is also called a **resolution**. You may want to ask your instructor what the current national high school or college topic is for debate. Each year one topic is chosen for interscholastic high school competition and one for college. You may want to debate those topics or some part of them.

HOW TO CHOOSE A TOPIC FOR DEBATE

Since two teams will be concerned with the choice of topic, consult your opponents to reach agreement on a subject for debate. Remember that one team will uphold the proposition under debate, while the other will argue against it. So, in choosing a topic, it should also be decided which team will debate affirmative (for the topic) and which will debate negative (against it).

In arriving at an agreement on the subject, be sure that all of you have an interest in the subject and that you can find information about it. If you are in doubt about the availability of source materials, check with your school and city librarians before making a final decision. One answer to the problem of what to debate is to ask your instructor to assign the subject and the side you will argue. The following are sample topics. Notice their structure: they all use the term "should be" and they all suggest a policy change:

1. Resolved: That the federal government should significantly increase social services to homeless individuals in the United States.
2. Resolved: That the federal government should initiate and enforce safety guarantees on consumer goods.
3. Resolved: That the federal government should guarantee comprehensive medical care for all citizens in the United States.
4. Resolved: That smoking should be prohibited by law.
5. Resolved: That students caught cheating should be expelled from school.
6. Resolved: That capital punishment should be abolished.

HOW TO PREPARE A DEBATE

The following outline briefly states what each speaker should do in each speech.

First Affirmative Constructive
1. State the resolution.
2. Define terms of resolution.
3. Present affirmative reasons for change.
4. Present proof for reasons for change.
5. Present affirmative plan.

First Negative Constructive
1. Explain basic negative approach.
2. Present negative position.
3. Argue affirmative definition of terms (optional).
4. Prove affirmative reasons for change are not significant.
5. Prove status quo can achieve affirmative reason for change without affirmative plan (inherency).

Second Affirmative Constructive
1. Attack negative position.
2. Rebuild affirmative reasons for change.
3. Answer all first negative attacks.
4. Present added advantages.

Second Negative Constructive
1. Extend (develop in light of opponent's attacks) negative position.
2. Attack affirmative plan as unworkable and undesirable.

First Negative Rebuttal
1. Extend on first negative constructive arguments in light of second affirmative responses.
2. Review reasons for change and why they are insufficient.

First Affirmative Rebuttal
1. Answer second negative attacks on plan.
2. Return to affirmative case to rebuild affirmative reason for change.

Second Negative Rebuttal
1. Review first negative attacks on reasons for change.
2. Return to plan attacks—show how plan is still unworkable and undesirable in light of first affirmative rebuttal.

Second Affirmative Rebuttal
1. Answer attacks on affirmative plan by proving it workable and desirable.

2. Return to case and emphasize reason for change.

As stated earlier in this chapter, a debate is really two or more opposing speeches to convince. Your purpose, then is to convince your audience that you are correct in your point of view. To refresh your memory about the speech to persuade, re-read Chapter 9.

Because a debate is an activity in which two colleagues team against two other colleagues, it is necessary that preparation for the contest be made jointly by each pair of debaters. This can best be done if the following suggestions are carried out:

1. Decide who will be the first speaker.

2. Make a mutual agreement that both colleagues will search for materials to prove your side of the question. Later these materials can be exchanged to help each of you to strengthen your arguments.

3. Begin your hunt for information on your subject. Whenever you find something pertinent, take notes on it. Be sure to be able to give the exact reference for the information. Record the following items: The author's name and qualifications, the name of the article, the name of the magazine, newspaper, or book in which you found the item, and the exact date of publication. Take your notes on four-inch by six-inch cards; then at the top of each card write briefly what the notes on that card concern. For instance, on a health care topic, labels might be: cost of care, uninsured, or Canadian system.

4. Take only complete and exact quotes. It is very important in a debate to have accurate information. Therefore, when quoting sources copy the information exactly as it appears in the publication. Don't leave anything out or add anything. You could set yourself up for an attack by the opposition if you do not take the quotation exactly as it is written.

I. Divide your entire case into four parts. These parts are called stock issues. An affirmative must prove all issues; a negative can win by disproving any one of the issues.

A. **HARM**—This shows a need for the specific proposal you are offering by showing some harm is currently happening that needs to be solved.

B. **INHERENCY**—This shows that there is something that currently exists in our present system that prevents us from solving the harm. You must show the harm is inherent. For example in a topic that would ask for the right of doctors to prescribe marijuana for medical purposes, we have a law that is in the present system that states that marijuana use is a federal offense. Therefore, the law prevents the present system from solving the problem.

C. **PLAN**—You have to come up with a plan of action to solve the harm you identify. In other words, you need a solution to the problem, and you need to show that solution works.

D. **DISADVANTAGES**—You need to show that there will not be problems that happen (disadvantages) if we accept your solution.

II. Your finished affirmative case should be set up as follows:

A. Introduce the topic's importance and state resolution.

B. Define your terms. If you are arguing that compulsory military training should be established in the United States, you must tell what you mean by "compulsory." Will anyone be excepted? What does "military training" mean? Does it refer to the infantry, the air force, or a technical school for nuclear specialists? In other words, state exactly what you are talking about.

C. Show that your proposal is needed (stock issue of harm).

1. To prove the need give examples, illustrations, opinions of authorities, facts, and analogies which all point to the need for your proposition. Give enough of these proofs to establish your point.

D. Show that we cannot solve the problem in the present system.

E. Show that your proposition is practical (it will work). Give proofs as you did to establish your need in point C, above.

F. Show that your proposal is desirable (its results will be beneficial). That there will be no disadvantages to it. Give proofs as you did in point C, above.

G. Summarize your speech, then close it by stating your belief in your proposal.

III. Negative colleagues should set up their case as follows:

A. Prepare material that denies that there is a problem.

B. Prepare to defend the fact that the present system can take care of any problem on its own, assuming one exists.

C. Find reasons the affirmative solution will not work.

D. Prepare material that shows problems or disadvantages that would occur if the affirmative plan is adopted.

Note: All your arguments need to be presented in constructive speeches. The rebuttal speeches are used to provide further support for your arguments, to deny the opposition's arguments, and to summarize why you are winning.

IV. Rebuttal is easy if you follow a plan.

A. In refuting points, try to run the debate. Take the offensive. This is easy but you must follow a plan. The plan is to take your main speech point by point. Reiterate the first point you made, tell what the opposition did to disprove it; then give more evidence to re-establish it. Now take you second point, do exactly the same thing over again. Continue this strategy throughout your rebuttal and close with a summary, followed by a statement of your belief in the soundness of your proposal.

Do not talk about points brought up by your opponents, except as you refer to them while you re-emphasize your own points. You must carry out this plan of advancing your own case or you will be likely to confuse yourself and your audience. Refuse to be budged from the consideration of your plan for advancing your own case.

B. The final speech by each side in the debate should be the strongest. Each side needs to prove why they should win the debate. Concentrate on those points you are winning. Remember, the affirmative needs to win all the stock issues and the negative need win only one.

V. The points (**stock issues**) listed above apply to both affirmative and negative speakers. When each team tries to run the debate, that is, take the offensive, there is a real argument. Because each plays upon their own case, the two proposals and their arguments are easily followed.

VI. Colleagues should plan their cases together and rehearse them together. They should have their material so well in mind that they make little reference to their notes, except when bringing up objections raised by the opposition. Practice should be continued until a student feels complete mastery of the material. They should not memorize a debate speech word for word. A speaker should know the sequence of points and the evidence to prove the point. Besides this, they need a well-planned introduction and conclusion.

HOW TO PRESENT A DEBATE

A debater's attitude should be one of confidence but not "cockiness." Debaters should be friendly, firm, polite, and very eager to be understood. A sense of humor is helpful if well applied.

Movement, gestures, and use of notes should be done without awkwardness. Posture should be one of ease and alertness. The voice should be conversational in quality, earnest, and sincere. Everyone should hear it easily.

When debaters rise to speak they should address the audience and opponents. No more is needed. Many debaters utter trite, stereotyped phrases which would be better left unsaid. The debater should make a few introductory remarks about the occasion, the audience, and pleasure of debating a timely question. They should move into the debate by defining the terms. This should all be done informally and sincerely in a communicative manner. There is no reason why a debate should be a formal, cold, stilted, unfriendly affair.

After a debate is concluded, it is customary and advisable for the teams to rise, walk to the center of the room, and shake hands.

HOW A DEBATE IS CONDUCTED

1. The two teams sit at tables on opposite sides of the room facing the audience.

2. A timekeeper sits on the front row in the audience. The timekeeper signals the debaters by raising time cards. If the two card is up, this means that the speaker has two minutes left. When time is "up," the stop card will be raised. The speaker should stop speaking within ten seconds after the final signal.

3. One, three, or five judges may be used. They are provided with ballots which carry spaces in which to write their decisions. After a debate is concluded, the judges, without consultation, immediately write their decision.

4. Debaters may refer to their teammates by name, or as "my colleague." Opponents may be referred to by name or as "my opponent" or "the first nega-tive speaker" or "the second affirmative speaker" or "the negative" if that is their side of the debate. Debaters may refer to themselves as "we," or "my colleague and I."

QUESTIONS TO HELP YOU IN EVALUATING OTHERS' SPEECHES

1. Did the speech achieve its intended result? Did it inform, persuade, entertain, etc. as the speaker intended?

2. Was the speech clearly and effectively organized?

3. Did the introduction catch your attention?

4. Did the speaker give you a reason why the speech was important to you personally?

5. Was the speech delivered well with good posture, appropriate gestures, eye contact, and rate and volume of speech.

6. Did the speech contain sufficient and appropriate supporting materials?

7. Was the conclusion effective? Remember: When critiquing a speech, be positive, take time to comment on good points as well as areas for improvement.

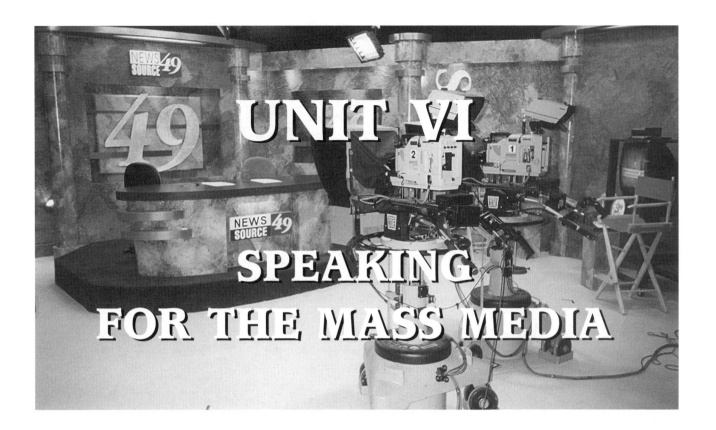

UNIT VI

SPEAKING

FOR THE MASS MEDIA

Speaking for broadcast by the mass media amplifies the usual concerns of the speaker's relationship to the audience in a couple of important ways. First, the actual audience receiving the message is potentially much larger than one that would fill any single auditorium. This means that tailoring a message to such an audience can be significantly more challenging because the parameters, or limits, of their needs or concerns are more difficult to define.

Second, a mass media broadcast—unlike many public address situations—will be directly influenced by economic interests of the broadcast station and its advertisers. In order to maintain the opportunities to use the mass media, financial support for the programming must be obtained and sustained. Therefore, the speaker must pay even more attention to his or her relationship to the audience in order to persuade them that they want to have access to such messages, no matter what the content of those messages may be.

These considerations provide students with opportunities to build their audience analysis skills, their abilities to write and edit messages for precision, and their listening skills. Therefore, this unit is included in this text to offer students assignments that will allow them to apply many of the speaking skills introduced in previous units to the entirely different contexts of mass media, and to observe the important distinctions such shifts in contexts can make to the development of the presentation.

The unit begins with a chapter on *The Radio Commercial* which introduces the student to the demands of persuading an audience to buy a product (such as in Chapter 13 on *The Sales Talk*) while tightly organizing that message into a precisely timed script, coordinating dramatic elements and any background sounds necessary to capture the audience's attention and imagination. Unlike *The Sales Talk*, the radio format of this assignment brings the added challenge of persuading the audience without the benefit of most of the nonverbal forms of communication available to public address speakers.

Chapter 36, *The In-Depth News Report Interview*, draws upon interviewing skills discussed in previous units, but places the interview itself—not just the results of the interview—in the public context. The student serves as a representative of the larger public who may be wishing to conduct the interview themselves. It requires the student to build on basic research skills to be as fully informed on the topic of the interview as possible, to develop critical listening skills to determine what questions to ask the interviewee, and to seek to maintain the role of facilitator instead of participant during the broadcast.

In the next chapter, *The Film/TV Program Review* students are assigned to present an analysis and critique of a mass media-based program. This requires the researching and developing of an understanding of the different elements of composition that go into a non-print media production. Drawing upon analytical skills introduced in the chapter on *The Book Review*, students using this assignment will again determine the various purposes of such reviews, this time tailoring the review to the needs and interests of the mass mediated audience.

The unit concludes with an assignment on *Radio/Television Commentary* in which a news reporter or selected viewer prepares and delivers a subjective statement on one side of a controversial issue of interest to a mass media audience. The selection of such topics, development of the subjective viewpoint, and the presentation and delivery in a mass media format offers each student the chance to rehearse persuasive skills from earlier chapters. In this assignment, however, the focus of student efforts should be heavily directed toward audience analysis and adaptation, carefully selecting and applying the various persuasive elements to the mass audience situation.

Mass media provide the public speaker with a significant change in speaking contexts from other public address situations. These assignments are designed to help students understand the impact of such contextual changes on communication skill demands, and to help them develop communication behavior flexibility by adapting basic speaking competencies to these different environments.

CHAPTER 35

THE RADIO COMMERCIAL

Time limits: 1 minute.

Speaking notes: A full script of the commercial, complete with all voices, pauses, and sound effects indicated, and a notation of each 5-second interval of the material.

Sources of information: Two or more. List them at the end of your script.

Outline of speech: None is required for instructor.

Question: Is speaking over the radio the same as speaking in person?

Answer: No. Radio speech depends on voice alone, and has no body language for the listener to see.

 Key Words:
Auditory appeals
Dialogue
Dramatic story line
Multivoiced
Univocal

Student Expectations: In completing this assignment, each student will:
➤ *Create a media presentation to fit a given time limit*
➤ *Assess effectiveness of various auditory message designs*
➤ *Coordinate a multifaceted project*
➤ *Identify and develop a dramatic story line*

PURPOSE OF THIS ASSIGNMENT

Hour-long radio dramas are a thing of the past in America today. However, producing a dramatic radio commercial can provide the student with some valuable communication skills once learned through those dramas including analyzing a message for its maximum auditory impact, coordination of several voices and sound effects, creating a **dramatic story line** that sells a product, and developing a very concise message due to severe time constraints. Such skills provide a unique opportunity for self-expression, enhance one's understanding of the listening process, and provide the student with a chance to practice making precise, but complete, language choices.

EXPLANATION OF THE RADIO COMMERCIAL

Radio commercials take a variety of forms, but this assignment is designed to focus on presenting a brief drama, or enactment, that illustrates why an audience should buy a certain selected product.

A radio commercial is characterized by musical backgrounds, involved sound effects, and a lack of stage action (nonverbals) by the players. The various parts are read rather than memorized. An announcer may be used to narrate or describe the scene, and usually delivers the closing call for action. The purpose of the radio commercial is to persuade an audience to buy a product based on **auditory appeals** only.

Because your words will be read directly from a full script, you will be able to concentrate on the following aspects of delivery: a pleasing voice, correct pronunciation, clear enunciation, proper English grammar, and cooperation with all who make the broadcast.

SELECTING A RADIO COMMERCIAL TOPIC

Select a product you would like to sell through a radio commercial. You will need some background information on the product such as scientific studies of its effectiveness, or testimony from credible sources your audience will easily recognize in order to lend credibility to your product. Keep in mind that your audience is very diverse and your choice of product should appeal to a wide range of people.

HOW TO PREPARE A RADIO COMMERCIAL

Once you have selected the product you wish to advertise, you will need to choose an appropriate format for your commercial. A **univocal** ad is one that depends solely on one voice delivering the message. This format would be the one closest to delivering a speech in other assignments you have had in this text. In a **multivoiced** commercial, two or more voices are used to deliver the message, both speaking directly to the listeners, not to each other. A **dialogue** commercial features multiple voices carrying on a conversation in which the selected product is the topic being discussed between them. Finally, a dramatized commercial adds appropriate sound effects to the dialogue conversation in order to "act out" the scene.

After selecting the format, gather all the appropri-

Radio advertising has a wide reach because radios are accessible at times and in places, such as a car, that televisions aren't.

ate resource materials and identify the key message, or thesis statement, you wish to convey by the end of the ad. When you have selected the essential information required (what the product is, how it works, when to use it, where it is available, advantages of this product over others, etc.) prepare the script keeping in mind the principles of good organization discussed in earlier chapters of this text. Remember, this is a *persuasive* message above all else.

The next step in preparing your radio commercial is to carefully time the script, noting at which point each five seconds passes. You will likely need to adjust your script to fit the assigned time limit. Once you have done this, show the completed script to your instructor for approval. When your script is approved, rehearsals begin. Practice performing your script into a tape recorder and reviewing it for possible improvements. Do this several times until the delivery is flawless.

HOW TO PRESENT A RADIO COMMERCIAL

Even though a radio audience will be very large and include a wide variety of people, listeners would most likely hear your presentation in small groups or as individuals. Therefore, you should imagine that you are presenting your commercial to a small group of people.

In presenting your commercial, avoid rustling papers in any way. Be sure you do not cough, sneeze, or clear your throat. Speak into the microphone from a uniform distance; do not shout into the mike. Ten inches from the mike is an adequate distance in most cases. You may use gestures if you like, to add vitality to your presentation. However, be careful not to hit the microphone while doing so.

Because radio is audio only, your presentation will need plenty of animation, clarity, force and emphasis to build and maintain interest. Your rehearsals with the tape recorder will show you the importance of these qualities.

*   This assignment was constructed with the help of information found in "Radio Commercials," from Peter B. Orlik, *Broadcast Copywriting*, Copyright © 1986 by Allyn & Bacon. Adapted by permission.

CHAPTER 36

THE IN-DEPTH NEWS REPORT INTERVIEW

Time limit: 5 minutes.

Speaking notes: Interview questions and background data on interviewee.

Sources of information: Two or more, including the person being interviewed. List them at the end of your outline.

Outline of interview: Prepare a 75-100 word complete sentence outline.

Question: What is the difference between conducting a live interview and reporting information obtained in an earlier interview?

Answer: In the live interview, listeners are able to hear the facts, reasons, or opinions directly from the interviewee and draw their own conclusions about that person's ideas.

Key Words:
Clarifying
Conversationality
Facilitator
Monitor

Student Expectations: In completing this assignment, each student will:
➤ *Analyze audience interest in a speaker or topic*
➤ *Research topic and prepare interview questions tailored to audience interests*
➤ *Facilitate the flow of a dialogue*
➤ *Monitor an ongoing interview to fit a given time limit*

PURPOSE OF THIS ASSIGNMENT

Interviewing someone for your own information (as in the assignment in Chapter 16) is different from interviewing someone for a group of listeners. The audience analysis must include those who are unable to ask the questions. Your task as an interviewer is more complex because first, you will need to know nearly as much about your subject as the person you are interviewing; and second, you will need to structure the questioning so that the interviewee discusses the information and opinions in a manner that is easy for the audience to follow. This assignment will introduce you to these complexities and give you an opportunity to learn them by doing them.

EXPLANATION OF THE IN-DEPTH NEWS REPORT INTERVIEW

A radio or television news interview is not a discussion. Therefore, the interviewer must avoid offering an opinion on the subject at hand. The interviewer's opinion is irrelevant here. The objective of the interview is to allow the interviewee to present his or her ideas to the listeners as openly as possible. The interviewer serves solely as a **facilitator** and must not agree, disagree, or comment in any substantive way upon the information offered by the one being interviewed.

Questions should be carefully prepared by the interviewer ahead of time, but the interview should not be rehearsed. Rehearsing the interview can take away the **conversationality** of the delivery. It can also give the listener the impression that the interview has been edited or censored, thus damaging the credibility of either or both.

HOW TO CHOOSE AN INTERVIEW TOPIC

For this assignment you will need to select a topic that is of interest to your audience and can be discussed by an authority who is willing to be interviewed. Look for topics of interest around your school and invite a teacher, coach, or administrator to be interviewed about it. Community policies that affect your audience may also be of interest; persons to interview may come from state or local government agencies. Avoid a person or group too distant to reach within a short amount of time.

HOW TO PREPARE FOR AN IN-DEPTH NEWS REPORT INTERVIEW

It is very important that you know what you wish to accomplish in the interview before you begin. As you determine the questions to be asked, you will need to place yourself in the role of the listener. From your research on the topic you have chosen, determine what are the main points to be covered. Prepare a list of questions and rank them from most important to least important so that if you should run low on time you have not missed the most important ones.

Next, determine the best way to phrase the questions in order to get the kind of answers you want. Who?, When?, and Where? questions ask for facts and have relatively short, specific answers. What?, How?, and Why? questions ask for facts, interpretations, and even opinions on the topic. Be sure you narrow the scope of your question enough to help the interviewee get to the points you are interested in hearing about. "Tell us what you do as principal," is too broad for a five-minute interview. A better question might be, "Tell us what is the worst thing about being principal of this school, in your opinion."

Once you have prepared the questions you wish to ask, get the specific information from your instructor on when and where the interview is to be conducted. With this in mind, refer to the section

of Chapter 16 titled *How to Prepare For an Interview* and follow the suggestions there.

HOW TO CONDUCT AN IN-DEPTH NEWS REPORT INTERVIEW

Start the interview by introducing yourself and your guest. Indicate to the audience what topic is to be discussed. State your questions courteously, tactfully, and directly.

It will be your responsibility to **monitor** the time throughout the interview. Do not assume you can go over the time limit and "edit out" parts of the interview later. Plan ahead to follow your schedule. You may wish to rehearse by interviewing a friend or parent who can help you role play so that you can get a feel for controlling the time. It is very important, however, that you do not become so absorbed with the timing that you do not listen to your interviewee. Something they say may be left unclear and it will be up to you to ask a follow-up or **clarifying** question.

When you are ready to wind up the interview, be sure you signal the end *only once*. If you indicate

A good interviewer puts the subject at ease to better ensure the audience gets the information it needs.

to the audience that, "Our last question today is..." then be sure it is truly your last question. If you say, "Finally,..." be sure it is your last question or point to be made. Conclude by thanking your interviewee, repeating his or her name and title, and restating your name as well.

Interviewing for a news report can help the student sharpen a sense of timing and audience analysis skills as well as provide practice in sharing a public speaking platform with others.

* This assignment was constructed with the help of information found in "Interviewing," from Robert McLeish, *The Technique of Radio Production. Copyright © 1978 by Butterworth- Heinemann.* Adapted by permission.

AN IN-DEPTH NEWS REPORT INTERVIEW
by Mark S. Redding

MSR: Today we welcome Dr. Susan Emel to Radioactive KNBY. Dr. Emel is the sponsor of the OWL group here on campus. Dr. Emel, you're the sponsor of the OWLs. Now that stands for...

Dr. E: It stands for Organization for Women Leaders.

MSR: And what do OWLs do ?

Dr. E: The primary purpose of the organization is to provide opportunities for women students to network with women in all types of leadership positions... to learn how they got into those positions and how they view women in leadership.

MSR: Wow, that's cool. So how did the organization get started?

Dr. E: Four students—Holly Davis, Heather Cessna, Stephanie Cauble, and Mary Tolman—and I attended a workshop held in St. Louis last summer, conducted by Center for American Women in Politics from Rutgers University. The goal of the workshop was to introduce college women from schools in the midwest to several women in leadership roles, and to encourage them to go back to their campuses and initiate some kind of ongoing service project that promotes leadership development in women. Our group, together with two students selected as alternates for the workshop, Cassie Haas and Stefanie Balzer, chose to start a networking organization for women on campus to connect with women leaders and discuss related issues.

MSR: How often do you have those discussions? What happens?

Dr. E: We have had two to three meetings each semester in which we have invited prominent women leaders to speak. This year we hosted Kansas' First Lady Linda Graves, Kansas' Attorney General Carla Stovall, and several women from the Kansas legislature, in addition to an outstanding woman professor here at Baker, Martha Harris. We also held two open business meetings for anyone interested in helping us plan.

MSR: You mentioned earlier that other schools attended the workshop last summer. Do you know if there are groups like this in other universities?

Dr. E: Yes. Although many schools came to the workshop and designed service projects of different kinds, one of the groups we became friends with was the group from Iowa State University. After returning home and laying the groundwork for our organization, we learned that they had started a similar group, AND had come up with a similar name! In April, some of our group went to their campus to hear featured speaker Anita Hill.

MSR: What has been the response from the members?

Dr. E: Well, Mark, we don't actually have formal membership, but we have had excellent responses from students on campus and women in the Baldwin community as well. Several students have joined our leadership team in making plans for the future.

MSR: And what about men?

Dr. E: Well, as a mater of fact, we have had men attend some of these presentations. But other times we have had only women attend.

MSR: Finally, we only have a minute left, is there anything else your group hopes to accomplish?

Dr. E: Yes, Mark, one of the most exciting things the OWL group has begun is a service project in which our students mentor young girls from the inner city. Through an association with the YWCA of Kansas City, Kansas, this spring several elementary and junior high girls form the Y came to Baker and followed our members around to classes, to lunch and to their jobs on campus to see what it was like to be in college. It was a very successful experience, and we hope to continue it next year.

MSR: Okay. Well, thanks for being on the show today we've been talking with Dr. Susan Emel, assistant professor of speech communication and sponsor of the OWL group here on campus. I'm your host, Mark Redding.

CHAPTER 37

THE FILM/TV PROGRAM REVIEW

Time limits: 3 minutes, exactly.

Speaking notes: Write out a full manuscript with 30-second time intervals indicated throughout the speech.

Outline of speech: None is required for instructor.

Question: What should you do if your speech is seriously over the time limit given?

Answer: Consider cutting out "flowery" sentences or making them simpler, reduce the number of examples used, and, if necessary, reduce the number of sub-points.

 Key Words:
Captive audience
Elements of composition
Formal review

Student Expectations: In completing this assignment, each student will:
➤ *Identify elements of program composition*
➤ *Draw conclusions about the effectiveness of those elements*
➤ *Determine levels of sensitivity in a captive audience to material being reviewed*
➤ *Present a complete assessment of a program within a given time limit*

PURPOSE OF THIS ASSIGNMENT

Many times people share opinions of films or television programs they have seen. A **formal review**, however, gives the listener a more complete picture of the reviewer's response to a program. Reviewing a program will help the student understand the complexities of film and television production, while giving experience in presenting one's ideas in a live broadcast setting. This assignment is designed to provide the student with an opportunity to present a critical evaluation of a popular film or television production to a widely varied audience.

EXPLANATION OF THE FILM/TV PROGRAM REVIEW

Though a review of a film or television program may begin with similar questions as a book review

(See Chapter 30) about plot, style, and the author, the film or TV program review must include assessment of many other production factors such as the quality of acting, directing, editing, etc. Like the book review, the purposes of the film/TV review may be to inform, to entertain, or to convince. The reviewer is expected to know the program very well, and to be able to present the review in an organized and interesting manner. Like the in-depth news report interview, the film/TV reviewer must anticipate the general interests of the audience and answer the questions they would be most likely to ask about the production. A film or TV program review is often consulted by an audience for its recommendation on whether or not the program is worth viewing. A reviewer must be prepared to offer such an assessment.

HOW TO CHOOSE A FILM/TV PROGRAM FOR REVIEW

As with topic selections in other assignments, the best choices for films or TV programs to review are usually ones with which you are familiar. In the case of this review, you may wish to view the program several times to complete your analysis, so a good suggestion would be to choose one you have access to see again. Class members should select programs from a variety of different film and TV genres.

Taking notes while viewing a movie or TV program is essential to writing a good review.

In the classroom setting your primary audience (your classmates and instructor) is known as a **captive audience** because they are obligated to listen to your speech for educational purposes. Such audiences might not otherwise choose to hear a review of a program they might find offensive. Because of this unique circumstance, you are ethically obligated to select a program for review that will minimize offending the captive audience's sensibilities. You must carefully consider a program's language, violence, and sexual situations before you select it for review. In some cases it is possible to review a controversial piece without offending the audience during the review. In other cases it is not. You must use your best judgment in selecting your program for review. Be sure to get your instructor's approval of your selection before proceeding with the development of your review.

HOW TO PREPARE A FILM/TV PROGRAM REVIEW

As with the book review, begin your preparation by determining the purpose of your speech. Once you have decided whether you wish to inform, persuade or entertain, begin the review with some information that will give the audience the context of the show's origin and development.

Within the body of the review, discuss the **elements of composition** in the piece. Judge and report on the quality of such things as the lighting, sound, editing, set, acting, plot or purpose of the program, camera movements, special effects. Determine whether these things add to the meaning of the program or detract from it.

Additionally, provide your audience with answers to questions you would anticipate they would like to know. Such questions may include: For whom is the program intended? What is the point of view of the program—does the main character profess a particular perspective on an issue of concern in the program? Does the program portray life realistically—why or why not? What is the message of the program? What kind of person would get the most out of this program? Would you watch it again? What effect, if any, did it have on your opinions or actions? Would you recommend this program to others?

In the broadcast review, it can be important to use a short video clip of the program you are discussing to illustrate one of your strongest points. However, if you choose to do this, you must carefully select the clip to be sure it illustrates your point very clearly and efficiently for the audience. You must also time the clip precisely so that it fits well within your time limit and does not intrude on the other important ideas you wish to convey in the review.

One of the best ways to master the above information is to view the program once for your own enjoyment. Then view it the second and third times looking for the information you wish to include in your review. You may wish to make a list of items to look for as you watch in order to be sure you have observed carefully all the items about which you will report.

HOW TO PRESENT A FILM/TV PROGRAM REVIEW

In presenting your review, speak clearly and at a very deliberate pace so that your listeners will be able to follow you. Pay careful attention to enunciation and pronunciation of your words. On radio, due to the lack of visuals, your voice will need to utilize animation, clarity, force, and emphasis to keep the audience interested in your ideas. For television, you will need to give some attention to posture, gestures, movement, and appearance.

Be sure you are speaking directly into the microphone, and for television, looking directly into the camera as if to make eye contact with your audience. Also for television, you should make a careful assessment of clothes that will look best, facial make-up, use of jewelry, etc. For both radio and TV you will need to become familiar with signals given to you by the stage manager in charge of the production. A visit to a radio or television station will reveal many methods used to make speeches more effective for broadcasting. Become acquainted with them before you make your presentation.

CHAPTER 38

RADIO/TELEVISION COMMENTARY

Time limit: See your instructor for the exact time.

Speaking notes: Unless your instructor directs otherwise, you will write out your speech word for word. A copy of your speech should be in the hands of your instructor at least one day before you are scheduled to speak.

Sources of information: Two or more. List them at the end of your written speech.

Outline of speech: None is required for instructor.

Q

Question: What does it mean to write in an "aural" style?

A

Answer: This means writing for a listener rather than a reader. This style uses simple sentences, an active voice, words of high connotative value, correct grammar, and a restricted vocabulary since listeners are less likely to be able to look up unfamiliar words in a dictionary while they are listening.

Key Words:
Commentary
Controversy
Vocal qualities

Student Expectations: In completing this assignment, each student will:
- ➤ *Identify opposing viewpoints on a selected topic*
- ➤ *Gather information on a topic of importance to a community of listeners/ viewers*
- ➤ *Use divergent thinking and originality to analyze and suggest solutions to a controversial topic*
- ➤ *Prepare a concise persuasive appeal to fit a given time limit*

PURPOSE OF THIS ASSIGNMENT

If one understands the preparation and presentation of media commentaries through first-hand knowledge and experience, one is much freer to identify, evaluate, and appreciate them as a media consumer. Such an experience will pose real problems while answering many questions for all who take part.

EXPLANATION OF RADIO/TELEVISION COMMENTARY

Commentaries are not always used by radio or television stations because they can be controver-

sial and the station may wish to avoid offending any listeners in any way. However, sometimes commentaries are broadcast as a public service to promote community discussion on particular topics of concern. A **commentary** is the airing of subjective views by news reporters or by selected viewers. (Subjective views presented by station owners or managers are called "editorials.")

Good commentaries have impact, are personal (making reference to the reporter), are timely, and involve **controversy**—a topic with at least two clearly defined and advocated points of view. In other words, they are quite similar to persuasive speeches.

HOW TO CHOOSE A TOPIC FOR A RADIO/ TELEVISION COMMENTARY

There are three levels for topics of public concern: national, statewide, and local. In order to maintain timeliness in your commentary, a good place to look for topics is from the media sources around you. Medical discoveries, governmental policies, social needs are all potential topics for a good commentary.

Some public issues are viable concerns over long periods of time and across all three levels, such as stereotypes in programming, violence in the media, TV ratings systems proposals, censorship/First Amendment issues, trying accused persons in the media before the courts do, etc.

Follow the principles discussed in earlier chapters for topic selection and review topic possibilities in earlier chapters as well for ideas.

Many television and radio stations include commentaries on local and national issues as a part of their newscasts.

HOW TO PREPARE A RADIO/TELEVISION COMMENTARY

All principles involving the preparation of the persuasive speech you intend to present apply here.

It is wise to review your work regarding those chapters. Give special attention to details and correctness. No excuses can be offered for errors when you have a printed copy lying before you. It should be double-spaced for easy reading.

The final preparation should be submission of your speech to the instructor for approval. After the preparation is completed, numerous rehearsals will be required before you are ready to step before the microphone. If possible you should practice with a microphone while a friend listens critically and offers suggestions for improvement. The use of a recording device for practice will greatly add to the quality of your speech. If desirable, after several rehearsals, you may write time signals in the margin of your paper to tell you where you should be at the end of two, three, or four minutes, etc.

HOW TO PRESENT A RADIO/TELEVISION COMMENTARY

Ordinarily, these speeches are presented with the thought that the audience will be scattered far and wide throughout the nation, possibly the world. They may be congregated in groups of two, three, or four, or there may be only one person in a home. Your presentation should be tempered to meet all situations. If you ask yourself how you would speak were you to step before these small groups of people in person, your type of presentation becomes quite clear. It should be remembered that if this is radio, only your voice will be heard. This calls particular attention to the dynamics of your **vocal qualities**. If you utilize television, then of course you are in full view for all to see and hear. This calls attention to posture, gestures, movement and appearance.

As mentioned in other media assignment chapters, avoid rustling your manuscript in any way. Do not cough, clear your throat, or shout into the mike. Keep a uniform distance from the mike at all times to prevent a sudden fading or sudden increase in volume.

* This assignment was constructed with the help of information found in "Announcements" and "News Programs," from Roger L. Walters, *Broadcast Writing: Principles and Practice.* Copyright © 1988 by McGraw-Hill, Inc.

The Roosevelt Room

THE PRESIDENT: Good morning. Something remarkable happened this week; something that can forever help parents, children and anybody who cares about what our children watch on television. We took an enormous step toward controlling the images of violence and bias that can enter our homes and disturb our children. Television is one of the most influential voices that can enter a home. It can be entertaining, enlightening and educating. But when it transmits pictures or words we wouldn't want our children to see and hear in real life, television can become an unwelcome intruder, one that parents have too often found too difficult to control.

In study after study, the evidence has steadily mounted that television violence is numbing and corrosive. It can have a destructive impact on young children. In my State of the Union speech, I challenged the members of Congress to give control back to parents. I asked them to require TVs to include the V-chip, a device that lets parents filter out programs they don't want to let into their homes and their children's lives. Congress answered that challenge and, three weeks ago when I signed the Telecommunications Bill into law, the V-chip also became law. Now it will be standard in new television sets sold in our country. We need this.

To make the V-chip work, I invited leaders of the media and entertainment industry to come to the White House to work with us to help our families. And this past Thursday I met with the leaders of the television networks, the production studios, the cable companies, actors, directors and writers. Their response was overwhelming, and our meeting was a great success.

For the first time ever, leaders of the television and entertainment industry have come together as one force and agreed to develop a rating system for their programming that will help parents to protect their children from violence and other objectionable content on television. They said this system will be in place by next January.

Like the movie ratings have done for 27 years, the ratings for television will help parents to guide their children's entertainment choices. The system will provide families with a standard they can rely on from show to show, from channel to channel. Parents are the best judges of what their children should and shouldn't see, and this new rating system will help them to make those critical judgments. The best programming director for our children is a parent.

At my meeting with the entertainment industry, we also discussed the need for more programming that is suitable for children, and that is educational and attractive to them. I want to preserve public broadcasting and the innovation it has brought in educational shows for children.

These days, a typical child will watch 25,000 hours of television before his or her 18th birthday. It's up to us whether these shows stimulate their minds or numb them. Let's build on the good shows that we have as models for educating and informing our children. I applaud the entertainment leaders for what they have done voluntarily. Through their action, they are being responsible for the product they produce, and they are showing greater concern for our American community and our children's future.

With the V-chip and the rating system, we mark a sea of change. We are harnessing technology, creativity and responsibility, bringing together parents, business and government to meet a major challenge to our society. After all, it doesn't do a family any good to have nice a television if the images it brings to our children erodes their values and diminishes their future.

We should look at this breakthrough as part of the bigger picture and as a lesson for even greater achievement. As I have said many times, this is an age of great possibility when more Americans will have more opportunities to live out their dreams than ever before. But we also know that this is a time of stiff challenges as well. If we are to meet those challenges, all of us must take our proper responsibility. Government must play a part, but only a part. Only if each of us measures what we do by basic standards of right and wrong, taking responsibility for our actions, moving us together, will we be able to move forward as a nation.

Let me say again—only if we work together in our businesses, our schools, our places of worship, our civic groups—will we transform our lives and our country. That is what I mean when I talk about corporate responsibility.

The actions of the television industry show us what can happen when visionary business leaders make a commitment to values and the common good as well as to the bottom line, and when they live up to their responsibilities as corporate citizens of our great country. I hope their example will be matched by the executives in other industries to address other problems and other challenges we face as a people. That means corporations helping to improve our schools, helping to connect them to the Information Superhighway, helping to demand high standards. That means corporations finding new ways to protect our environment even as they grow the bottom line and improve our economy.

That means businesses recognizing that workers are an asset, not a liability, and that a well-trained work force is any business's most important competitive edge. All these things demand a renewed commitment from business. And I am confident that the leaders of other industries will also rise to the challenge just the way the leaders of the entertainment industry did this week.

We can celebrate a giant step toward realizing the possibility of a great instrument of communication in the homes of our families. I believe we can meet our other challenges to the nation in the same way. We'll all want to stay tuned for that.

Thanks for listening.

GLOSSARY

Acceptance speech — A speech given in response to a formal nomination to office which is designed to establish the nominee as a competent leader in the minds of supporters and voters. May also refer to a speech given in response to the formal presentation of an award or gift which is designed to express sincere appreciation for the honor.

Action — The last step of the Motivated Sequence method of organizing speeches in which the speaker clearly and directly states what response is desired from the audience.

Adaptable — The ability to craft a speech to fit the needs of the occasion and the audience very closely with the intended message of the speaker.

Affirmative — The team or speaker in a debate who supports the topic under discussion.

After dinner speaking — A speech presented at the end of a meal which may have a serious purpose or be designed primarily for entertainment.

Amendment — A change in a bill or motion which adds to or deletes information.

Analogy — A comparison between two things. A literal analogy compares similar things, such as two boats. A figurative analogy compares things that function similarly but are not actually the same such as comparing a computer to the human brain.

Analysis of the audience — This process involves learning as much as possible about your listeners either by inferring basic information about their demographics, interests, and attitudes, or by doing a formal survey of them. This information is used to tailor the message more specifically to their needs.

Anecdote — A short story or recalling of an incident, usually humorous.

Anniversary speech — The purpose of this speech is to recall events of the past and to relate their importance to the present while indicating how they might serve as guides for the future.

Attention — The first step of the Motivated Sequence method of organizing speeches in which the speaker captures the focus and imagination of the listeners.

Audience — The group of listeners in any public speaking situation who make the communication transaction with the speaker complete.

Auditory appeals — persuasive messages designed to be attractive to the human sense of hearing.

Background data — General information about a company or person that gives the reader or interviewer a sense of the communication context for the interview. This could include information on the history of the company, what they produce and how they produce it, the management structure, career history of the interviewee, etc.

Bodily actions — See "Body language."

Body language — A type of nonverbal communication that involves use of the body such as gestures, posture, or movement.

Captive audience — a group of listeners in a public speaking setting who are not in attendance first and foremost for the pleasure of hearing the speaker, but are rather in attendance due to other requirements.

Character studies — The presentation of significant events in a person's life in terms of how the person responded to the events and how those events shaped who they became and what they valued; usually used in a speech of praise.

Chronological — Following an ordered pattern based on the flow of time; for example, from past to present to future.

Clarifying — Active listening technique of asking questions that invite the speaker to offer more specific information about statements being made, examples to illustrate the intended meaning, or definitions of terms and ideas.

Codes — Symbols, commonly agreed upon, used to express the thoughts, feelings, and meanings between people of a community; may be verbal or nonverbal.

Commemoration — To honor, remember, or recognize with a formal observation.

Commemorative — To have the nature of a commemoration.

Commencement address — Speech presented in honor of graduates at a commencement ceremony.

Commentary — A subjective analysis of one side or aspect of a controversial topic, presented in a mass media setting.

Common values — Identification of particular values held in mutual regard by the speaker and the audience.

Communication — Intentional or unintentional words, actions, or symbols which others interpret.

Communication apprehension — The natural nervousness that occurs when communicating with others, usually in a public setting; commonly called "stage fright."

Conclusion — The part of a speech which summarizes and emphasizes the speaker's main ideas.

Confidence — In public speaking, this refers to the attitude of the speaker that springs from being well-prepared and well-rehearsed, and inspires the audience to assign credibility to the speaker in return.

Constructive speech — The first speech given by a speaker in a debate which presents or builds a case for acceptance or rejection of a topic.

Context — The environment in which a communication transaction takes place, which has varying degrees of influence on the exchange of meanings.

Controversy — See "Debatable proposition."

Conversationality — The ability to make a well-planned public presentation flow at a rate and natural quality found in regular interpersonal conversation.

Convince — To persuade.

Cooperative effort — This is achieved when members of a group are successfully able to divide, combine, and present information together as a group to others.

Counterarguments — Arguments made in response to original arguments, usually presenting an opposing viewpoint.

Credibility — The quality or qualities of a speaker or of sources of information that an audience perceives as trustworthy, competent, and dynamic.

Criticisms — Feedback designed to benefit the communicator by helping the speaker understand how his or her messages are being perceived by others.

Cross-examine — In a debate, this is the process of asking the speaker questions to gain additional information and to clarify what the speaker said.

Debatable proposition — A proposal that has at least two clearly distinguishable (and often opposing) points of view in which the speakers have an interest; a controversy.

Debate — A contest in which the affirmative and negative sides of a proposition are advocated by opposing speakers.

Decoding — The process of interpreting a message.

Dedication speech — A speech of commemoration, usually part of a ceremony.

Demonstration — This speech features the physical display and assembly of steps in a process while explaining each along the way and reaching completion.

Dialogue — Conversation between two individuals.

Disadvantages — In debate, these are problems showing that a team's position is unworkable and undesirable.

Dramatic story line — The narrative or "plot" of a broadcast or film production.

Dynamic — The quality of a speaker's presentation style that indicates enthusiasm for the message and a confident delivery.

Elements of composition — The various aspects that combine to form the substance of a work of art; in film, for example, these would include acting, scriptwriting, costume and make-up, set design, etc.

Emotion — The feelings, or passions, of audience members.

Encoding — The process of constructing a message.

Entertain — To capture and hold the attention and imagination of the audience.

Ethics — Moral principles or values that guide the communicator in choosing and presenting ideas and materials to an audience.

Eulogy — A speech of praise that is delivered in honor or commemoration of someone living or dead.

Evidence — Materials offered to listeners in support of claims, including examples, testimony, statistics, visual aids, etc.

Extemporaneous — A speech given with an outline or a few notes.

Eye contact — To maintain connection with members of an audience by looking individuals in the eye while delivering a public address.

Facilitator — One whose function in a group discussion is primarily to keep the conversation flowing and focused on the announced topic.

Farewell speech — Formal remarks given in recognition of one's immanent departure.

Felicitations — Remarks designed to create feelings of happiness and goodwill.

Fields of experience — In the transactional model of communication, this refers to the sum of personal experiences each communicator brings to the communication exchange that influences the individual's perceptions of, and responses to, the communication process.

Formal review — A critique of a book, film, or other artistic endeavor that has been well prepared through clarity of purpose, thorough research, clear organization, and thoughtful language choices.

Forum — The exchange of questions and answers between a speaker and an audience.

Fundamentals of preparation — See the Prologue, "The Basics of Public Speaking."

Genre — A kind, or type, as of works of literature, art, etc.

Genuineness — Sincerity.

Gestures — Arm and hand movements used to illustrate a spoken message.

Goodwill — An attitude reflecting the belief that the speaker is charitable toward the audience; the view that the speaker has the audience's best interests at heart.

Harm — In debate, this is the problem which requires the proposed solution.

Homage — Showing respect or the worth of another person.

Humor — The art or skill of the speaker to evoke laughter from an audience.

Impromptu — A speech given with little or no advance preparation.

Incidental motions — In parliamentary procedure, these motions are neither privileged nor subsidiary, but may be required in the course of the proceedings. They have no precedence of order as the other categories of motions do.

Inform — To instruct; to provide information.

Inherency — In debate, this refers to any quality of the present system that prevents or inhibits the problem from being resolved.

Internal summaries — Brief restatements of key thoughts covered in significant sections of the speech, usually provided to the audience before moving on to another substantial segment of the speech.

Interview — A conversation between two or more people characterized by one party in particular being asked questions by the other(s) for the purposes of gaining information and clarification.

Introduction — The beginning of a speech which should get the audience's attention, give them a reason to listen, and introduce the topic.

Introductory statement — An opening statement of a speech that captures the essential purposes of a full introduction: getting the audience's attention, stating your topic and showing enthusiasm for it.

Keynote — Usually the first address at a conference, convention, or meeting that identifies key issues participants will address and generates enthusiasm for the work.

Lecture forum — A speech followed by a period of questions from the audience.

Lecture forum — An informative speech followed by a period of questions from the audience.

Logic — The use of careful reasoning which follows the formulas of standard classical critical thinking patterns such as deduction, induction, and reasoning by analogy.

Manuscript — A complete text of a speech that is used as speaking notes.

Messages — Meaningful information exchanged between two communicators.

Mood — In public speaking, this refers to the emotional environment in a speech setting as well as the emotional context of the topic and the speaker's delivery.

Motion — A formal proposal for action or change to be debated by selected speakers or by a group.

Multivoiced — Using several voices to communicate a single message; usually refers to radio or television productions.

Need — The second step in the Motivated Sequence method of organizing speeches in which the problem, or need for the plan, is fully discussed.

Negative — The team or person in a debate who opposes or disagrees with the resolution under discussion.

Noise — Interference of any kind that makes a communication transaction unsuccessful.

Nominating speech — This speech places the name of a candidate for office before the audience and offers reasons why voters should support that candidate.

Nonverbal communication — Any message not involving words such as gestures, tone of voice, facial expressions, or symbols.

Oral book review — A critique of a book presented in a speech format.

Oral interpretation — A spoken presentation of a written work emphasizing the emotional content of the piece as understood by the speaker.

Order of business — The sequence of topics to be addressed by a decision-making body.

Organizational method — A general model for coordinating main ideas and supporting materials in a way that can be easily followed or anticipated by an audience.

Outline — The main features of a speech usually presented in sentences, phrases, or single words.

Outlining — To write speech materials down in outline form.

Panel discussion — A group of people trying to solve a problem through discussion.

Pantomime — A performance involving only body language to tell a story.

Paraphrasing — Taking someone else's thoughts and putting them into your own words as a way of summarizing them.

Parliamentary procedure — A recognized procedure for conducting a business meeting in an orderly manner.

Persuasion — The process of influencing another to change, modify, or adopt an attitude or behavior.

Pet peeve — Something that upsets or disturbs you or causes you to react negatively.

Plagiarize — To take someone else's work and represent it as your own.

Plan — In debate, this refers to the proposed solution offered by a debate team to resolve the problem being debated.

Poise — To maintain a calm, steady, gracious, and assured manner.

Portfolio — A collection of works produced by the student, designed to illustrate the student's abilities and show the levels of accomplishment in development of communication skills.

Posture — The position of your body.

Precedence of motions — The established order of priority of parliamentary motions in relation to other possible motions that may be made.

Preparation — The process of planning and rehearsing the speech before the delivery of it in front of an audience.

Preparation time — In contest speaking, this is a strictly limited amount of time allowed for the collection and organization of materials into presentation-ready format.

Presentation speech — A speech (usually brief) made in honor of a recipient, which highlights the purpose of the award, its history and meaning, and the traits of the recipient that qualify that person to receive the award.

Problem-solving — The process of discussion, coordination of ideas, and development of agreement on ways to resolve a problematic situation.

Proofreading — The careful scrutiny of a written document, paying especially close attention to grammar, spelling, punctuation, and word choices.

Proposition — A topic for group discussion, sometime phrased in the form of a question.

Purpose — The goal of a presentation, or what the speaker hopes to accomplish by making the presentation.

Rebuttal speech — The second speech given by a debater which responds to the opponent's arguments.

Recapitulation — Restating a point or points.

Redundancy — The repetition of the same ideas or word choices in the same speech.

Rephrase — In a forum, this refers to the occasion when the speaker restates, condenses, or summarizes the meaning of an audience member's question before attempting to answer it.

Sales — The use of communication to persuade consumers to purchase goods or services.

Salutation — The expression of a courteous greeting in a speech, letter, or ceremony.

Satisfaction — The third step in the Motivated Sequence method of organizing speeches in which the solution to the problem presented earlier is discussed.

Self-disclosure — The act of revealing personal information about yourself that would otherwise remain unknown to listeners.

Signposts — Verbal signals within a speech that indicate a sequence of ideas to the audience. For example, "First,..." "Second,..." or "Next,..." etc.

Simile — When two unlike things are compared such as to say he is a bright light in my life.

Sources of information — Credible, professional, authoritative origins of facts, statistics, examples, quotations, and other materials used to develop a speech, such as national news publications or broadcasts, books, and personal interviews with experts on the topic.

Stage fright (speech anxiety) — See "Communication Apprehension."

Stock issues — The major requirements or issues an affirmative team must include in a constructive speech.

Succinct — Using few words; concise.

Summarizing statement — A single statement that serves the basic function of putting the speaker's previously spoken ideas in a brief form for review.

Symposium — A presentation involving several speakers each of whom discusses a different aspect of a problem.

Thesis — The major idea being discussed in a speech.

Toastmaster — The person who presides at a dinner and who is responsible for introducing guests, speakers, and programs.

Transitions — A connecting statement between two main ideas or sections of a speech, usually created by referring to the previously discussed idea and previewing the next idea to be discussed in the same sentence.

Tribute — See "Eulogy."

Univocal — Using only one voice.

Variety — A wide range of different approaches or options.

Verbal communication — A message which relies on the use of words, either spoken or written.

Visual aids — Photos, objects, models, transparencies, videos, and other means of assisting the audience to literally see what the speaker is talking about.

Visualization — The fourth step in the Motivated Sequence method of organizing speeches in which the speaker uses vivid imagery to help an audience imagine what the world would be like if the speaker's proposal is enacted (may also be used to help listeners imagine what could happen if the speaker's proposal is *not* enacted).

Vocal qualities — The various aspects of vocal delivery such as tone, rate, pitch, volume, and attractiveness of the voice.

APPENDIX A

SPEECHES FROM HISTORY

SPEECH
By Heinmot Tooyalaket (Chief Joseph) of the Nez Percés

The earth was created by the assistance of the sun, and it should be left as it was ... the country was made without lines of demarcation, and it is no man's business to divide it ... I see the whites all over the country gaining wealth, and see their desire to give us lands which are worthless ... The earth and myself are of one mind. The measure of the land and the measure of our bodies are the same. Say to us if you can say it, that you were sent by the Creative Power to talk to us. Perhaps you think the creator sent you here to dispose of us as you see fit. If I thought you were sent by the Creator I might be induced to think you had a right to dispose of me. Do not misunderstand me, but understand me fully with reference to my affection for the land. I never said the land was mine to do with as I chose. The one who has the right to dispose of it is the one who has created it. I claim a right to live on my land, and accord you the privilege to live on yours.

THE "GIVE ME LIBERTY OR GIVE ME DEATH" SPEECH
By Patrick Henry (1775)
*Delivered on March 23, 1775, before the Second Revolutionary Convention of Virginia,
in the old church in Richmond.*

No man thinks more highly than I do of the patriotism, as well as abilities, of the very worthy gentlemen who have just addressed the House. But different men often see the same subject in different lights; and, therefore, I hope it will not be thought disrespectful to those gentlemen, if, entertaining as I do opinions of a character very opposite to theirs, I shall speak forth my sentiments freely and without reserve. This is not time for ceremony.

The question before the House is one of awful moment to this country. For my own part, I consider it as nothing less than a question of freedom or slavery; and in proportion to the magnitude of the subject ought to be the freedom of the debate. It is only in this way that we can hope to arrive at truth, and fulfill the great responsibility, which we hold to God and our Country. Should I keep back my opinions at such a time, through fear of giving offense, I should consider myself as guilty of treason toward my country, and of act of disloyalty toward the Majesty of Heaven, which I revere above all earthly kings.

Mr. President, it is natural to man to indulge in the illusions of hope. We are apt to shut our eyes against a painful truth, and listen to the song of that siren, till she transforms us into beasts. Is this the part of wise men, engaged in a great and arduous struggle for liberty? Are we disposed to be of the number of those, who having eyes, see not, and having ears, hear not, the things which so nearly concern their temporal salvation? For my part, whatever anguish of spirit it may cost, I am willing to know the whole truth; to know the worst, and to provide for it.

I have but one lamp by which my feet are guided, and that is the lamp of experience. I know of no way of judging of the future but by the past. And judging by the past, I wish to know what there has been in the conduct of the British ministry for the last ten years to justify those hopes with which gentlemen have been pleased to solace themselves and the House. Is it that insidious smile with which our petition has been lately received? Trust it not, sir; it will prove a snare to your feet. Suffer not yourselves to be betrayed with a kiss. Ask yourselves how this gracious reception of our petition comports with those warlike preparations which cover our water and darken our land. Are fleets and armies necessary to a work of love and reconciliation? Have we shown ourselves so unwilling to be reconciled that force must be called in to win back our love? Let us not deceive ourselves, sir. These are the implements of war and subjugation; the last arguments to which kings resort.

I ask gentlemen, sir, what means this martial array, if its purpose be not to force us to submission? Can gentlemen assign any other possible motive for it? Has Great Britain any enemy in this quarter of the world to call for all this accumulation of navies and armies? No, sir, she has none. They are meant for us: they can be meant for no other. They are sent over to bind and rivet upon us those chains which the British ministry have been so long forging. And what have we to oppose to them? Shall we try argument? Sir, we have been trying that for the last ten years. Have we anything new to offer upon the subject? Nothing. We have held the subject up in every light of which it is capable; but it has been all in vain.

Shall we resort to entreaty and humble supplication? What terms shall we find which have not been already exhausted? Let us not, I beseech you, sir deceive ourselves longer. Sir, we have done everything that could be done, to avert the storm which is now coming on. We have petitioned; we have remonstrated; we have supplicated; we have prostrated ourselves before the throne, and have implored its interposition to arrest the tyrannical hands of the ministry and Parliament. Our petitions have been slighted; our remonstrances have produced additional violence and insult; our supplications have been disregarded, and we have been spurned, with contempt, from the foot of the throne!

In vain, after these things, may we indulge the fond hope of peace and reconciliation. There is no longer any room for hope. If we wish to be free—if we mean to preserve inviolate those inestimable privileges for which we have been so long contending—if we mean not basely to abandon the noble struggle in which we have been so long engaged, and which we have pledged ourselves never to abandon, until the glorious object of our contest shall be obtained—we must fight! I repeat it, sir, we must fight! An appeal to arms to the God of Hosts is all that is left us!

They tell us, sir, that we are weak—unable to cope with so formidable an adversary. But when shall we be stronger? Will it be the next week, or the next year? Will it be when we are totally disarmed, and when a British guard shall be stationed in every house? Shall we gather strength by irresolution and inaction? Shall we acquire the means of effectual resistance by lying supinely on our backs and hugging the delusive phantom of hope, until our enemies shall have bound us hand and foot?

Sir, we are not weak if we make a proper use of those means which the God of nature has placed in our power. Three millions of people armed in the holy cause of liberty, and in such a country as that which we possess, are invincible by any force which our enemy can send against us. Besides, sir, we shall not fight our battles alone. There is a just God who presides over the vigilant, the active, the brave. Besides, sir, we have no election. If we were base enough to desire it, it is now too late to retire from the contest. There is no retreat but in submission and slavery! Our chains are forged! Their clanking may be heard on the plains of Boston! The war is inevitable—and let it come! I repeat it, sir, let it come!

It is in vain, sir, to extenuate the matter. Gentlemen may cry, Peace, Peace—but there is no peace. The war is actually begun! The next gale that sweeps from the north will bring to our ears the clash of resounding arms! Is life so dear, or peace so sweet, as to be purchased at the price of chains and slavery? Forbid it, Almighty God! I know not what course others may take, but as for me, give me liberty or give me death!

ON THE FEDERAL CONSTITUTION
By Benjamin Franklin (1787)
From a speech in Philadelphia before the Constitutional Convention of 1787.

(The Constitution was adopted only after much debate. In the following speech one well-known individual expressed his feelings about signing the document.)

I CONFESS that I do not entirely approve of this Constitution at present; but, sir, I am not sure I shall never approve of it, for, having lived long, I have experienced many instances of being obliged, by better information or fuller consideration, to change opinions even on important subjects, which I once thought right, but found to be otherwise. It is therefore that, the older I grow, the more apt I am to doubt my own judgment of others. Most men, indeed, as well as most sects in religion, think themselves in possession of all truth, and that wherever others differ from them, it is so far error. Steele, a Protestant, in a dedication, tells the pope that the only difference between our two churches in their opinion of the certainty of their doctrine is, the Romish Church is infallible, and the Church of England is never in the wrong. But, though many private persons think almost as highly of their own infallibility as of that of their sect, few express it so naturally as a certain French lady, who, in a little dispute with her sister said: "But I meet nobody but myself that is always in the right."

In these sentiments, sir, I agree to this Constitution with all its faults—if they are such—because I think a general government necessary for us, and there is no form of government but what may be a blessing to the people if well administered; and I believe, further, that this is likely to be well administered for a course of years, and can only end in despotism, as other forms have done before it, when the people shall become so corrupted as to need despotic government, being incapable of any other. I doubt, too, whether any other convention we can obtain may be able to make a better Constitution; for, when you assemble a number of men, to have the advantage of their joint wisdom, you inevitably assemble with those men all their prejudices, their passions, their errors of opinion, their local interests, and their selfish views. From such an assembly can a perfect production be expected?

It therefore astonishes me, sir, to find this system approaching so near to perfection as it does; and I think it will astonish our enemies, who are waiting with confidence to hear that our counsels are confounded like those of the builders of Babel, and that our States are on the point of separation, only to meet hereafter for the purpose of cutting one another's throats. Thus I consent, sir, to this Constitution, because I expect no better, and because I am not sure that it is not the best. The opinions I have had of its errors I sacrifice to the public good. I have never whispered a syllable of them abroad. Within these walls they were born, and here they shall die. If every one of us, in returning to our constituents, were to report the objections he has had to it, and endeavor to gain partisans in support of them, we might prevent its being generally received, and thereby lose all the salutary effects and great advantages resulting naturally in our favor among foreign nations, as well as among ourselves, from our real or apparent unanimity. Much of the strength and efficiency of any government, as well as of the wisdom and integrity of its governors. I hope, therefore, for our own sakes, as a part of the people, and for the sake of our posterity, that we shall act heartily and unanimously in recommending this Constitution wherever our influence may extend, and turn our future thoughts and endeavors to the means of having it well administered.

On the whole, sir, I can not help expressing a wish that every member of the convention who may still have objections to it, would, with me, on this occasion, doubt a little of his own infallibility, and, to make manifest our unanimity, put his name to this instrument.

THE "HOUSE DIVIDED AGAINST ITSELF" SPEECH
By Abraham Lincoln (1858)

If we could first know where we are, and whither we are tending, we could better judge what to do, and how to do it. We are now far into the fifth year since a policy was initiated with the avowed object, and confident promise, of putting an end to slavery agitation. Under the operation of that policy, that agitation not only has not ceased, but has constantly augmented. In my opinion, it will not cease until a crisis shall have been reached and passed. "A house divided against itself cannot stand."

I believe this government cannot endure permanently half slave and half free. I do not expect the Union to be dissolved; I do not expect the house to fall; but I do expect that it will cease to be divided. It will become all one thing, or all the other.

Either the opponents of slavery will arrest the further spread of it, and place it where the public mind shall rest in the belief that it is in the course of ultimate extinction; or its advocates will push it forward till it shall become alike lawful in all States, old as well as new, North as well as South. Have we no tendency to the latter condition? Let any one who doubts carefully contemplate that now almost complete legal combination—piece of machinery, so to speak—compounded of the Nebraska doctrine and the Dred Scott decision.

Put this and that together, and we have another nice little niche, which we may, ere long, see filled with another Supreme Court decision, declaring that the Constitution of the United States does not permit a State to exclude slavery from its limits. And this may especially be expected if the doctrine of "care not whether slavery be voted down or voted up," shall gain upon the public mind sufficiently to give promise that such a decision can be maintained when made.

Such a decision is all that slavery now lacks of being alike lawful in all the States. Welcome or unwelcome, such decision is probably coming, and will soon be upon us, unless the power of the present political dynasty shall be met and overthrown. We shall awake to the reality, instead, that the Supreme Court has made Illinois a slave State. To meet and overthrow that dynasty is the work before all those who would prevent that consummation. That is what we have to do. How can we best do it?

There are those who denounce us openly to their own friends, and yet whisper to us softly that Senator Douglas is the aptest instrument there is with which to effect that object. They wish us to infer all, from the fact that he now has a little quarrel with the present head of the dynasty; and that he has regularly voted with us on a single point, upon which he and we have never differed. They remind us that he is a great man and that the largest of us are very small ones. Let this be granted. "But a living dog is better than a dead lion." Judge Douglas, if not a dead lion, for this work, is at least a caged and toothless one.

How can he oppose the advance of slavery? He does not care anything about it. His avowed mission is impressing the "public heart" to care nothing about it. A leading Douglas Democratic newspaper thinks Douglas's superior talent will be needed to resist the revival of the African slave trade. Does Douglas believe an effort to revive that trade is approaching? He has not said so. Does he really think so? But if it is, how can he resist it? For years he has labored to prove it a sacred right of white men to take negro slaves into the new Territories. Can he possibly show that it is less s sacred right to buy them where they can be bought cheapest? And unquestionably they can be bought cheaper in Africa than in Virginia.

He has done all in his power to reduce the whole question of slavery to one of a mere right of property; and as such, how can he oppose the foreign slave trade? How can he refuse that trade in that "property" shall be "perfectly free," unless he does it as a protection to the home production? And as the home producers will probably ask the protection, he will be wholly without a ground of opposition.

Senator Douglas holds, we know, that a man may rightfully be wiser today than he was yesterday—that he might rightfully change when he finds himself wrong. But can we, for that reason run ahead, and infer that he will make any particular change, of which he himself has given no intiation? Can we safely base our action upon any such vague inference?

Now, as ever, I wish not to misrepresent Judge Douglas' position, question his motives, or do aught that can be personally offensive to him. Whenever, if ever, he and we can come together on principle, so that our cause may have assistance from his great ability, I hope to have interposed no adventitious obstacle. But clearly, he is not now with us—he does not pretend to be, he does not promise ever to be.

Our cause, then, must be entrusted to, and conducted by, its own undoubted friends—those whose hands are free, whose hearts are in the work—who do care for the result. Two years ago the Republicans of the nation mustered over thirteen hundred thousand strong. We did this under the single impulse of resistance to a common danger.

With every external circumstance against us, of strange, discordant, and even hostile elements, we gathered from the four winds, and brave all then, to falter now?—now, when that same enemy is wavering, dissevered, and belligerent! The result is not doubtful. We shall not fail—if we stand firm, we shall not fail. Wise counsels may accelerate, or mistakes delay it; but, sooner or later, the victory is sure to come.

ON WOMAN'S RIGHT TO VOTE
by Susan B. Anthony (1873)

This is an except of Anthony's speech which was delivered several times around the county in which she was arrested (but not confined) in 1873. Her speech so swayed potential jurors in her favor that the judge was forced to move the trial to another county and detain Anthony behind bars. She was found guilty of voting in the presidential election of 1872, and fined one hundred dollars. She refused to pay the fine and never did pay it.

FRIENDS AND FELLOW CITIZENS: I stand before you tonight under indictment for the alleged crime of having voted at the last presidential election, without having a lawful right to vote. It shall be my work this evening to prove to you that in thus voting, I not only committed no crime, but, instead, simply exercised my citizen's rights, guaranteed to me and all United States citizens by the National Constitution, beyond the power of any State to deny. The Preamble of the Federal Constitution says:

"We, the people of the United States, in order to form a more perfect union, establish justice, insure domestic tranquility, provide for the common defense, promote the general welfare, and secure the blessings of liberty to ourselves and our posterity, do ordain and establish this Constitution for the United States of America."

It was we, the people, not we, the white male citizens; nor yet we, the male citizens; but we, the whole people, who formed the Union. And we formed it, not to give the blessings of liberty, but to secure them; not to the half of ourselves and the half of our posterity, but to the whole people—women as well as men. And it is downright mockery to talk to women of their enjoyment of the blessings of liberty while they are denied the use of the only means of securing them provided by this democratic-republican government—the ballot.

For any State to make sex a qualification that must ever result in the disfranchisement of one entire half of the people is to pass a bill of attainder, or an ex post facto law, and is therefore a violation of the supreme law of the land. By it the blessings of liberty are forever withheld from women and their female posterity. To them this government has no just powers derived from the consent of the governed. To them this government is not a democracy. It is not a republic. It is an odious aristocracy; a hateful oligarchy of sex; the most hateful aristocracy ever established on the face of the globe; an oligarchy of wealth, where the rich govern the poor. An oligarchy of learning, where the educated govern the ignorant, or even an oligarchy of race, where the Saxon rules the African might be endured; but this oligarchy of sex, which makes father, brothers, husband, sons, the oligarchies over the mother and sisters, the wife and daughters of every household—which ordains all men sovereigns, all women subjects, carries dissension, discord and rebellion into every home of the nation.

Webster, Worcester and Bouvier all define a citizen to be a person in the United States, entitled to vote and hold office.

The only question left to be settled now is: Are women persons? And I hardly believe any of our opponents will have the hardihood to say they are not. Being persons, then, women are citizens; and no State has a right to make any law, or to enforce an old law, that shall abridge their privileges or immunities. Hence, every discrimination against women in the constitutions and laws of the several States is today null and void, precisely as in every one against negroes.

THEIR FINEST HOUR
By Winston Churchill (1940)
The excerpt contains the conclusion only. The speech was delivered to the House of Commons, London, England, then broadcast June 18, 1940, in the early stages of World War II.

The Battle of France is over. I expect that the Battle of Britain is about to begin. Upon this battle depends the survival of Christian civilization. Upon it depends our own British life, and the long continuity of our institutions and our Empire. The whole fury and might of the enemy must very soon be turned on us. Hitler knows that he will have to break us in this Island or lose the war. If we can stand up to him, all Europe may be free and the life of the world may move forward into broad, sunlit uplands. But if we fall, then the whole world, including the United States, including all that we have known and cared for, will sink into the abyss of a new Dark Age made more sinister, and perhaps more protracted, by the lights of perverted science. Let us therefore brace ourselves to our duties, and so bear ourselves that, if the British Empire and its Commonwealth last for a thousand years, men will still say, "This was their finest hour."

INAUGURAL ADDRESS
By John F. Kennedy (1961)
Delivered on January 20, 1961 in Washington, D.C.

Vice President Johnson, Mr. Speaker, Mr. Chief Justice, President Eisenhower, Vice President Nixon, President Truman, Reverend Clergy, Fellow Citizens: We observe today not a victory of party but a celebration of freedom—symbolizing an end as well as a beginning—signifying renewal as well as change. For I have sworn before you and Almighty God the same solemn oath our forebears prescribed nearly a century and three quarters ago.

The world is very different now. For man holds in his mortal hands the power to abolish all forms of human poverty and all forms of human life. And yet the same revolutionary beliefs for which our forebears fought are still at issue around the globe—the belief that the rights of man come not from the generosity of the state but from the hand of God.

We dare not forget today that we are the heirs of that first revolution. Let the word go forth from this time and place, to friend and foe alike, that the torch has been passed to a new generation of Americans—born in this century, tempered by war, disciplined by a hard and bitter peace, proud of our ancient heritage—and unwilling to witness or permit the slow undoing of those human rights to which this nation has always been committed, and to which we are committed today, at home and around the world.

Let every nation know, whether it wishes us well or ill, that we shall pay any price, bear any burden, meet any hardship, support any friend or oppose any foe to assure the survival and the success of liberty. This much we pledge—and more.

To those old allies whose cultural and spiritual origins we share, we pledge the loyalty of faithful friends. United, there is little we cannot do in a host of cooperative ventures. Divided, there is little we can do—for we dare not meet a powerful challenge at odds and split asunder. To those new states whom we welcome to the ranks of the free, we pledge our word that one form of colonial control shall not have passed away merely to be replaced by a far more iron tyranny. We shall not always expect to find them supporting our view. But we shall always hope to find them strongly supporting their own freedom—and to remember that, in the past, those who foolishly sought power by riding the back of the tiger ended up inside.

To those people in the huts and villages of half the globe struggling to break the bonds of mass misery, we pledge our best efforts to help them help themselves, for whatever period is required—not because the Communists may be doing it, not because we seek their votes, but because it is right. If a free society cannot help the many who are poor, it cannot save the few who are rich.

To our sister republics south of our border, we offer a special pledge—to convert our good words into good deeds—in a new alliance for progress—to assist free men and free governments in casting off the chains of poverty. But this peaceful revolution of hope cannot become the prey of hostile powers. Let all our neighbors know that we shall join with them to oppose aggression or subversion anywhere in the Americas. And let every other power know that this hemisphere intends to remain the master of its own house.

To that world assembly of sovereign states, the United Nations, our last best hope in an age where the instruments of war have far outpaced the instruments of peace, we renew our pledge of support—to prevent it from becoming merely a forum for invective—to strengthen its shield of the new and the weak—and to enlarge the area in which its writ may run.

Finally, to those nations who would make themselves our adversary, we offer not a pledge but a request: That both sides begin anew the quest for peace, before the dark powers of destruction unleashed by science engulf all humanity in planned or accidental self-destruction.

We dare not tempt them with weakness. For only when our arms are sufficient beyond doubt can we be certain beyond doubt that they will never be employed. But neither can two great and powerful groups of nations take comfort from our present course—both sides overburdened by the cost of modern weapons, both rightly alarmed by the steady spread of the deadly atom, yet both racing to alter that uncertain balance of terror that stays the hand of mankind's final war.

So let us begin anew—remembering on both sides that civility is not a sign of weakness, and sincerity is always subject to proof. Let us never negotiate out of fear. But let us never fear to negotiate. Let both sides explore what problems unite us instead of belaboring those problems which divide us. Let both sides, for the first time, formulate serious and precise proposals for the inspection and control of arms—and bring the absolute power to destroy other nations under the absolute control of all nations. Let both sides seek to invoke the wonders of science instead of its terrors.

Together let us explore the stars, conquer the deserts, eradicate disease, tap the ocean depths and encourage the arts and commerce. Let both sides unite to heed in all corners of the earth the command of Isaiah—to "undo the heavy burdens... [and] let the oppressed go free." And if a beachhead of cooperation may push back the jungle of suspicion, let both sides join in creating a new endeavor: not a new balance of power, but a new world of law, where the strong are just and the weak secure and the peace preserved.

All this will not be finished in the first one hundred days. Nor will it be finished in the first one thousand days, nor in the life of this administration, nor even perhaps in our lifetime on the planet. But let us begin.

In your hands, my fellow citizens, more than mine, will rest the final success or failure of our course. Since this country was founded, each generation of Americans has been summoned to give testimony to its national loyalty. The graves of young Americans who answered the call to service surround the globe.

Now the trumpet summons us again—not as a call to bear arms, though arms we need—not as a call to battle, though embattled we are—but a call to bear the burden of a long twilight struggle, year in and year out, "rejoicing in hope, patient in tribulation"—a struggle against the common enemies of man: Tyranny, poverty, disease and war itself.

Can we forge against these enemies a grand and global alliance, North and South, East and West, that can assure a more fruitful life for all mankind? Will you join in that historic effort?

In the long history of the world, only a few generations have been granted the role of defending freedom in its hour of maximum danger.

I do not shrink from this responsibility—I welcome it. I do not believe that any of us would exchange places with any other people or any other generation. The energy, the faith, the devotion which we bring to this endeavor will light our country and all who serve it—and the glow from that fire can truly light the world.

And so, my fellow Americans: Ask not what your country can do for you—ask what you can do for your country.

My fellow citizens of the world: Ask not what America will do for you, but what together we can do for the freedom of man.

DEMOCRATIC CONVENTION KEYNOTE ADDRESS
By Barbara Jordan (1976)
Delivered July 12, 1976 in New York City. (Reprinted with permission from Vital Speeches of the Day, Vol. 42, No. 21, August 21, 1976.)

One hundred and forty-four years ago, members of the Democratic Party first met in convention to select a Presidential candidate. Since that time, Democrats have continued to convene once every four years and draft a party platform and nominate a Presidential candidate. And our meeting this week is a continuation of that tradition.

But there is something different about tonight. There is something special about tonight. What is different? What is special? I, Barbara Jordan, am a keynote speaker.

A lot of years passed since 1832, and during that time it would have been most unusual for any national political party to ask that a Barbara Jordan deliver a keynote address... but tonight here I am. And I feel that notwithstanding the past that my presence here is one additional bit of evidence that the American Dream need not forever be deferred.

Now that I have this grand distinction what in the world am I supposed to say? I could easily spend this time praising the accomplishments of this party and attacking the Republicans, but I don't choose to do that. I could list the many problems which Americans have.

I could list the problems which cause people to feel cynical, angry, frustrated: problems which include lack of integrity in government; the feeling that the individual no longer counts; the reality of materials and spiritual poverty; the feeling that the grand American experiment is failing or has failed. I could recite these problems, and then I could sit down and offer no solutions. But I don't choose to do that either.

The citizens of America expect more. They deserve and they want more than a recital of problems.

We are a people in a quandary about the present. We are a people in search of our future. We are a people in search of a national community. We are a people trying not only to solve the problems of the present—unemployment, inflation—but we are attempting on a larger scale to fulfill the promise of America. We are attempting to fulfill our national purpose; to create and sustain a society in which all of us are equal.

Throughout our history, when people have looked for new ways to solve their problems, and to uphold the principles of this nation, many times they have turned to political parties. They have often turned to the Democratic Party.

What is it, what is it about the Democratic Party that makes it the instrument that people use when they search for ways to shape their future? Well I believe the answer to that question lies in our concept of governing. Our concept of governing is derived from our view of people. It is a concept deeply rooted in a set of beliefs firmly etched in the national conscience of all of us. Now what are these beliefs?

First, we believe in equality for all and privileges for none. This is a belief that each American regardless of background has equal standing in the public forum, all of us. Because we believe this idea so firmly, we are an inclusive rather than an exclusive party. Let everybody come.

I think it no accident that most of those emigrating to America in the 19th century identified with the Democratic Party. We are a heterogeneous party made up of Americans of diverse backgrounds.

We believe that the people are the source of all governmental power; that the authority of the people is to be extended, not restricted. This can be accomplished only by providing each citizen with every opportunity to participate in the management of the government. They must have that.

We believe that the government which represents the authority of all the people, not just one interest group, but all the people, has an obligation to actively, underscore actively, seek to remove those obstacles which would block individual achievement... obstacles emanating from race, sex, economic condition. The government must seek to remove them.

We are a party of innovation. We do not reject our traditions, but we are willing to adapt to changing circumstances, when change we must. We are willing to suffer the discomfort of change in order to achieve a better future. We have a positive vision of the future founded on the belief that the gap between the promise and reality of America can one day be finally closed. We believe that.

This my friends, is the bedrock of our concept of governing. This is a part of the reason why Americans have turned to the Democratic Party. These are the foundations upon which a national community can be built.

Let's all understand that these guiding principles cannot be discarded for short-term political gains. They represent what this country is all about. They are indigenous to the American idea. And these are principles which are not negotiable.

In other times, I could stand here and give this kind of exposition on the beliefs of the Democratic Party and that would be enough. But today that is not enough. People want more. That is not sufficient reason for the majority of the people of this country to vote Democratic. We have made mistakes. In our haste to do all things for all people, we did not foresee the full consequences of our actions. And when the people raised their voices, we didn't hear. But our deafness was only a temporary condition, and not an irreversible condition.

Even as I stand here and admit that we have made mistakes I still believe that as the people of America sit in judgment on each party, they will recognize that our mistakes were mistakes of the heart. They'll recognize that.

And now we must look to the future. Let us heed the voice of the people and recognize their common sense. If we do not, we not only blaspheme our political heritage, we ignore the common ties that bind all Americans.

Many fear the future. Many are distrustful of their leaders, and believe that their voices are never heard. Many seek only to satisfy their private work wants. To satisfy private interests.

But this is the great danger America faces. That we will cease to be one nation and become instead a collection of interest groups: city against suburb, region against region, individual against individual. Each seeking to satisfy private wants.

If that happens, who then will speak for America? Who then will speak for the common good? This is the question which must be answered in 1976. Are we to be one people bound together by common spirit sharing in a common endeavor or will we become a divided nation?

For all of its uncertainty, we cannot flee the future. We must not become the new puritans and reject our society. We must address and master the future together. It can be done if we restore the belief that we share a sense of national community, that we share a common national endeavor. It can be done.

There is no executive order; there is no law that can require the American people to form a national community. This we must do as individuals and if we do it as individuals, there is no President of the United States who can veto that decision.

As a first step, we must restore our belief in ourselves. We are a generous people so why can't we be generous with each other? We need to take to heart the words spoken by Thomas Jefferson: "Let us restore to social intercourse that harmony and that affection without which liberty and even life are but dreary things."

A nation is formed by the willingness of each of us to share in the responsibility for upholding the common good. A government is invigorated when each of us is willing to participate in shaping the future of this nation.

In this election year we must define the common good and begin again to shape a common future. Let each person do his or her part. If one citizen is unwilling to participate, all of us are going to suffer. For the American idea, though it is shared by all of us, is realized in each one of us.

And now, what are those of us who are elected public officials supposed to do? We call ourselves public servants but I'll tell you this: we as public servants must set an example for the rest of the nation. It is hypocritical for the public official to admonish and exhort the people to uphold the common good if we are derelict in upholding the common good. More is required of public officials than slogans and handshakes and press releases. More is required. We must hold ourselves strictly accountable. We must provide the people with a vision of the future.

If we promise as public officials, we must deliver. If we as public officials propose, we must produce. If we say to the American people it is time for you to be sacrificial; sacrifice. If the public official says that we (public officials) must be the first to give. We must be. And again, if we make mistakes, we must be willing to admit them. We have to do that. What we have to do is strike a balance between the idea that government should do everything and the idea, the belief, that government ought to do nothing. Strike a balance.

Let there be no illusions about the difficulty of forming this kind of a national community. It's tough, difficult, not easy. But a spirit of harmony will survive in America only if each of us remembers that we share a common destiny. If each of us remembers, when self-interest and bitterness seem to prevail, that we share a common destiny.

I have confidence that we can form this kind of national community. I have confidence that the Democratic Party can lead the way. I have that confidence. We cannot improve on the system of government handed down to us by the founders of the Republic, there is no way to improve upon that. But what we can do is to find new ways to implement that system and realize our destiny.

Now, I began this speech by commenting to you on the uniqueness of a Barbara Jordan making the keynote address. Well I am going to close my speech by quoting a Republican President and I ask you that as you listen to these words of Abraham Lincoln, relate them to the concept of a national community in which every last one of us participates: "As I would not be a slave, so I would not be a master. This expresses my idea of Democracy. Whatever differs from this, to the extent of the difference is no Democracy."

APPENDIX B

CONTEMPORARY SPEECHES

OPPORTUNITIES FOR HISPANIC WOMEN
It's Up to Us
by Janice Payan (1990)

Thank you. I felt as if you were introducing someone else because my mind was racing back ten years, when I was sitting out there in the audience at the Adelante Mujer conference. Anonymous. Comfortable. Trying to relate to our "successful" speaker, but mostly feeling like Janice Payan, working mother, glad for a chance to sit down.

I'll let you in on a little secret. I still am Janice Payan, working mother. The only difference is that I have a longer job title, and that I've made a few discoveries these past ten years that I'm eager to share with you.

The fist is that keynote speakers at conferences like this are not some sort of alien creatures. Nor were they born under a lucky star. They are ordinary Hispanic women who have stumbled onto an extraordinary discovery.

And that is: Society has lied to us. We do have something up here! We can have not only a happy family but also a fulfilling career. We can succeed in school and work and community life, because the key is not supernatural powers, it is perseverance. Also known as hard work!

And God knows Hispanic women can do hard work!!! We've been working hard for centuries, from sun-up 'til daughter-down!

One of the biggest secrets around is that successful Anglos were not born under lucky stars, either. The chairman of my company, Jack MacAllister, grew up in a small town in eastern Iowa. His dad was a teacher; his mom was a mom. Jack worked, after school, sorting potatoes in the basement of a grocery store. Of course I realize, he could have been hoeing them, like our migrant workers.

Nevertheless, Jack came from humble beginnings. And so did virtually every other corporate officer I work with. The major advantage they had was living in a culture that allowed them to believe they would get ahead. So more of them did.

It's time for Hispanic women to believe we can get ahead, because we can. And because we must. Our families and workplaces and communities and nation need to reach our full potential. There are jobs to be done, children to be raised, opportunities to be seized. We must look at those opportunities, choose the ones we will respond to, and do something about them.

We must do so, for others. And we must do so, for ourselves. Yes, there are barriers. You're up against racism, sexism, and too much month at the end of the money. But so was any role model you choose.

Look at Patricia Diaz-Denis. Patricia was one of nine or ten children in a Mexican-American family that had low means, but high hopes. Her parents said Patricia should go to college. But they had no money. So, little by little, Patricia scraped up the money to send herself.

Her boyfriend was going to be a lawyer. And he told Patricia, "You should be a lawyer too, because nobody can argue like you do!" Well, Patricia didn't even know what a lawyer was, but she became one—so successful that she eventually was appointed to the Federal Communication Commission in Washington, D.C.

Or look at Toni Panteha, a Puerto Rican who grew up in a shack with dirt floors, no father, and often no food... But through looking and listening, she realized the power of community—the fact that people with very little, when working together, can create much.

Dr. Panteha has created several successful institutions in Puerto Rico, and to me, she is an institution. I can see the wisdom in her eyes, hear it in her voice, wisdom far beyond herself, like Mother Teresa.

Or look at Ada Kirby, a Cuban girl whose parents put her on a boat for Miami. Mom and Dad were to follow on the next boat, but they never arrived. So Ada grew up in an orphanage in Pueblo, and set some goals, and today is an executive director at U.S. West's research laboratories.

Each of these women was Hispanic, physically deprived, but mentally awakened to the possibilities of building a better world, both for others and for themselves.

Virtually every Hispanic woman in America started with a similar slate. In fact, let's do a quick survey. If you were born into a home whose economic status was something less than rich...please raise your hand.

It's a good thing I didn't ask the rich to raise their hands. I wouldn't have known if anyone was listening.

All right. So you were not born rich. As Patricia, Toni and Ada have shown us, it doesn't matter. It's the choices we make from there on, that make the difference.

If you're thinking, "that's easy for you to say, Payan," then I'm thinking: "little do you know..."

If you think I got where I am because I'm smarter than you, or have more energy than you, you're wrong.

If I'm so smart, why can't I parallel park?

If I'm so energetic, why do I still need eight hours of sleep a night?

And I mean need. If I hadn't had my eight hours last night, you wouldn't even want to hear what I'd be saying this morning!

I am more like you and you are more like me than you would guess.

I'm a third generation Mexican-American... born into a lower middle class family right here in Denver. My parents married young; she was pregnant. My father worked only about half the time during my growing-up years. He was short on education, skills, and confidence. There were drug and alcohol problems in the family. My parents finally sent my older brother to a Catholic high school, in hopes that would help him. They sent me to the same school to watch him. That was okay.

In public school I never could choose between the "Greasers" and the "Soshes." I wanted desperately to feel that I "belonged." But I did not like feeling that I had to deny my past to have a future.

Anybody here ever feel that way?

Anyway, the more troubles my brother had, the more I vowed to avoid them. So, in a way, he was my inspiration. As Viktor Frankl says, there is meaning in every life.

By the way, that brother died after returning from Vietnam.

I was raised with typical Hispanic female expectations. In other words: if you want to do well in life, you'd better... Can anybody finish that sentence?

Right!

Marry well.

I liked the idea of loving and marrying someone, but I felt like he should be more than a "meal ticket." And I felt like I should be more than a leech. I didn't want to feel so dependent.

So I set my goals on having a marriage, a family and a career. I didn't talk too much about those goals, so nobody told me they bordered on insanity for a Hispanic woman in the 1960s.

At one point, I even planned to become a doctor. But Mom and Dad said, "wait a minute. That takes something like 12 years of college."

I had no idea how I was going to pay for four years of college, let alone 12. But what scared me more than the cost was the time: In 12 years I'd be an old woman.

Time certainly changes your perspective on that.

My advice to you is, if you want to be a doctor, go for it!

You may be several years older when you finish, but by that time you'd be several years older if you don't finish college, too.

For all my suffering in high school, I finished near the top of my graduating class. I dreamed of attending the University of Colorado, at Boulder. You want to know what my counselor said? You already know. That I should go to business college for secretaries, at most.

But I went to the University of Colorado, anyway. I arranged my own financial aid: a small grant, a low paying job, and a big loan.

I just thank God that this was the era when jeans and sweatshirts were getting popular. That was all I had!

I'm going to spare you any description of my class work, except to say that it was difficult—and worth every painful minute. What I want to share with you is three of my strongest memories—and strongest learning experiences—which have nothing to do with books.

One concerns a philosophy professor who, I was sure, was a genius. What I liked best about this man was not the answers he had—but the questions. He asked questions about the Bible, about classic literature, about our place in the universe. He would even jot questions in the margins of our papers. And I give him a lot of credit for helping me examine my own life.

I'm telling you about him because I think each of us encounters people who make us think—sometimes painfully. And I feel, strongly, that we should listen to their questions and suffer through that thinking. We may decide everything in our lives is just like we want it. But we may also decide to change something.

My second big "non-book" experience was in UMAS—the United Mexican American Students. Lost in what seemed like a rich Anglo campus, UMAS was an island of familiarity: people who looked like me, talked like me, and felt like me.

We shared our fears and hopes and hurts—and did something about them. We worked hard to deal with racism on campus, persuading the university to offer Chicano studies classes. But the more racism we experienced, the angrier we became.

Some members made bombs. Two of those members died. And I remember asking myself: "Am I willing to go up in smoke over my anger? Or is there another way to make a difference?"

We talked a lot about this, and concluded that two wrongs don't make a right. Most of us agreed that working within the system was the thing to do. We also agreed not to deny our Hispanic heritage: not to become "coconuts"—brown on the outside and white on the inside—but to look for every opportunity to bring our culture to a table of many cultures.

That outlook has helped me a great deal as a manager, because it opened me to listening to all points of vies. And when a group is open to all points of view, it usually chooses the right course.

The third experience I wanted to share from my college days was the time they came nearest to ending prematurely. During my freshmen year, I received a call that my mother had been seriously injured in a traffic accident. Both of her legs were broken. So was her pelvis.

My younger brother and sister were still at home. My father was unemployed at the time, and I was off at college. So who do you think was elected to take on the housework? Raise your hand if you think it was my father.

No???

Does anybody think it was me?

I am truly amazed at your guessing ability.

Or is there something in our Hispanic culture that says the women do the housework?

Of course there is.

So I drove home from Boulder every weekend; shopped, cleaned, cooked, froze meals for the next week, did the laundry, you know the list. And the truth is it did not occur to me until some time later that my father could have done some of that. I had a problem, I was part of the problem.

I did resist when my parents suggested I should quit school It seemed better to try doing everything than to give up my dream. And it was the better choice. But it was also very difficult.

Which reminds me of another experience. Would it be too much like a soap opera if I told you about a personal crisis? Anybody want to hear a story about myself that I've never before told in public?

While still in college, I married my high school sweetheart. We were both completing our college degrees. My husband's family could not figure out why I was pursuing college instead of kids, but I was. However, it seemed like my schoolwork always came last.

One Saturday night I had come home form helping my Mom, dragged into our tiny married-student apartment, cooked a big dinner for my husband, and as I stood there washing the dishes, I felt a teardrop trickle down my face.

Followed by a flood.

Followed by sobbing.

Heaving.

If you ranked crying on a scale of 1 to 10, this was an 11.

My husband came rushing in with that... you know... that "puzzled-husband" look. He asked me what was wrong.

Well, it took me awhile to figure it out, to be able to put it into words. When I did they were 12 words:

"I just realized I'll be doing dishes the rest of my life."

Now, If I thought you'd believe me, I'd tell you my husband finished the dishes. He did not. But we both did some thinking and talking about roles and expectations, and, over the years, have learned to share the domestic responsibilities. We realized that we were both carrying a lot of old, cultural "baggage" through life.

And so are you.

I'm not going to tell you what to do about it. But I am going to urge you to realize it, think about it, and even to cry over the dishes, if you need to. You may be glad you did. As for me, what have I learned from all this?

I've learned, as I suggested earlier, that Hispanic women have bought into a lot of myths through the years. Or at least I did. And I want to tell you now, especially you younger women, the "five things I wish I had known" when I was 20, 25, even 30. In fact, some of these things I'm still learning at 37.

Now for that list of "five things I wish I had known."

First: I wish I had known that I—like most Hispanic women—was underestimating my capabilities.

When I first went to work for Mountain Bell, which has since become U.S. West Communications, I thought the "ultimate" job I could aspire to would be district manager. So I signed up for the courses I knew would help me achieve and handle that kind of responsibility. I watched various district managers, forming my own ideas of who was most effective—and why. I accepted whatever responsibilities and opportunities were thrown my way, generally preparing myself to be district manager.

My dream came true.

But then it almost became a nightmare. After only eighteen months on the job, the president of the company called me and asked me to go interview with his boss—the president of our parent company. And the next thing I knew, I had been promoted to a job above that of district manager.

Suddenly, I was stranded in unfamiliar territory. They gave me a big office at U.S. West headquarters down in Englewood, where I pulled all the furniture in one corner. In fact, I sort of made a little "fort." From this direction, I could hide behind the computer. From that direction, the plants. From over here, the file cabinet. Safe at last.

Until a friend from downtown came to visit me. She walked in, looked around, and demanded to know: "What is going on here? Why was your door closed? Why are you all scrunched up I the corner?"

I had all kinds of excuses.

But she said, "You know what I think? I think you're afraid you don't deserve this office!"

As she spoke, she started dragging the plants away from my desk. For a moment, I was angry. Then afraid. Then we started laughing, and I helped her stretch my furnishings—and my confidence.

And it occurred to me that had I pictured, from the beginning, that I could become an executive director, I would have been better prepared. I would have pictured myself in that big office. I would have spent more time learning executive public speaking. I would have done a lot of things. And I began to do them with my new, expanded vision of becoming an officer—which subsequently happened.

I just wish that I had known, in those early years, how I was underestimating my capabilities.

I suspect that you are, too.

And I wonder" What are you going to do about it?

Second: I wish I had known that power is not something others give you.

It is something that comes form within yourself... and which you can then share with others.

In 1984, a group of minority women at U.S. West got together and did some arithmetic to confirm what we already knew. Minority women were woefully under-represented in the ranks of middle and upper management. We had a better chance of winning the lottery. We gathered our courage and took our case to the top. Fortunately, we found a sympathetic ear. The top man told us to take our case to all the officers.

We did. But we were scared. And it showed. We sort of "begged" for time on their calendars. We apologized for interrupting their work. Asked for a little more recognition of our plight. And the first few interviews went terribly.

Then we realized: we deserve to be on their calendars as much as anyone else does. We realized that under-utilizing a group of employees is not an interruption of the officers' work—it is the officers' work. We realized that we should not be asking for help—we should be telling how we could help.

So we did.

And it worked. The company implemented a special program to help minority women achieve their full potential. Since then, several of us have moved into middle and upper management, and more are on the way.

I just wish we had realized, in the beginning, where power really comes from. It comes from within yourself... and you can then share with others.

I suspect you need to be reminded of that, too.

And I wonder: What are you going to do about it?

Third: I wish I had known that when I feel envious of others, I'm really just showing my lack of confidence in myself.

A few years ago, I worked closely with one of my co-workers in an employee organization. She is Hispanic. Confident. Outgoing. In fact, she's so likable I could hardly stand her !

But as we worked together, I finally realized: She has those attributes; I have others. And I had to ask myself: do I want to spend the time it would take to develop her attributes, or enjoy what we can accomplish by teaming up our different skills? I realized that is the better way .

I suspect that you may encounter envy from time to time.

And I wonder: What are you going to do about it?

Fourth: I wish I had realized that true success is never something you earn single-handed.

We hear people talk about "networking" and " community" and "team-building." What they mean is an extension of my previous idea: We can be a lot more effective working in a group than working alone.

This was brought home to me when I was president of my Hispanic employees' organization at U.S. West Communications. I wanted my administration to be the best. So I tried to do everything myself, to be sure it was done right. I wrote the newsletter, planned the fund-raiser, scheduled the meetings, booked the speakers, everything.

For our big annual meeting, I got the chairman of the company to speak. By then the other officers of the group were feeling left out. Come to think of it, they were left out.

Anyway, we were haggling over who got to introduce our big speaker. I was determined it should be me, since I so "obviously" had done all the work.

As it turned out, I missed the big meeting altogether. My older brother died. And I did a lot of painful thinking. For one thing: I was glad my team was there to keep things going while I dealt with my family crisis. But more important: I thought about life and death and what people would be saying if I had died.

Would I prefer they remember that "good ol' Janice sure did a terrific job of arranging every last detail of the meeting?" Or that "we really enjoyed working with her? Together, we did a lot."

All of us need to ask ourselves that question from time to time.

And I wonder: What are you going to do about it?

Hispanic women in America have been victims of racism, sexism, and poverty for a long, long time.

I know, because I was one of them. I also know that when you stop being a victim is largely up to you.

I don't mean you should run out of here, quit your job, divorce your husband, farm out your kids or run for President of the United States.

But I do mean that whatever you can dream, you can become.

A couple of years ago, I came across a poem by an Augsburg College student, Devoney K. Looser, which I want to share with you now.

I wish someone had taught me long ago
How to touch mountains
Instead of watching them from breathtakingly safe distances.
I wish someone had told me sooner
That cliffs are neither so sharp nor so distant nor so solid as they seemed.
I wish someone had told me years ago
That only through touching mountains can we reach peaks called beginnings, endings or exhilarating points of no return.
I wish I had learned earlier that ten fingers and the world shout more brightly from the tops of mountains
While life below only sighs with echoing cries.
I wish I had realized before today
That I can touch mountains
But now that I know, my fingers will never cease to climb

Please, my sisters, never, ever, cease to climb.

Adelante Mujer

INAUGURAL ADDRESS AS PRINCIPAL CHIEF OF THE CHEROKEE NATION
By: Wilma P. Mankiller (1992)

This extemporaneous speech was presented from notes and later transcribed and edited by Chief Mankiller's staff. It is used with permission from Chief Mankiller.

I'd like to thank Congressman Mike Synar for the very nice introduction. He has been a tremendous help to the Cherokee Nation during the time that I have been in office and we appreciate his leadership.

I'm sure that Deputy Chief John Ketcher and I, and this Tribal Council feel the same degree of gratitude to you who have supported us during this past election, either by voting for us, saying prayers for us, or just being there when we needed you. I also would like to express my personal gratitude for the support you have given me the last eight years I have been in office.

During the time, I have received a lot of honors and recognition, much of it undeserved. Much of it should have gone to the employees, to the Tribal Council, or to the citizens of the Cherokee Nation. But honors and awards are meaningless in comparison to the gratitude I feel and the tremendous honor that I feel when I think about the fact that you elected me to represent you and the Cherokee Nation. No honor I could have ever received in the past or in the future is greater than that honor. I appreciate that and will always remember it.

Today is a day for celebration, not just because we end one term of office and begin a new term. It's a time for celebration because the Cherokee Nation still has a strong, viable tribal government. Not only do we have a government that has continued to exist, but we have a tribal government that is progressing and getting stronger. We have managed to move forward in a very affirmative way. Given our history of adversity, I think it is a testament to our tenacity, individually and collectively, that we have been able to keep the Cherokee government's voice alive since time immemorial.

Basically, what we are doing is keeping the face of the Cherokee Nation government alive. At times in our history and most particularly around the turn of the century, that flame dimmed considerably. Many people have gone before us, some just completed serving, and the people we have elected today will tend that flame and make sure that the Cherokee Nation continues.

Around the turn of the century when there was a concerted attempt to abolish the Cherokee Nation, no one ever gave up the dream of having the Cherokee Nation revitalized. People would walk to each other's homes in the rural communities, people rode horses, they went to churches and went to ceremonial grounds, and met in little community groups, old men and women, and talked about ways to keep the government alive. And it worked.

Our people by many standards are outwardly very acculturated. People say we are very progressive. But I don't think any tribe in this country, no matter how traditional that tribe might be, has fought more valiantly or more passionately for the right to self-governance and tribal sovereignty than the Cherokee Nation. In fact, much of Indian law that other tribes rely on relative to tribal sovereignty is based on a Cherokee case that went to the U.S. Supreme Court.

After the tragic forced removal of our people from our homelands in the southeast, we had incredible devastation, bitter division, loss of lands, lives, government, economy, and everything we had ever known. When the last contingent arrived in April of 1839, we began immediately to establish a government for our people and a community. That's very important for those of us who are charged with that responsibility today to remember. Our ancestors fought valiantly to make sure that this government did survive.

The U.S. government promised us, in exchange for land and many lives in the southeast, that we could live here in Indian Territory without interference forever. Believing that, we began in 1839 to rebuild a strong viable Cherokee tribal government. We built schools, for both men and women. We built, in fact, the first schools west of the Mississippi, very remarkable first schools, Indian or non-Indian, west of the Mississippi. We built schools for the education of women, which was a very radical idea for the time. We re-established a judicial system in Indian Territory. We built beautiful institutions of government, some of which still stand today. They're now the oldest buildings in what is now Oklahoma. We printed newspapers in Cherokee and English. We built an economic system and began to rebuild our government.

Around the turn of the century our tribal government was again devastated, and the flame that I spoke about earlier was dimmed. When Oklahoma came into being, our tribal government was diminished significantly. Our schools were closed down. Our tribal judicial system was stopped. Most importantly to our people, land we had held in common was allotted out in individual allotments. The Allotment Act precipitated some of the worst cases of land abuse and land fraud in the history of Indian-U.S. relations which is well documented by Angie Debo's literature. Despite all that, our people clung to the idea of some sense of destiny and control over their lives and continued as a culturally distinct group of people and government.

From 1906 to 1971, the chiefs of the Cherokee Nation were appointed by the president of the United States. However, during this period there were always Cherokees meeting and talking about revitalizing the Cherokee government. In 1971 with the election of Chief W. W. Keeler, we saw the first step towards again revitalizing and rebuilding the Cherokee Nation.

The best argument I could make for the existence of tribal government is to compare where our people were in the last century when we, in essence, were more literate than our non-Indian neighbors to the period from 1906 to 1971, when there was no tribal government. By the time we had our first election after statehood in 1971, our people had some of the lowest education attainment scores in the state. They were living in dilapidated housing, without jobs, and were in very poor health. They had lost a sense of control over their lives as a result of external factors.

In 1971 when Chief Keeler began revitalizing the Cherokee Nation, he started it in a storefront here in Tahlequah. The tribe had very little income and resources, and in many cases none beyond what Chief Keeler would take out of his own pocket and use to help people. Since 1971, we have grown to the point that we now employ about 900 people. There is an annual budget of $52 million. We have forty separate organizations with volunteers working in various communities. We have begun to have an impact, at long last, in turning around some of the educational attainment levels. We have begun to have an impact on housing, health care, and many other issues. All the progress that we have made in the last twenty years has been by our own hard work and determination. Mike spoke about my hard work and determination, but I don't think that is a characteristic that I have by myself. I think it is a mark of the character of our people. Unlike some tribes, we didn't have marketable natural resources. Whatever we have done in the last twenty years, we've done through our own absolute determination to make sure that the Cherokee Nation existed and survived.

I wanted to share a little of our history with you because I think that it's important to put what is happening today in perspective. Those of us who were sworn in today, and who were elected, are temporary people. If you look at the totality of Cherokee history, we're not going to be here for a very long time. And it is our job to keep that flame going and to do everything within our power to make sure that we have a responsible and honest tribal government that you can be proud of, that listens to you and advocates for you. I also wanted to take a minute to remember all the people, our ancestors, and people that have gone before us who have worked here to preserve the Cherokee Nation. It is not just these people here on the stage who are responsible for the preservation of the Cherokee Nation. Its communities, its culture, and its heritage. It's up to all of us, every tribal member to take part in making sure that we survive into the 21ˢᵗ century as a culturally distinct group of people. Every Cherokee, whether full-blood or mixed-blood, whether rich or poor, whether liberal or conservative, has a responsibility to honor our ancestors by helping to keep our government, or communities and our people very strong.

The Cherokee Nation really is not, as people always seem to think, those buildings south of town or any of our field offices or the clinics. The Cherokee Nation is wherever Cherokee people are. That is the Cherokee Nation. The people are the Cherokee Nation.

My style of leadership, and what I hope I have brought to the Cherokee Nation, is to build communities, families, and people and not just build buildings and monuments. The words "tribal sovereignty" and "self-governance" are meaningless unless the people are actively involved and are able to participate in all aspects of the government.

And so today we celebrate this transition from one term of office to the next; the move from electing our Tribal Council at large to a system of electing our council by districts. And we should celebrate the fact that despite everything that has happened to us as a people we have indeed survived. We should celebrate the fact that we are here and we still have many attributes of our culture that are very strong.

If you look at the problems we've faced and are facing in their totality, it is almost overwhelming. We face a crisis in education. We face a crisis in health care, housing needs, jobs, and basic infrastructure. There are still people in our tribe who do not have the basic minimal services that all Americans, I think, should have. But we have never been better equipped to deal with all these issues and problems. We are equipped because we are positive and we believe in our people, and because we believe in our ability to have some control over our lives. We are equipped because we believe that we have reached a point where we have been able to start trusting our own thinking again. We have a professional staff, active community support, and a good set of newly elected tribal leaders who are ready to deal with all these issues in a very aggressive way.

During the last two decades with Chief Swimmer, Chief Keeler, and myself, we have made some headway in dealing with all these problems and I am proud to say that I have been a part of that. But I also think that we have a long, long way to go. So I would ask our staff, and our tribal members, and also the people who have been elected to recommit yourselves to grappling with these problems with as much force as you can. Let's really roll up our sleeves and try to turn them around. Let's use this next four years for activism, advocacy and hard work and see if we can really have an impact.

I would also ask the tribal employees, the tribal citizens, and the council to get out of their offices and out of their homes and talk with people. Learn what's going on in the communities. Listen to people. Interact with people. Get involved. Too often we hear from people who have an axe to grind or a complaint. Let's hear from people who want to do some volunteer work. Let's hear from people who want to provide some public service. Let's hear from people that want to join the team, and let's all hold hands, figuratively, and see what we can do to turn things around. We have made progress. I think we are an excellent organization. I am very proud to be associated with this organization. But we have to do more. We have to do more when we have the dropout rate we have. We have to do more when our people don't have access to health care that they need. We have to do more when we still have people in eastern Oklahoma who have to live in extremely poor housing or without indoor plumbing. That's unconscionable. And I don't think that we should stand for it. We should collectively figure out some way to do as much as we can and work as hard as we can to try to turn things around.

I also want to pay special tribute to the Delawares and the Shawnees who have come into our tribe by treaty. It is very difficult for a tribe which has its separate history, a separate language, and a separate culture to find their niche within the Cherokee Nation umbrella. The Delawares and Shawnees are led by competent, responsible, honest people. They are doing many things in collaboration with the Cherokee Nation. I spent a lot of time reaching out to those organizations because of their particular situation and working with them and I think it is very important to acknowledge that they are also part of the Cherokee Nation and the collective Cherokee family. And I am very proud of that.

Finally, I'd like to tell my family how much I appreciate their support and for all they have had to put up with. I've missed so many ball games, family reunions, and family dinners. I got an irate letter from a California Cherokee who was extremely upset because he had come to visit in Oklahoma and I hadn't seen him. In fact he said he hadn't seen me in six months. I wrote him a letter and told him that I haven't seen my mother in about three months. My family has been very forgiving of me for missing a lot of those things. I'd like to also especially thank my brother Don, who just a little more than a year ago donated a kidney to me. Without that I certainly wouldn't have been able to run for election and withstand the rigors of a campaign and then look forward to four more years in office.

I would like to thank all of you for taking the time to share this day with us. My feeling toward the Cherokee people is one of friendship and love. And that love and friendship has been returned to me a thousand fold over the past eight years. The relationship that I have developed with many of you and people everywhere has been one of the most rewarding things that has ever happened to me. I appreciate it, and I leave with you and give back to you a strong sense of friendship and love as we begin this new term. There is a lot of hard work to do. We're ready to do it in the most positive and forward thinking way we can.

I'd also like to congratulate the people here. I will say it again that working with this past council was unbelievable. It was an excellent Tribal Council and represents a tremendous loss of experience and diversity. The new council is going to have a hard act to follow, but I think it is up to the task. It's a group of people that I think that you will be proud of. With that, we are ready to go back to work. Thank you very much.

OUR FIRST AMENDMENT RIGHTS IN CYBERSPACE
by Senator Patrick Leahy (1996)
Delivered at the Media Institute Friends and Benefactors Banquet
October 22, 1996. Text taken from http://www. senate.gov/~leahy/g.htm

I am deeply honored to be the recipient of the Freedom of Speech Award. Long before I got the nickname "CyberSenator," and long before I ever began using the Internet, I was a confirmed Dead Head. Following John Perry Barlow to this podium is the closest I'll come to a Dead Head experience this year, so I'm doubly pleased to be here tonight.

Let me tell you another reason why this award has special meaning to me. My parents published a weekly newspaper and owned a printing business while I was growing up in Vermont. They instilled in me an enduring respect for the First Amendment and our rights to free speech, to practice the religion of our choice—or no religion at all—and to associate with whom we want. These rights are the surest footing for a sound democracy.

When a dynamic new technology like the Internet explodes onto the scene, some cultural indigestion is inevitable. The exhilarating freedom to speak that is part and parcel of the Internet invites more speech and more participation, and wherever there is such freedom, there will be some who abuse it. Computer technology and the Internet make it easier to gossip, search, collect and dispense personal information without knowledge or consent and to do it on an unprecedented scale.

What we need in the on-line world is to cultivate an ethic of self-restraint to check these temptations to invade privacy or to venture into other excesses. What the on-line world patently does not need are government restraints to limit speech freedom on the Internet.

Unfortunately, our free speech rights on the Internet have been under siege. The same Congress that promised to get government off our backs passed the Communications Decency Act to regulate on-line speech.

The CDA imposes far-reaching new federal criminal penalties on Americans for exercising their free speech rights on-line, including on the Internet. This law was recognized to be seriously flawed and unconstitutional every place but where it counted—in the Congress of the United States. And, it passed overwhelmingly.

Specifically, the Communications Decency Act penalizes with two-year jail terms and large fines any-one who transmits indecent material to a minor, or displays or posts indecent material in areas where a minor can see it.

An e-mail message to a teenager with a four-letter swear word would violate this law. So, too, would posting in a Usenet discussion group, on electronic bulletin boards, or in a chat room accessible to children, any quote from the racier parts of some of the great works of literature. Information on AIDS, birth control or prison rape could all be out of bounds on the Internet. Advertisements that would be perfectly legal in print could subject the advertiser to criminal liability if circulated online.

Of course, in the borderless world of the Internet, enforcement of the Communications Decency Act, or other speech restrictions, also presents stark practical problems. And then there is the definitional issue. The CDA targets speech that is either, quote, "indecent," or, quoting again, "patently offensive." What strikes some as "indecent" or "patently offensive" may look very different to others in another part of the country, let alone the world. Now, I might find some of the speeches that Phil Gramm gives on the Senate Floor to be patently offensive, quote, unquote, but some others would disagree with me about that. Given these cultural, social and regional differences, the end result is to leave in the hands of the most aggressive prosecutor in the least tolerant community the power to set standards for what every other Internet user may say on-line. This will have a significant chilling effect on all the speech that is put online, including the speech between consenting adults.

The myth is that Members of Congress passed the CDA because most do not use and do not understand the Internet. That was certainly part of it. There still are some policy makers here and there who think a computer monitor is simply a TV on the fritz!

Unfortunately, ignorance about the Internet is only a partial excuse. The First Amendment has always provided fertile ground for demagoguery and political posturing. Just look at the number of times Congress has voted on flag burning bans and on legislation to control the content of TV and cable programming.

The United States is certainly not alone in its efforts to censor the Internet. As the *Washington Post* opined yesterday, the governments of China, Singapore, Iran and Burma have all taken steps to maintain control of their citizens by controlling what their citizens may access on the Internet.

As these issues are raised and debated around the globe, the United States—with the oldest and most effective constitutional protections of free speech anywhere—is uniquely situated to provide cultural leadership in answering these questions.

The Internet is a home-grown American technology that has swept the world. Americans should take the high ground to protect the future of the Internet and fight censorship efforts springing up here at home and around the globe. Instead of championing the First Amendment, however, responses such as the Communications Decency Act trample the principles of free speech and free flow of information that have fueled the growth of democracy around the world.

Make no mistake, there is a global battle being waged over what the Internet will look like in the near and distant future. Many of the heroes of this battle have formed a coalition to make it easy for us to identify them. Organized by the Center for Democracy and Technology, America OnLine, the American Library Association, Microsoft, the Recording Industry Association of America and others, the Citizens Internet Empowerment Coalition won a stunning victory when the CDA was declared unconstitutional in Philadelphia in June. I was proud to support their effort with a declaration. We are all counting on them to win the case before the Supreme Court this term.

Even if we win this case—and my legislation to wipe the books clean of the CDA is then able to pass—the battle over First Amendment rights in Cyberspace will simply shift to other areas. For example, the debate over the extent to which we can engage in anonymous communications over the Internet looms as one of the future First Amendment battles in cyberspace.

The Supreme Court has made crystal clear that speaking anonymously is protected by the First Amendment and that "anonymity is a shield from the tyranny of the majority." Indeed, our freedom to speak anonymously on the Internet is one way to protect our privacy, and is particularly important for those Internet users who access sensitive information anonymously to avoid stigma or embarrassment.

Yet, a Justice Department official has testified that our ability to have anonymous communications in cyberspace poses problems for law enforcement that may generate proposals to restrict our ability to communicate anonymously over the Internet.

Vigilant defense of freedom of thought, opinion and speech will be crucially important as the Internet graduates from infancy and on to adolescence and maturity. Members of Congress each are sworn custodians of the Constitution during our brief terms in office. We were given a Bill of Rights that has served to protect our rights and speech for more than two centuries. We should provide no less to our children and grandchildren, who are growing up with computers and the Internet. For the Internet to fulfill its promise as a communications medium, we need to give it the full breadth of protection under the First Amendment.

AMERICAN HISPANIC POPULATION
Reaching New Heights, Seeking New Horizons
by SOL TRUJILO
President, CEO, US West Communication Group
Delivered to the U.S. Hispanic Chamber, Denver, Colorado, September 20, 1996.

Thank you, Sharon. Good morning and welcome to Denver for those of you from out of town. It's an honor to have the 17th Annual United States Hispanic Chamber of Commerce convention here in my new hometown. I'm happy to see so many of my old friends here today. It's also exciting to see so many new faces.

US WEST Communications has been a member of the USHCC from the beginning back in 1979. The growth and success since those early days have been extremely gratifying. I am proud of our association.

And of course that success is due to all of you, the entrepreneurs and small business owners being honored here this morning.

I must say I swell with pride and satisfaction at your accomplishments. Too many of us have been told... "You can't, you shouldn't, you won't." But many of you didn't listen or found a way over or under or around those obstacles and you did it! You can, you should, you will and you did!

So to all of you here today, let me say congratulations on your successes. I'd also like to thank you for your successes because your example will inspire more success.

You are sending a very strong message to other "would-be" entrepreneurs that they can because you did. And the "can-do" message is a very important message for us to deliver, especially to our young people.

These are exciting times. There's a lot of change in the air not just for the Hispanic Community, but for all Americans and especially for the business community.

I know it is early in the morning, but I would like to take a few minutes here to take a serious look at some of the larger issues that have brought us here today.

I've noted that this year's theme is "Reaching New Heights."

I would like to add a co-equal theme. Let's call it "Seeking New Horizons." Now let me tell you what I am thinking about here and I can do it like Stephen Covey, with Seven Basic Points.

Let's begin with the idea of "Reaching New Heights." That's a theme I can endorse. It has a forward spin. It sends a message to our young people and to the outside world that we have made tremendous progress and that we are reaching for more.

And we have made tremendous progress. Now, here is the first of my seven points:
Point #1: Our numbers are large and growing. That's important because numbers count in a democracy because people vote. And numbers count in business because people buy things.

So our increasing numbers give us growing influence in the polling booth and growing influence in the market place.

Let me just give one example: By the year 2010, experts predict that Hispanics will be the largest minority group in the U.S., with more than 20% of the nation's population. That's 1 of every 5 people.

America's Hispanic population by itself will be larger than most of America's major trading partners. In a nation governed by the principles of democratic capitals, those numbers represent a tremendous opportunity. We should use this opportunity wisely.

Point #2: Our success in the world of business is well established. I am not talking here only about Hispanic leaders who have made it to the Board Room or the executive suites of large corporations. That is happening. That is good. And it will happen at a faster rate in the future.

What I am talking about is explosion in the number of Hispanic owned businesses. The number of these small and midsized enterprises has more than doubled since 1987. These include:

An astonishing 76% growth from 1987 to 1992, from less than half a million (490,000) to nearly a million (863,000). And Jose Ninio tells me that the number will be close to 2 million by the year 2000.

In Los Angeles County alone, Latino-owned firms have increased by 700 percent over the past two decades, three times the over all Latino population growth rate. Statewide the number of Latino owned firms has exploded from around 70,000 in 1982 to an estimated 280,000 in 1996.

These numbers don't surprise me. I'll tell you why. I was the founding president of US West Small Business Services.

And it was during my days with the USW small business group that I first began to see the reality of these big numbers we all use. Every time I went out to meet customers I found hard working Hispanic entrepreneurs, trying to make things work in the world of business.

Some were what I call "Pilgrims"—people just looking for a new way of life. They weren't trying to start the next Hewlett Packard or the next Intel or Netscape. They were just trying to make a better living for themselves and their families, to buy a home, to send their kids to the community college or the university, to take care of their parents because those are the kinds of things that are important to our community.

I also encountered more than a few hard chargers. I call them "Swashbucklers." They were going to change the world, create new markets, get rich. And some I came to know will succeed. I'm sure of that.

So let's really try to understand what is happening in our community. The fact is we are a hard working people with a culture that values learning, loyalty, performance and personal responsibility.

Guess what! Those are precisely the qualities that are required to win in the New Economy and that's why our community is doing so well, by any measure, by any standard of comparison. And that is why "Reaching New Heights" is an appropriate theme because we can and we are doing it.

Point #3: The Hispanic community is a powerful and growing economic force. Hispanic purchasing power has quadrupled since 1980, going from about $53 billion to more than $195 billion. Again, Jose says it will be over $200 billion by the year 2000.

That level of purchasing power exceeds the Gross State Product of the entire state of Michigan or Massachusetts. It's almost three Colorados!

Hispanic purchasing power is nearly double the GDP of Argentina and is larger than every other nation in Central and South America with the single exception of Brazil

Growing numbers of business people in the U.S. understand these numbers. They know how important our market is. We also need to understand how important it is and see it as a source of strength and self-confidence. Why? Because a free market will respond to a market of our size and wealth with products and services that we need and want.

Point #4: Our prospects are good. More Hispanics are graduating from high school.

More are going to college or other institutions that provide post-secondary education. The U.S. Department of Labor has predicted that the growth of the Hispanics in the workplace will be up by more than one-third (37%) by the year 2005. Once again, we are reaching new heights, and that's the way it should be.

So, as you can see, I am in agreement with your primary theme, "Reaching New Heights."

But let's talk for a minute about "Seeking New Horizons." I want to do this because I believe we need to look out beyond ourselves and beyond our community.

Let me be frank. Sometimes, I think we spend too much time looking inward. Too much time talking about ourselves and our community. Too much time thinking about our problems in the world when we should be engaging in the larger world, making things happen for our families, our businesses and our community.

Every community has problems. But whatever our problems may be, we have a history of achievement and a supportive culture that tells us that we can make things work especially in the New Economy in which we find ourselves.

So, when I talk about "Seeking New Horizons," I am thinking about all the things that are going on out there and the opportunities they create for us. Let me just tick off a few to finish my Seven Points.

Point #5: America is a strong family based entrepreneurial economy.

There are 22 million business enterprises in the U.S.

Only14,000 have more than 500 employees.

The other 21 million plus are sole proprietorships, partnerships, and small and midsized business enterprises.

This is a world where we have already succeeded. We need to work hard to give our young people the confidence so they, too, can succeed.

And we need to look at our own business practices and see what we can do to create new opportunities for ourselves and our kids. Let me give you an example.

When I was head of small business for USW, I also established a Small Office/Home Office market unit. We called it the "SOHO group." Its purpose is to serve the growing numbers of Americans who work at home. Today, 41 million people work at home some time during the week and more than 12 million work at home full time.

These so-called SOHO workers include many in our community and they have many problems that are created by people like us, you and me not just people "out there."

Let me give you some examples. If you are a SOHO worker and part of the most rapidly growing segment of our domestic economy your problems are endless. They include:

- bankers who are reluctant to give loans
- merchant accounts are hard to come by
- difficulties leasing anything; space, copiers and other equipment.
- office supply stores won't give credit
- temp agencies won't send people
- insurance companies won't insure
- zoning laws won't permit home offices
- neighborhood covenants won't permit FedEx or other delivery trucks
- telephone companies are often required by government tariffs to charge you more for a phone that is also used for business purposes.

Now, these are all problems that many in this room can do something about. But first we have to wake up to the new world out there, a new world that includes new ways of living and working that requires each of us to change how we do business

We all must keep up with the change. General Electric CEO Jack Welch once said, "When the rate of change on the outside begins to exceed the rate of change on the inside, the end is in sight."

That is a good warning for each of us, for all our businesses and many entrepreneurs in our community are facing obstacles because we, as business leader, haven't changed our business practices to keep up with changes in the market place. The result? We hurt our business and we hurt our community.

Point #6: International commerce is a key feature of America's New Economy and is a major opportunity for the Hispanic community.

I know it's fashionable in some quarters both on the Left and on the Right to question the value of America's overseas trade. The enemies of trade call it "globalization." But, believe me, that is a short sighted view for Americans and especially Hispanic Americans.

Let me just give you some numbers to put things into perspective: how many people know that global trade has grown from less than $100 billion in 1945 to more than $4.0 trillion, that exports represent the most rapidly growing marketplace for American goods and services, and that exports create jobs as each $1.0 billion of exports creates 19,000 to 24,000 jobs depending on the industry; how many people realize that the U.S. is the largest trading nation in the world, not Japan or Germany, and that much or our post-WWII prosperity and economic power has been because of our pre-eminent trade position?

How many people realize that export jobs are growing at twice the rate of jobs in the rest of the domestic economy; and that export jobs are good jobs because export jobs pay about 17% more than domestic economy jobs.

How many people realize that NAFTA has been a huge success, serving to stabilize trade volatility between the U.S. and Mexico at a time of severe economic crisis in Mexico.

And, let's not forget, as Mexico recovers and increases its standard of living there will be reduced pressures for illegal immigration.

And let us also remember that Mexico's prosperity will also lead to increased trade with the outside would and especially with the Pacific Rim and that large volumes of that trade will be moved on an inter-modal land bridge that extends from Los Angeles to Brownsville, Texas and includes important border gateways such as San Diego, Nogales, El Paso, and Laredo.

Bottom line: All Americans, and not the least Hispanic Americans, have a big stake in the success of NAFTA and the success of Mexico. So far, I believe, we are on the right course.

And let's also understand that the expanding global marketplace also includes small and midsized companies, where Hispanics have been very successful. Example: In 1970, 805 of U.S. exports came form less than 1.0% of its companies; companies like Boeing, General Electric, General Motors and Caterpillar. No longer.

A recent Department of Commerce report shows that 50% of U.S. exports measured by dollar value are now achieved by companies under 500 employees.

A report by MIT's business guru David Birch shows that, measured by exporters (i.e., the size of company doing the exporting), 50% of U.S. exports are by companies under 100 employees and in some Western states it gets as high as 81%.

These studies clearly show for the U.S. the rapidly increasing role of small and medium sized business in international trade.

So, what's the punch line? It's this: There are huge opportunities for export growth by small and midsized enterprises (SMEs) and especially for Hispanic owned SMEs run by people who speak the language and share the culture of potential customers in the second most rapidly growing market in the world: the 500 million people who live in Mexico and in Central and South America, nearly all of whom speak Spanish and share our culture.

And there is another important lesson I learned when I was head of small business, and it is this: The biggest international trade problems of small business are things like letters of credit, paperwork, compliance with international quality standards, etc. I call this know-how.

The second is strategic intelligence, mostly about new market opportunities or new technologies that could make an enterprise more productive, and the third is access to international contacts and networks. I call this know-who.

Now stop and think about it. Almost every one of these challenges is a problem that can be addressed through cooperation, through a group like a local Hispanic chamber or World Trade Center or partnership with a larger business. My point is this. Even in seemingly esoteric areas like international commerce, we can solve our own problems if we just call on the institutional and other resources that we already have at our disposal.

Point #7: Since we are in a political season, let's also note that not all minorities share the same political beliefs.

I think it is interesting and noteworthy that Hispanics have not allowed themselves to be coopted by either of the two major political parties. Many of us vote Democrat. A lot of us vote Republican. Too many of us do not vote al all.

But I think we have gained strength by playing the game of American politics the way the Anglos play: We vote our interests and our perspectives. And in the process, we are courted by both parties.

And we do have many different interests, as business people and different perspectives as Hispanics.

Some of us, more than 60 percent, are Mexican-Americans.

Others (13) are Puerto Ricans or Cubans (5%).

The rest of us, about 20% all together come from Central and South America or Spain.

But we still share a language, and we all share a culture that values, as Congressman Bill Richardson has said, "a work-hard mentality, pride, self-reliance, intact families, church, neighborhood."

We have contacts throughout the world, in a world that increasingly rewards energy, connections and hard work.

So, what's the bottom line? It's this. Some of our leaders and much of the media focus on the problems in our community. But we have a lot going for us on the asset side of the page. That's why I appreciate the opportunity you've given me today to look at the asset side. I think we need to do that more.

I am not a Pollyanna. I know there is a liability side of the page, and I am ready to tackle tough problems that we face in the community.

But let me tell you this: Bad cases make bad law. As Franklin Roosevelt said in his First Inaugural, "Where there is no vision, the people will perish."

We need to spend more time on our vision. We need to spend more time on the "good cases." We need to look outward, to new horizons and new possibilities in order to make things better where it really counts: in our homes and communities.

Most importantly, we need to identify and celebrate the "good cases" as a legacy to our children, to the next generation, so that their success and their achievements can exceed ours. That's the real test of success for Hispanic Americans.

Thank you for listening. I am deeply honored by your invitation to come here today. And I am very proud of the achievements you represent.

A MESSAGE TO SADDAM HUSSEIN
United States Senate
by Senator Bob Torricelli (1997)

Mr. President, almost 10 years ago I had an opportunity in visiting Baghdad to meet with Saddam Hussein and members of his cabinet.

I went to Iraq because of a brutal and seemingly endless conflict between the armies of Iran and Iraq that were consuming hundreds of thousands of lives. Like many people in our Government, I was concerned about how this would impact the region, and whether, indeed, it threatened world peace. I left Baghdad with unmistakable impressions of Saddam Hussein who continued to influence my own judgment, and which I revisit now that we are on the verge of yet another conflict with the army of Iraq.

President Hussein knew little of the Western World, and profoundly misunderstood the United States. Because we are a good and a decent people willing to engage in dialogue, it was interpreted as a lack of resolve; a failure of will.

It was for these reasons when President Bush sent American forces to the Persian Gulf that I was proud as a Member of the House of Representatives to be the Democratic sponsor of the war resolution.

In the years since American men and women triumphed in the Persian Gulf War to uphold the will of the United Nations and serve the best traditions of our country, the Saddam Hussein that I met on that day has not only not changed; he remarkably seems to have learned very little.

His rape and pillage of Kuwait is now known to have included not simply combatants but thousands of innocent Kuwaiti citizens. Six years after his retreat from Kuwait he continues to hold 620 unaccounted for Kuwaiti civilians. Upon his retreat he torched the land with oil fires and sullied the water, creating the largest oilspill and oil fires in history.

In 1988, he employed mustard gas against his own people killing more than 5,000 Kurds.

The Saddam Hussein that America met in the Persian Gulf War was not an isolated departure from good judgment. It was part of a long record of brutality against his own people and his neighbors.

Today we are on the verge of yet another conflict with Saddam Hussein, because not only is there a long tradition of such irresponsible international behavior but because nothing seemingly has changed.

In 1992, he violated the terms of the gulf war cease-fire by moving antiaircraft missiles into northern and southern Iraq. The world responded. The coalition held. And more than 100 United States, British, and French planes fired on missile stations.

A year later—in 1993—still not having learned the price of his misjudgments, Saddam Hussein ordered an attempt on the life of former President George Bush. President Bush was visiting Kuwait. Not only was Saddam Hussein not humbled in the face of the victor; he planned an assassination leading to an American military response against his intelligence headquarters.

In 1994, he sent battalions of Iraqis 20 miles north of the Kuwaiti border. Again, the United States needed to respond and 40,000 troops were again sent to the Persian Gulf.

And, last year, despite a willingness by the United Nations to begin easing sanctions in order to ease the pain on the Iraqi people in a food for oil program that was instituted, Saddam Hussein responded by military attack against the Kurds in the town of Erbil needing a response with the oil for food program.

There are few comparisons in contemporary history of any leader in any government that has so routinely miscalculated at the disadvantage of his government and himself.

The Saddam Hussein that I met a decade ago may not have understood much about the world, or his place in it, the relative power of his country as opposed to potential adversaries, the use of technology, his measure of international will—his misunderstanding of the United States may have been legendary—but it is almost unbelievable that with these annual confrontations, this extraordinary record of miscalculations, that virtually nothing seems to have been learned.

What more is necessary to be understood about the resolve of the United States? This Government is clearly prepared to pay the price to maintain the peace in the Middle East. This country has a deep determination to deny Saddam Hussein every and all classes of weapons of mass destruction.

The United States will provide leadership for international response when necessary, but clearly is both capable and willing to act unilaterally if required.

What is it, Saddam Hussein, that you do not understand about the world resolve? And what is it about us that could still be unclear?

Last month, this long and extraordinary record of miscalculation added yet another chapter. Saddam Hussein barred access to U.N. weapons inspectors under the pretext that they included American citizens. He challenged the right of the United States to be a part of the inspection teams of the United Nations, and asked rhetorically by what right we would be present.

Saddam Hussein, it comes to mind that the United States has about 500,000 reasons why we have a right to participate and will demand full compliance—a reason for every man and woman that left family, friends and home to put their lives on the line in the Persian Gulf war to end your occupation of Kuwait. And those 500,000 reasons have not yet run their course. They will stand for a long time.

The record since the United Nations began the inspections to ensure compliance with its resolutions has not been without success.

Since 1991, U.N. inspectors have found and destroyed more illegal weapons in Iraq than were destroyed during the entire Persian Gulf war. Surveillance cameras to monitor weapons activities were installed. This is a regime imposed by the United Nations of weapons inspection that has and can yield real results. But, as we now stand on the verge of yet another military confrontation, it is necessary to face the unmistakable and painful truth that there is no reason to believe that anything has changed in Baghdad.

This week, the *Washington Times* revealed that Saddam Hussein has been intending to buy five electronic warfare systems that would allow him to detect and destroy radar-evading aircraft.

The weapons markets of the world have routinely been contacted by Iraqi agents and representatives still seeking military technology.

This is important lest we fail to understand that the strategy of frustrating U.N. inspectors and noncompliance is not happening in a vacuum. It is part of an ongoing strategy to restore military capability.

The lessons of the Persian Gulf war and our experience through our sacrifices have yielded more than simply the destruction of these weapons. There is another great lesson that the Persian Gulf war has left the United States, the United Nations and the international community. It is, first, that the international community is capable of acting in concert for common purpose, but it is also that there is by definition a class of nations with leaders who are easily identifiable who are so irresponsible by their actions, who act in such contempt of international normal standards of conduct and international law that the international community will take it upon itself to deny them aspects of their own sovereignty.

Of all the things that Saddam Hussein failed to learn about us and our resolve and our capability or the international community's ability to act in concert it is the single lesson that is the foundation of the current crisis. Saddam Hussein will not be allowed to have weapons of mass destruction or wage war on his own people or regain great military capability because as a consequence of the Persian Gulf War and the invasion of Kuwait, the international community has decided to deny him that sovereign right of other nations to possess certain weapons and conduct their own affairs today, tomorrow and potentially forever.

It is not only a lesson of the Persian Gulf war; it is a gift of this generation to succeeding generations that something has been learned by the history of the 20th century. And the primary pupil of this lesson will be Saddam Hussein, in life or in death, today or tomorrow, one way or another.

I know every Member of this Senate, indeed, the entire U.S. Government, is in prayerful hope that military confrontation is avoided. In an age when military weapons hold such power and the destructive capability is so great, conflict must always be avoided when possible. That is our nature. It speaks well of our people that this is our resolve.

Saddam Hussein, with so many miscalculations, so many mistakes that caused so much harm for your people, do not miscalculate again.

There is in this Senate, I know, nothing but affection for the people of Iraq, an abiding hope that there will be a day when not only we can meet them again in friendship but the members of this Senate may vote to send an ambassador of good intention and good will to Baghdad to normalize relations. Between this day and that is either the learning of a fundamental lesson by Saddam Hussein against all odds and all experience or that the people of Iraq take their future in their hands against extraordinary odds and regain responsible leadership.

I do not know, Mr. President, how this crisis will be resolved. Indeed, no one could predict. Only that somehow we be understood and that somehow the United Nations obtain the strength and resolve to see its judgments fulfilled. All the frustration of these years and all the sacrifice from the international community can still have real meaning if this lesson will be learned not simply by Saddam Hussein but by all the dictators, all the despots to come who would abuse their people and wage war. If we can stand together here, finally have the lesson learned, all this will have had real meaning.

Mr. President, I yield the floor.

APPENDIX C

FORMS

📁 Speech Outlines & Resource Information Forms

📁 Students Interest Inventory

📁 Speech Critique Form (any kind of speech)

📁 Informative Speech Forms (2)

📁 Persuasive Speech Forms (2)

📁 Peer Speech Evaluation

📁 Panel Discussion Evaluation Form

📁 Symposium Evaluation Form

📁 Student Congress (Resolution and Bill Forms)

📁 Individual Speaking Event Ballot

📁 Debate Ballot

Construct a neat, complete sentence outline on this sheet and hand it to your instructor when you rise to speak. Your instructor may wish to write criticisms of the outline and speech in the margins.

Type of speech:_____Name:_____

Number of words in outline:_____Date:_____

Purpose of this speech: (What do you want your audience to learn, to think, to believe, to feel, or do because of this speech?)

_____

_____

TITLE:

INTRODUCTION:

BODY:

CONCLUSION:

Instructor's comments may concern choice of topic, development of ideas, organization, language use, personal appearance, posture, physical activity, sources, and improvement.

(Write sources of information on back of sheet.)

SOURCES FROM LITERATURE

Fill out sources' requirements completely. Write "none listed" if an author's name or copyright date is not listed.

1. Author's name_____

   Title of book or magazine used_____

   Title of article in above book or magazine _____

   Chapter and/or pages read_____

   Date of above publication_____

2. Author's name_____

   Title of book or magazine used_____

   Title of article in above book or magazine _____

   Chapter and/or pages read_____

   Date of above publication_____

3. Author's name_____

   Title of book or magazine used_____

   Title of article in above book or magazine_____

   Chapter and/or pages read _____

   Date of above publication_____

INTERVIEW SOURCES

1. Person interviewed_____Date of interview_____

   Position, occupation, and location_____

   Why is he/she a reliable source? Be specific._____

_____

2. Person interviewed_____Date of interview_____

   Position, occupation, and location_____

   Why is he/she a reliable source? Be specific._____

_____

PERSONAL EXPERIENCE OF SPEAKER

1. Tell (1) when, (2) where, and (3) the conditions under which you became an authority on subject matter in your

speech:_____

_____

SPEECH OUTLINE

Construct a neat, complete sentence outline on this sheet and hand it to your instructor when you rise to speak. Your instructor may wish to write criticisms of the outline and speech in the margins.

Type of speech:_____Name:_____

Number of words in outline:_____Date:_____

Purpose of this speech: (What do you want your audience to learn, to think, to believe, to feel, or do because of this speech?)

_____

_____

TITLE:

INTRODUCTION:

BODY:

CONCLUSION:

Instructor's comments may concern choice of topic, development of ideas, organization, language use, personal appearance, posture, physical activity, sources, and improvement.

(Write sources of information on back of sheet.)

SOURCES FROM LITERATURE

Fill out sources' requirements completely. Write "none listed" if an author's name or copyright date is not listed.

1. Author's name_____

   Title of book or magazine used_____

   Title of article in above book or magazine _____

   Chapter and/or pages read_____

   Date of above publication_____

2. Author's name_____

   Title of book or magazine used_____

   Title of article in above book or magazine _____

   Chapter and/or pages read_____

   Date of above publication_____

3. Author's name_____

   Title of book or magazine used_____

   Title of article in above book or magazine_____

   Chapter and/or pages read _____

   Date of above publication_____

INTERVIEW SOURCES

1. Person interviewed_____Date of interview_____

   Position, occupation, and location_____

   Why is he/she a reliable source? Be specific._____

   _____

2. Person interviewed_____Date of interview_____

   Position, occupation, and location_____

   Why is he/she a reliable source? Be specific._____

   _____

PERSONAL EXPERIENCE OF SPEAKER

1. Tell (1) when, (2) where, and (3) the conditions under which you became an authority on subject matter in your

speech:_____

_____

SPEECH OUTLINE

Construct a neat, complete sentence outline on this sheet and hand it to your instructor when you rise to speak. Your instructor may wish to write criticisms of the outline and speech in the margins.

Type of speech:_____Name:_____

Number of words in outline:_____Date:_____

Purpose of this speech: (What do you want your audience to learn, to think, to believe, to feel, or do because of this speech?)

_____

_____

TITLE:

INTRODUCTION:

BODY:

CONCLUSION:

Instructor's comments may concern choice of topic, development of ideas, organization, language use, personal appearance, posture, physical activity, sources, and improvement.

(Write sources of information on back of sheet.)

SOURCES FROM LITERATURE
Fill out sources' requirements completely. Write "none listed" if an author's name or copyright date is not listed.

1. Author's name_____

   Title of book or magazine used_____

   Title of article in above book or magazine _____

   Chapter and/or pages read_____

   Date of above publication_____

2. Author's name_____

   Title of book or magazine used_____

   Title of article in above book or magazine _____

   Chapter and/or pages read_____

   Date of above publication_____

3. Author's name_____

   Title of book or magazine used_____

   Title of article in above book or magazine_____

   Chapter and/or pages read _____

   Date of above publication_____

INTERVIEW SOURCES

1. Person interviewed_____Date of interview_____

   Position, occupation, and location_____

   Why is he/she a reliable source? Be specific._____

   _____

2. Person interviewed_____Date of interview_____

   Position, occupation, and location_____

   Why is he/she a reliable source? Be specific._____

   _____

PERSONAL EXPERIENCE OF SPEAKER

1. Tell (1) when, (2) where, and (3) the conditions under which you became an authority on subject matter in your

speech:_____

_____

SPEECH OUTLINE

Construct a neat, complete sentence outline on this sheet and hand it to your instructor when you rise to speak. Your instructor may wish to write criticisms of the outline and speech in the margins.

Type of speech:_____Name:_____

Number of words in outline:_____Date:_____

Purpose of this speech: (What do you want your audience to learn, to think, to believe, to feel, or do because of this speech?)

_____

_____

TITLE:

INTRODUCTION:

BODY:

CONCLUSION:

Instructor's comments may concern choice of topic, development of ideas, organization, language use, personal appearance, posture, physical activity, sources, and improvement.

(Write sources of information on back of sheet.)

SOURCES FROM LITERATURE

Fill out sources' requirements completely. Write "none listed" if an author's name or copyright date is not listed.

1. Author's name_____

   Title of book or magazine used_____

   Title of article in above book or magazine _____

   Chapter and/or pages read_____

   Date of above publication_____

2. Author's name_____

   Title of book or magazine used_____

   Title of article in above book or magazine _____

   Chapter and/or pages read_____

   Date of above publication_____

3. Author's name_____

   Title of book or magazine used_____

   Title of article in above book or magazine_____

   Chapter and/or pages read _____

   Date of above publication_____

INTERVIEW SOURCES

1.Person interviewed_____Date of interview_____

   Position, occupation, and location_____

   Why is he/she a reliable source? Be specific._____

_____

2.Person interviewed_____Date of interview_____

   Position, occupation, and location_____

   Why is he/she a reliable source? Be specific._____

_____

PERSONAL EXPERIENCE OF SPEAKER

1.Tell (1) when, (2) where, and (3) the conditions under which you became an authority on subject matter in your

speech:_____

_____

SPEECH OUTLINE

Construct a neat, complete sentence outline on this sheet and hand it to your instructor when you rise to speak. Your instructor may wish to write criticisms of the outline and speech in the margins.

Type of speech:_____Name:_____

Number of words in outline:_____Date:_____

Purpose of this speech: (What do you want your audience to learn, to think, to believe, to feel, or do because of this speech?)

_____

_____

TITLE:

INTRODUCTION:

BODY:

CONCLUSION:

Instructor's comments may concern choice of topic, development of ideas, organization, language use, personal appearance, posture, physical activity, sources, and improvement.

(Write sources of information on back of sheet.)

SOURCES FROM LITERATURE

Fill out sources' requirements completely. Write "none listed" if an author's name or copyright date is not listed.

1. Author's name_____

   Title of book or magazine used_____

   Title of article in above book or magazine _____

   Chapter and/or pages read_____

   Date of above publication_____

2. Author's name_____

   Title of book or magazine used_____

   Title of article in above book or magazine _____

   Chapter and/or pages read_____

   Date of above publication_____

3. Author's name_____

   Title of book or magazine used_____

   Title of article in above book or magazine_____

   Chapter and/or pages read _____

   Date of above publication_____

INTERVIEW SOURCES

1. Person interviewed_____Date of interview_____

   Position, occupation, and location_____

   Why is he/she a reliable source? Be specific._____

   _____

2. Person interviewed_____Date of interview_____

   Position, occupation, and location_____

   Why is he/she a reliable source? Be specific._____

   _____

PERSONAL EXPERIENCE OF SPEAKER

1. Tell (1) when, (2) where, and (3) the conditions under which you became an authority on subject matter in your

speech:_____

_____

SPEECH OUTLINE

Construct a neat, complete sentence outline on this sheet and hand it to your instructor when you rise to speak. Your instructor may wish to write criticisms of the outline and speech in the margins.

Type of speech:_____Name:_____

Number of words in outline:_____Date:_____

Purpose of this speech: (What do you want your audience to learn, to think, to believe, to feel, or do because of this speech?)

_____

_____

TITLE:

INTRODUCTION:

BODY:

CONCLUSION:

Instructor's comments may concern choice of topic, development of ideas, organization, language use, personal appearance, posture, physical activity, sources, and improvement.

(Write sources of information on back of sheet.)

SOURCES FROM LITERATURE

Fill out sources' requirements completely. Write "none listed" if an author's name or copyright date is not listed.

1. Author's name_____

   Title of book or magazine used_____

   Title of article in above book or magazine _____

   Chapter and/or pages read_____

   Date of above publication_____

2. Author's name_____

   Title of book or magazine used_____

   Title of article in above book or magazine _____

   Chapter and/or pages read_____

   Date of above publication_____

3. Author's name_____

   Title of book or magazine used_____

   Title of article in above book or magazine _____

   Chapter and/or pages read _____

   Date of above publication_____

INTERVIEW SOURCES

1. Person interviewed_____Date of interview_____

   Position, occupation, and location_____

   Why is he/she a reliable source? Be specific._____

   _____

2. Person interviewed_____Date of interview_____

   Position, occupation, and location_____

   Why is he/she a reliable source? Be specific._____

   _____

PERSONAL EXPERIENCE OF SPEAKER

1. Tell (1) when, (2) where, and (3) the conditions under which you became an authority on subject matter in your

   speech:_____

   _____

SPEECH OUTLINE

Construct a neat, complete sentence outline on this sheet and hand it to your instructor when you rise to speak. Your instructor may wish to write criticisms of the outline and speech in the margins.

Type of speech:_____Name:_____

Number of words in outline:_____Date:_____

Purpose of this speech: (What do you want your audience to learn, to think, to believe, to feel, or do because of this speech?)
_____

_____

TITLE:

INTRODUCTION:

BODY:

CONCLUSION:

Instructor's comments may concern choice of topic, development of ideas, organization, language use, personal appearance, posture, physical activity, sources, and improvement.

(Write sources of information on back of sheet)

SOURCES FROM LITERATURE

Fill out sources' requirements completely. Write "none listed" if an author's name or copyright date is not listed.

1. Author's name_____

   Title of book or magazine used_____

   Title of article in above book or magazine _____

   Chapter and/or pages read_____

   Date of above publication_____

2. Author's name_____

   Title of book or magazine used_____

   Title of article in above book or magazine _____

   Chapter and/or pages read_____

   Date of above publication_____

3. Author's name_____

   Title of book or magazine used_____

   Title of article in above book or magazine_____

   Chapter and/or pages read _____

   Date of above publication_____

INTERVIEW SOURCES

1. Person interviewed_____Date of interview_____

   Position, occupation, and location_____

   Why is he/she a reliable source? Be specific._____

   _____

2. Person interviewed_____Date of interview_____

   Position, occupation, and location_____

   Why is he/she a reliable source? Be specific._____

   _____

PERSONAL EXPERIENCE OF SPEAKER

1. Tell (1) when, (2) where, and (3) the conditions under which you became an authority on subject matter in your

speech:_____

_____

STUDENT'S INTEREST INVENTORY
(Complete this at the beginning of the course and use it to help you develop speech topic ideas).

1. Where have you lived since you were born?

_____

_____

2. What interesting places have you visited?

_____

_____

3. What musical instruments do you play?

_____

_____

4. What sports events do you view or participate in?

_____

_____

5. What is your family's ethnic background?

_____

6. What customs (holiday or otherwise) are unique to your family's ethnic background?

_____

_____

7. What do you do in your spare time?

_____

_____

8. What skills do you have? (computer software design, repairing cars, sewing, etc.)

_____

_____

9. What historical event do you want to know more about?

_____

_____

10. What invention or machine would you like to understand how it works?

_____

_____ (over)

11. What is the biggest problem you think is facing individuals your age?

_____

_____

12. What is the biggest problem facing your school?

_____

_____

13. What is the biggest problem facing your city, town, or area?

_____

_____

14. What is the biggest problem facing your country?

_____

_____

15. What is the biggest problem facing the world?

_____

_____

16. What is one topic on which you enjoy arguing your point of view?

_____

_____

17. What is something you could teach someone else about?

_____

_____

18. What is the most difficult decision you ever had to make?

_____

_____

19. What is the most humorous memory you have?

_____

_____

20. What would you like to talk about that people have to listen to?

_____

_____

SPEECH CRITIQUE FORM
(Any type of speech)

TYPE OF SPEECH_____

NAME _____

TOPIC _____

	Needs Work	Good	Excellent	Comments

1. ORGANIZATION

	Needs Work	Good	Excellent	Comments
Introduction				
Body clearly organized				
Conclusion				

2. DELIVERY

	Needs Work	Good	Excellent	Comments
Proper posture				
Appropriate gestures				
Appropriate rate & volume				
Poise				
Eye contact				

3. CONTENT

	Needs Work	Good	Excellent	Comments
Use of supporting material				
Appropriate for assignment				
Appropriate language				
Adapted to the audience				

COMMENTS:

GRADE_____

SPEECH EVALUATION FORM: Informative Speech

NAME_____   TOTAL POINTS/GRADE_____

TOPIC _____

Criteria	Comments
I. Topic: A. Original B. Appropriate for purpose and audience C. Substantive D. Narrowed sufficiently	
II. Introduction: A. Captured attention B. Stated thesis C. Related topic to audience D. Established credibility E. Previewed main points F. Provided transition to body	

III. Body:
 	
A. Organized main points effectively
B. Included transitions between main points
C. Included adequate supporting materials
in terms of:
    1. Relevance to audience
    2. Number of sources
    3. Identification of sources
    4. Ability to accomplish purpose
D. Used visual aids appropriately
    1. Clear explanations
    2. Neat, easy-to-see design
    3. Relevant to purpose and audience
E. Used language appropriate to:
    1. Topic
    2. Audience	

(over)

IV. **Conclusion:**

    A. Restated thesis
    B. Summarized main points
    C. Ended with a memorable final thought

V. **Delivery:**

    A. Used adequate and inclusive eye contact
    B. Used effective vocal delivery (appropriate rate and volume, clear articulation, varied inflection, and no vocal fillers)
    C. Used effective physical delivery (posture, gestures, movement)
    D. Contributed to credibility by emphasizing speaker's sincerity, confidence, and dynamism

VI. **Time Limit:**_____ **Length of Speech**_____

VII. **Outline:**

    A. Includeed specific purpose
    B. Included thesis statement
    C. Followed rules for numeration and indentation
    D. Used sentences
    E. Typewritten
    F. Included bibliography of speech sources

General Comments:

INFORMATIVE SPEECH WITH VISUAL AID

NAME_____   **DATE**_____

TOPIC_____

	Needs Work	Good	Excellent	Comments
1. ORGANIZATION				
Introduction				
Body clearly organized				
Conclusion				
2. VISUAL AID				
Appropriate to content				
Easily seen				
Used effectively				
3. DELIVERY				
Proper posture				
Appropriate gestures				
Appropriate rate, volume				
Poise				
Eye contact				

COMMENTS:

GRADE_____

PERSUASIVE SPEECH

NAME_____ DATE_____

TOPIC_____

	Needs Work	Good	Excellent	Comments
1. ORGANIZATION				
Introduction				
Body clearly organized				
Conclusion				

	Needs Work	Good	Excellent	Comments
2. PERSUASIVENESS				
Approach to topic				
Language				
Supporting material				
Organization				

	Needs Work	Good	Excellent	Comments
3. DELIVERY				
Proper posture				
Appropriate gestures				
Appropriate rate & volume				
Vocal variety & energy				
Poise				
Eye contact				

COMMENTS:

GRADE_____

SPEECH EVALUATION FORM: Persuasive Speech

NAME_____   TOTAL POINTS/GRADE_____

TOPIC _____   DATE_____

Criteria	Comments
I. Topic: A. Original B. Appropriate for purpose and audience C. Substantive D. Narrowed sufficiently	
II. Introduction: A. Captured attention B. Stated thesis C. Related topic to audience D. Established credibility E. Previewed main points F. Provided transition to body	

III.   Body:
 	
A. Organized main points effectively
       to persuade
B. Included transitions between main points
C. Constructed effective argument for
       position in terms of:
       1. Appropriateness for topic and
            audience
       2. Clear logic
       3. Quantity of evidence
       4. Quality of evidence
       5. Number of sources
       6. Identification of sources
       7. Use of appeals to emotions,
            values, motivations
D. Used visual aids appropriately
       1. Clear explanations
       2. Neat, easy-to-see design
       3. Relevant to purpose and audience
E. Used language appropriate to:
       1. Topic
       2. Audience	

(over)

IV. **Conclusion:**

    A. Restated thesis
    B. Summarized main points
    C. Ended with a memorable final thought

V. **Delivery:**

    A. Used adequate and inclusive eye contact
    B. Used effective vocal delivery (appropriate rate and volume, clear articulation, varied inflection, and no vocal fillers)
    C. Used effective physical delivery (posture, gestures, movement)
    D. Contributed to credibility by emphasizing speaker's sincerity, confidence, and dynamism

VI. **Time Limit:**_____ **Length of Speech**_____

VII. **Outline:**

    A. Includeed specific purpose
    B. Included thesis statement
    C. Followed rules for numeration and indentation
    D. Used sentences
    E. Typewritten
    F. Included bibliography of speech sources

General Comments:

PEER SPEECH EVALUATION

The student listener should conscientiously complete the form and hand it to the instructor who will give it to the student speaker.

SPEAKER_____**DATE**_____

SUBJECT_____

	Poor	Very Weak	Weak	Fair	Adequate	Good	Very Good	Excellent	Superior	Comments
	1	2	3	4	5	6	7	8	9	
1. Introduction										
2. Clarity of purpose										
3. Choice of words										
4. Bodily action–gesture–posture										
5. Eye contact & facial expression										
6. Vocal expression										
7. Desire to be understood										
8. Poise & self-control										
9. Adapting material to audience										
10. Organization of material										
11. Conclusion										

PANEL DISCUSSION EVALUATION FORM

TOPIC_____

TOTAL POINTS/GRADE_____

Preparation and research into causes and effects

PARTICIPANTS:	Needs work	Acceptable	Excellent	Comments
1.				
2.				
3.				
4.				
5.				
6.				

Determination of standards for the solution

PARTICIPANTS:	Needs work	Acceptable	Excellent	Comments
1.				
2.				
3.				
4.				
5.				
6.				

Generation of possible solutions with advantages and disadvantages

PARTICIPANTS:	Needs work	Acceptable	Excellent	Comments
1.				
2.				
3.				
4.				
5.				
6.				

Coordination of ideas with group members to reach agreement on one solution

PARTICIPANTS:	Needs work	Acceptable	Excellent	Comments
1.				
2.				
3.				
4.				
5.				
6.				

(over)

Suggestions for putting selected solution into action

PARTICIPANTS:	Needs work	Acceptable	Excellent	Comments
1.				
2.				
3.				
4.				
5.				

Delivery Skills

PARTICIPANTS:	Needs work	Acceptable	Excellent	Comments
1.				
2.				
3.				
4.				
5.				

Overall Effect

PARTICIPANTS:	Needs work	Acceptable	Excellent	Comments
1.				
2.				
3.				
4.				
5.				

Time limit_____**Length of presentation**_____

General Comments:

SYMPOSIUM EVALUATION FORM

TOPIC_____

TOTAL POINTS/ GRADE_____

Clear, logical division of topic into distinct but related areas

PARTICIPANTS:	Needs work	Acceptable	Excellent	Comments
1.				
2.				
3.				
4.				
5.				

Preparation and research of area presented

PARTICIPANTS:	Needs work	Acceptable	Excellent	Comments
1.				
2.				
3.				
4.				
5.				

Observation of time limits assigned

PARTICIPANTS:	Needs work	Acceptable	Excellent	Comments
1.				
2.				
3.				
4.				
5.				

Delivery — Movements, vocal qualities, eye contact

PARTICIPANTS:	Needs work	Acceptable	Excellent	Comments
1.				
2.				
3.				
4.				
5.				

Overall effectiveness

PARTICIPANTS:	Needs work	Acceptable	Excellent	Comments
1.				
2.				
3.				
4.				
5.				

General comments on the back.

RESOLUTION FOR STUDENT CONGRESS

Resolution Title: _____

_____

WHEREAS, _____

_____

WHEREAS, _____

_____

WHEREAS, _____

_____

WHEREAS, _____

_____

BE IT RESOLVED BY _____

THAT:

1

2

3

4

5

6

7

8

This resolution introduced by _____

BILL FOR STUDENT CONGRESS

Bill Title: _____

BE IT ENACTED BY _____

_____

THAT:

1

2

3

4

5

6

7

8

9

10

11

12

13

14

15

16

17

This bill introduced by_____

INDIVIDUAL SPEAKING EVENT BALLOT

Event _____ Contestant's Code _____

Contestant's Name _____

Instructions: This can be used for extemporaneous speaking and oral interpretation. After hearing all speakers in a section, rank each 1 through 8 — the best receiving the ranking of 1. No two contestants can receive the same rank. Circle the correct number. Rate each speaker on a scale of 1-25. The same rating may be given to more than one contestant. Circle the correct number. Sign all ballots and place in the envelope provided.

Rank:
(circle one)　　1　　　2　　　3　　　4　　　5　　　6　　　7　　　8

Rating:
(circle one)　　1 2 3 4 5　　　6 7 8 9 10　　　11 12 13 14 15　　　16 17 18 19 20
　　　　　　　　poor　　　　　fair　　　　　good　　　　　very good

　　　　　　　　　　21 22 23 24 25
　　　　　　　　　　excellent

_____

Judge's signature

Comments:

DEBATE BALLOT

ROUND _____ ROOM _____ AFFIRMATIVE (Code No.) _____ NEGATIVE (Code No.) _____

JUDGE'S INSTRUCTIONS

Rank each of the debaters 1, 2, 3, 4. The most effective speaker will receive the ranking of 1, and so on. No two speakers may receive the same ranking. The team with the lowest total rankings must win (e.g. 1 and 2; or 1 and 3). In a case where one team receives a 1 and a 4 and the other team receives a 2 and a 3, either team may win. No ties may be given. Each debater's performance should also be rated according to its quality. The same rating may be given to two or more debaters. The following scale will be used.

1 2 3 4 5	6 7 8 9 10	11 12 13 14 15	16 17 18 19 20	21 22 23 24 25	26 27 28 29 30
Poor	Fair	Good	Very Good	Excellent	Superior

	Rank (1-4)	Rating (1-30)			Rank (1-4)	Rating (1-30)
1st Aff	_____	_____	_____	1st Neg	_____	_____	_____
2nd Aff	_____	_____	_____	2nd Neg	_____	_____	_____

In my opinion, the better debating was done by the _____

(Affirmative or Negative)

_____

Judge's signature

_____

Reasons for Decision